Politics and the History Curriculum

Politics and the History Curriculum
The Struggle over Standards in Texas and the Nation

Edited by
Keith A. Erekson

palgrave
macmillan

POLITICS AND THE HISTORY CURRICULUM: THE STRUGGLE OVER STANDARDS IN TEXAS AND THE NATION
Copyright © Keith A. Erekson, 2012.

Softcover reprint of the hardcover 1st edition 2012 978-1-137-00893-0

All rights reserved.

First published in 2012 by PALGRAVE MACMILLAN® in the United States—a division of St. Martin's Press LLC, 175 Fifth Avenue, New York, NY 10010.

Portions of Chapter 8 appeared originally in *Christian American and the Kingdom of God*. Copyright 2009 by the Board of Trustees of the University of Illinois. Used with permission of the University of Illinois Press.

The Texas travel slogan is a registered trademark and is used by permission of the Office of the Governor of the State of Texas.

Figures 1 and 6 were photographed by Chris Caselli, courtesy of the Texas Freedom Network.

Figures 3, 4, and 10 are used by permission of Laura Muñoz, Jesús F. de la Teja, and David Fisher, respectively.

Figure 7 comes from the Texas Administrative Code, Chapter 13 Texas Essential Knowledge and Skills for Social Studies, Subchapter C High School.

All other figures are courtesy the Library of Congress, Prints and Photographs Division, Washington, DC.

Where this book is distributed in the UK, Europe and the rest of the world, this is by Palgrave Macmillan, a division of Macmillan Publishers Limited, registered in England, company number 785998, of Houndmills, Basingstoke, Hampshire RG21 6XS.

Palgrave Macmillan is the global academic imprint of the above companies and has companies and representatives throughout the world.

Palgrave® and Macmillan® are registered trademarks in the United States, the United Kingdom, Europe and other countries.

ISBN 978-1-349-43587-6   ISBN 978-1-137-00894-7 (eBook)
DOI 10.1057/9781137008947

Library of Congress Cataloging-in-Publication Data is available from the Library of Congress.

A catalogue record of the book is available from the British Library.

Design by Scribe Inc.

First edition: June 2012

To all the

students and teachers

impacted by the Texas standards

Contents

List of Illustrations		ix
Preface		xi

Part I: Rewriting History in Texas

1	Culture War Circus: How Politics and the Media Left History Education Behind *Keith A. Erekson*	3
2	"As Texas Goes, So Goes the Nation": Conservatism and Culture Wars in the Lone Star State *Gene B. Preuss*	19
3	Hijacks and Hijinks on the US History Review Committee *Laura K. Muñoz and Julio Noboa*	41
4	A Voice Crying in the Wilderness? An Expert Reviewer's Experience *Jesús F. de la Teja*	61
5	Negotiating for Quality: Taking a Proactive Approach to Achieve a Positive Outcome *Stephen Cure*	75
6	Moving the Liberal-Minority Coalition Up the Education Pipeline *Emilio Zamora*	89

Part II: Analysis and Alternatives

7	Names, Numbers, and Narratives: A Multicultural Critique of the US History Standards *Julio Noboa*	105

8	Why Do We Think of America as a Christian Nation? *Richard T. Hughes*	127
9	Neo-Confederate Ideology in the Texas History Standards *Edward H. Sebesta*	149
10	A Missed Opportunity for World History in Texas *David C. Fisher*	171
11	Standards before Standardization: The Affiliated Schools Program, 1885–1917 *Linda J. Black*	195
12	A Perfect Storm in Austin and Beyond: Making the Case —and Place—for US History in Texas and the Nation *Linda K. Salvucci*	213
Notes on Contributors		231
Appendix for Teachers		233
Appendix for Policy Makers		235
Index		237

Illustrations

Figure 1	The Texas State Board of Education	2
Figure 2	Cold War roots of the recent debate	18
Figure 3	The US History Review Committee speaks out	40
Figure 4	Guidelines for the expert reviewers	60
Figure 5	Tejanos in the Battle of the Alamo	74
Figure 6	Protesting the new standards	88
Figure 7	Changes to the standard on civil rights	102
Figure 8	Washington at prayer?	126
Figure 9	A new victory for the Lost Cause	148
Figure 10	Parting the cloud of Western civilization	170
Figure 11	An alternative to high stakes testing	194
Figure 12	A revolutionary grab bag	212
Table 1	Women and minority individuals in the eighth- and eleventh-grade US history standards	108
Table 2	The Standards' Significant Individuals during the American Revolution	217

Preface

During 2010, the revision of the Texas K-12 social studies standards made national and international headlines. The process of education reform enacted by politicians and pastors drew as much attention as their controversial conclusions about the religion of the founding fathers, American exceptionalism, and the rewriting of historical narratives. The public meetings of the Texas State Board of Education and the changes proposed by its members drew commentary from media outlets across the political spectrum—Fox News, the *Wall Street Journal*, the *Washington Post*, *USA Today*, the Public Broadcasting Corporation, CNN, *The New York Times*, and Comedy Central. *The Guardian* (London) ran several stories, the Danish Broadcasting Corporation sent a reporter and cameraman to Austin, and the *Al Jazeera* network provided a mutedly ironic analysis of Texas authoritarianism. Journalists, talking heads, educators, historians, and humorists joined the fray. Much of the coverage was sensational, most squeezed the process into a narrow culture war storyline, few saw the process within any larger context, and nearly all moved quickly away to the next breaking story.[1]

There are several reasons the debates in Texas matter to all Americans, and they are more complex and more far-reaching than typically reported in media coverage of the controversy. For example, countless accounts oversimplified the nature of textbook publishing to allege that because Texas is such a large market for textbooks its decision would impact many other states. The truth in this statement is that Texas was the largest statewide adopter of K-12 textbooks—most states permit local decisions, and California adopts statewide only through middle school. The real secret of Texas influence, however, has been its adoption of books with relatively generic text accompanied by Texas-specific sidebars, thereby allowing the core text to be reused by other states that simply substitute the sidebar material.[2] Of far more consequence are numerous other underexplored themes that will be unraveled in the following pages: the tangled and powerful mixture of politics, media, and education in the United States; the strategies, successes, and fragility of nationwide conservative political networks; the suitability of the Texas standards for serving as a blueprint for education reforms in other states and the nation.

The purpose of this volume is to set the debate over the Texas social studies standards within a broader context, both in terms of previous education reform and in terms of future impact on teachers and students, in Texas and the nation. This volume does not provide a line-by-line review of the standards, though many portions will undergo close scrutiny. It rejects a simplistic culture war reading of the entire process while recognizing that politics and cultural differences influenced the process and the final product in numerous ways.[3]

Part I explores the process of revising the standards and rewriting history. Keith A. Erekson provides an overview of the revision process that untangles the ways that politics and the media employed the culture war storyline within the spectacle of a media circus. Gene B. Preuss traces the connections between anticommunists in the 1960s and conservatives in Texas and the nation. The next four chapters document the activities of participants in the recent education reform process in Texas. Laura K. Muñoz and Julio Noboa examine their experience as members of the embattled US history review committee, Jesús F. de la Teja reflects on his service as an expert reviewer, Stephen Cure describes how the Texas State Historical Association avoided the limelight to improve the standards, and Emilio Zamora documents the grassroots mobilization of liberal activist groups and suggests that an expanded effort will be needed as conservative politicians set their sights on reforming higher education.

Part II analyzes the final standards produced by the revision process. Julio Noboa subjects the US history standards to a multicultural critique, Richard T. Hughes examines the religiosity of America's founders and the origins of the myth of "Christian America," Edward H. Sebesta reveals the infusion of neo-Confederate ideology, and David C. Fisher scrutinizes the emphasis on Western civilization in the world history standards. Finally, as alternatives to the politicized curriculum of the Lone Star State in the twenty-first century, Linda J. Black resurrects a model of collaborative reform employed by Texans during the Progressive Era, and Linda K. Salvucci contrasts the recent Texas reforms with the parallel process and product in Colorado, setting both states within the context of the modern "crisis" of history education in the nation.

The contributors to this volume are all teachers and scholars who closely followed the two-year revision process, participated in a variety of ways, and share a stake in the education of Texas students and the future of education in the nation. We are not dispassionate because we care deeply about the future of Texas and its children. We do all strive to be depoliticized, believing that the excessive emphasis on politics throughout the process left teachers and students impoverished. Among the contributors will be found Texans who fish, own guns, served in the military, attend church every Sunday, and vote (for Republicans, Democrats, and independent candidates). We also teach in schools and universities, participate in historical associations, and read and write about improving history education. Many of the contributors met one another at state board of education meetings or academic conferences, but each contribution was crafted individually. Throughout the text history receives the lion's share of the attention. This is appropriate because it generated most of the controversy throughout the process and because it serves as the backbone of the state's social studies curriculum, with Texas history taught in fourth and seventh grades; US history in fifth, eighth, and eleventh; and world history in tenth.

This volume will not rehash the stale, ideologized arguments that floated in the media during the first half of 2010. Instead, we aspire to set that narrow debate within a broader context in order both to reflect more meaningfully on what transpired and draw important lessons for the future. By looking for the bigger picture, this volume aims to assist future educators, administrators, and policy makers by providing a clear analysis of what happened and why, along with sensible recommendations for future efforts at teaching and policy making. Specific recommendations are presented in two special appendices for teachers and policy makers. As an estimated nine million Texas children grow up in the state's public schools over the coming decade, we hope that perhaps something we write here can improve teaching in the classrooms, policy making in the halls of power, and the value of history in public life.

Notes

1. "Texas Looks to Rewrite History," *Al Jazeera*, April 9, 2010. For an archive of media coverage see TEKS *Watch*, hosted by the Center for History Teaching & Learning at the University of Texas at El Paso, *http://tekswatch.utep.edu*.
2. Brian Thevenot, "Texas Textbooks' National Influence Is a Myth," *Texas Tribune*, March 26, 2010.
3. The Texas social studies standards were first established in 1998 with a provision to revise them every decade. During 2009–10, seven drafts were proposed and reviewed before the final draft was filed on August 23, 2010. All of the drafts were posted on the Texas Education Agency's website, *http://www.tea.state.tx.us/index2.aspx?id=3643*, with varying titles, numbering systems, and dates. Adding to the confusion, both the original and final versions are published as part of the Texas Administrative Code at *http://ritter.tea.state.tx.us/rules/tac/chapter113/ch113c.html*. For the purposes of this volume, citations will simply reference grade level, section, standard, and date. Thus, TEKS.11.c.1.A (7/31/09) refers to the July 31, 2009, draft for eleventh grade, section c, standard 1A; TEKS (7/31/09) refers to the entire draft. Drafts are dated 1998 (original), July 31, 2009, October 17, 2009, January 2010, March 2010, May 2010, and August 23, 2010 (final). In similar manner, minutes of the Texas State Board of Education meetings are published online with varying titles and formats at *http://www.tea.state.tx.us/index4.aspx?id=5173*; citations in the notes refer simply to the date.

PART I

Rewriting History in Texas

Figure 1 The Texas State Board of Education
The Texas State Board of Education sits in a ring (top), flanked by representatives of the media and witnesses offering public testimony. Outside, demonstrators surround a gaggle of cameras.

CHAPTER 1

Culture War Circus
How Politics and the Media Left History Education Behind

Keith A. Erekson

The scene in downtown Austin, Texas, felt very much like a circus. Television vans lined both sides of the streets, their satellite dishes poking skyward like robotic giraffes from train cars. Reporters invited one and all to step right up and pitch a sound bite worthy of the evening news. College students in bright T-shirts juggled protest signs and printed flyers. Music piping in from some unseen source put a bounce in the step of the crowds filing toward the glass doors of the big top—the William B. Travis Building, meeting place of the Texas State Board of Education. No ticket was required for entrance, but by nine o'clock in the morning the room's seats and aisles were packed. On the agenda were proposed changes to the state's social studies standards, the blueprint that would guide future revisions of public school textbooks, standardized tests, and teacher certification requirements. To the right, cameras rolled and journalists typed; to the left, witnesses waited to deliver their prepared testimony; in the center sat the publicly elected members of the board of education, their desks arranged in the shape of a ring. Though the board's 15-hour meeting on May 19, 2010, may not have been the "greatest show on Earth," it proved to be the longest, and it dominated headlines around the nation and world for one engrossing week.

Inside the meeting, the media circus became suffused with culture war politics. First, a former US Secretary of Education criticized the proposed changes as inadequate for twenty-first-century students. Then two Republican state congressmen praised the proposals as just right for Texas before two Democrats offered the opposite conclusion. The leader of a national civil rights organization walked the tightrope between identifying specific errors in the proposed standards and admitting that he had not actually read them. When the hearing stopped for lunch, the state's most visible conservative activist group staged a rally in which its director assembled a crowd of elderly white folks, placed miniature flags in their hands, pushed a college professor and a black woman to the front, and coached everyone to smile for the assembled cameras. The state's most visible liberal activist organization was likewise present, though subdued in the wake of the death threat delivered recently to its leader. Politics, media, history, and education seemed to dissolve into a foggy blur. Is it possible to disentangle them?

Local, national, and international coverage almost invariably cast the events in Texas as simply the latest chapter in America's ongoing culture wars. An amorphous metaphor that has grown in analytical application over the past three decades, the culture war storyline posits a polarized public that is ideologically and inseparably divided over issues ranging from abortion to multiculturalism, gun control to gay marriage, evolution to the environment. When applied to public debates over history, the moniker has been used to frame issues related to the exhibit of the *Enola Gay* at the Smithsonian museum, the development of national standards for history education, and the display of the Confederate flag. In the recent attempts at education reform in Texas, the culture war narrative focused on disputes that a bloc of Christian conservatives on the board brought to the discussion of César Chávez, Christmas, and separation of church and state.[1]

The metaphors of "culture war" and "media circus" ultimately prove both useful and distracting. On the one hand, both were clearly part of the events that unfolded in Texas. Members of the state board of education and countless commentators described their actions within a culture war storyline while the media regularly offered up a circus-like barrage of images and provocative statements. Indeed, employing a circus metaphor can help sort out the numerous participants in the process. On the other hand, the metaphors also obscure relevant contexts, minimize contemporary stakes, and ignore future impacts. Most significantly, the Texas social studies reform process reveals the perils of blending politics, media, and education. The media focused on politics and persuasion, whereas it should have paid attention to power and to principles of sound teaching and learning. Skills necessary for success in college and careers were ignored. In the end, the pursuit of a culture war in Texas shifted attention away from education reform at the time when it was needed most.

Making Sense of the Circus

The public hearing in Austin was only the most televisable part of the formal revision of the state's social studies standards, which extended from January 2009 through August 2010. It began with review committees composed of educators and citizens, who were joined by board-appointed "expert witnesses," including two ministers whose comments quickly drew media attention. Three meetings—in January, March, and May 2010—invited public testimony before the state board of education (SBOE), a group of 15 politicians whose discussions were often reduced in the media to sound bites taken from the comments of the board's former chair—a man passionate about education reform, Christian fundamentalism, and dentistry. In addition to these formal participants, reporters, pundits, activists, teachers, historians, and late-night comedians chimed in.

At one level, a circus metaphor *can* help us make sense of the various participants and their relation to the process of changing the state's curriculum. The three rings of the Texas education reform circus can be characterized by persuasion, performance, and power. Most Texans and Americans learned about the revision process through the ring of persuasion. Though commonly characterized simply as "the media," there were actually a variety of voices attempting to be heard via numerous media formats. The ring of persuasion was dominated by journalists, which included regular reporters from state news organizations who attended every meeting and analyzed every decision as well as cherry pickers from national and international media outlets, who dropped in for the public meetings. The writings and interviews of these journalists prompted responses from readers (sometimes more than a thousand comments) as well as opinion pieces and letters to editors. In general, coverage by large in-state news organizations was the most thorough and accurate; small inaccuracies in outsider reports or editorials often ballooned in the blogosphere. Professional associations representing historians, social studies teachers, and librarians as well as activist groups advocating for civil liberties and Hispanic farm workers issued public statements. Political activist groups—from the liberal Texas Freedom Network to the conservative Liberty Institute—held press conferences and issued press releases. Student groups from various institutions staged rallies and organized to deliver testimony. Two caucuses of the state legislature—the Mexican American Legislative Caucus and the Texas Conservative Coalition—held their own hearings and mobilized members and supporters. Organizations and individuals made statements and organized protests via YouTube, Facebook, and blogs. In all, thousands of Americans raised their voices in the ring of persuasion.[2]

The culture war circus also featured a ring of performance. The first performers were review committees of schoolteachers, district administrators, and college professors who applied for selection by the SBOE. Appointed one per grade in elementary and middle school social studies and one per subject area in high school, the committees contained four to nine members who were tasked with analyzing the state's then-current social studies standards (adopted in 1998) and making recommendations for improvement. The review committees were later joined by "expert reviewers," six individuals appointed by and accountable to the board. The experts required nomination only by two members of the SBOE, a lightweight selection process that produced two ministers, two historians, a geography educator, and a legal scholar. Finally, the board invited the general public to submit written feedback via fax and email or to testify at one of three public hearings. This invitation drew out both concerned citizens and representatives of interested organizations and institutions. For the most part, these performers addressed their commentary to the SBOE, though they were also interviewed, quoted, and challenged in the ring of persuasion.

The rings of persuasion and performance were merely sideshows, however, to the ring of power. When the SBOE holds its meetings, representatives of the ring of persuasion sit to the audience's right and witnesses in the ring of performance sit and speak on the left. The very architecture of the meeting room focuses attention onto the ring of power in the center, 15 desks arrayed in a circle so that board members can face each other while turning their backs on the persuaders, the performers, and the public. Board members are elected to represent 15 equipopulous regions across the state—regions that shift every ten years with census results just like legislative districts. As a result of a lengthy process that unfolded over several decades, this 15-member board possessed sole power to define and change the state's education standards in 2010. Furthermore, the Texas Education Code grants the state board of education statutory authority over the standards, meaning that the final draft carries the force of law after three public hearings (and without any additional action on the part of the legislature).

Board members are elected to their positions by voters because, in theory, Texans want to maintain "local control" over their children's education. In practice, the electoral process produced three attorneys, three who work in real estate, and one each with experience in investing, software engineering, editing, community volunteering, and dentistry. The remaining four had ties to the education establishment as paid consultants or caseworkers. Only one of the 15 brought extensive experience as a classroom teacher. In the landscape of Texas educational institutions, the board stands apart from, but collaborates with, the Texas Education Agency, which is filled with political appointees and paid public servants. The board adopts rules and establishes policies that affect more than 4.7 million students and 640,000 employees in more than 8,300 schools and 1,200 districts across the state of Texas. Funding for Texas education is controlled by the state legislature, but the board oversees the state's multibillion-dollar Permanent School Fund, which is used to purchase textbooks and, in recent years, to offset holes in the state budget. In theory, this is complex, but in reality it is simple: all power to design the education standards and standardized tests rests in the hands of the 15 board members in the ring of power.[3]

The ring of power largely controlled the activities in the ring of performance. The board set the agenda for meetings, gave the charges to the reviewers, overruled proposals that it did not like, and made amendments whenever it wanted. All performers—whether review committee members, expert reviewers, or concerned citizens—were selected, appointed, or invited to perform by the SBOE. Thus there was really only one side to the "debate"—that which the SBOE wished to hear. When the board-appointed expert reviewers disagreed with one another, the board piously lifted itself above the squabble of "experts" to make the "right" decision. The board criticized the "liberal" teachers on the world history committee for removing Christmas and the "liberals" on the US history committee for calling the United States imperialistic. But when the board was criticized for omitting Hispanics, members defended themselves by pointing to the work of those same committees.

The role of the public appeared largely ceremonial. Those citizens who used their public testimony to criticize the board could be dismissed without further question. When citizens brought a list of specific issues, the board complained that the individual did not understand the bigger picture. When citizens spoke about larger issues of interpretation or education, the board demanded the identification of a specific error in the standards. The board never required itself to respond to public comments, so it is difficult to track the public's influence. Board members certainly could not integrate the testimony of those who spoke at the final meeting—one day before the final draft was approved. The board made approximately one hundred amendments at its January meeting, more than a hundred more in March, and yet more in May, none of which was subjected to the same level of formal analysis that had previously been required of the review committees or expert reviewers. In the midst of the revision process—and outside the four-year electoral cycle—the SBOE was effectively accountable to no one.

The ring of power also exerted a profound influence over the debates in the ring of persuasion. From the outset, the board used a list of the names in the 1998 standards as the yardstick for their changes. Each significant new draft of changes was accompanied by an updated list indicating which names were added, removed, or unchanged. Dozens of journalists took the bait and wrote countless articles about who was in or out. Several of the board members also narrated their actions within a culture war storyline that pitted conservatives against liberals. The board was challenging the "liberal bias" of textbooks, "standing up to so-called experts," and correcting the errors of history. Most in the media ate up this story with delight, staging interviews with both liberals and conservatives, inviting guests to speak with "outrage" and "come with a passion."

Happy to encourage these conversations, the board obstructed the release of other information about the process by posting updates randomly across two different websites. Important announcements lay buried on one site, meeting agendas were posted elsewhere, and instructions for public testimony were loaded online with no link from either site. The accessibility of the laundry list of names coupled with the culture war narrative channeled public debates into a narrow analysis of the politics of board members or of the persons added and removed.

All three rings of simultaneous action filled television screens with a variety of activities and presented the feel of a free-flowing democratic process. Yet no matter how many opinion pieces or YouTube videos were created by college professors or middle school students, the simple fact remained that the SBOE exercised sole authority over revising the standards. No matter how colorful or energetic or spontaneous a circus may appear, we cannot lose track of the fact that it is planned, rehearsed even; perhaps this is too much to say of the SBOE, but their level of power gives the metaphor credence. The exercise of power should not be lost within the commotion of a culture war circus.

What the Circus Obscured

If the circus metaphor helps make sense of the variety of participants in this culture war, it also obscures the past contexts and contemporary stakes of the public debate over history, education, and politics. One crucial contextual omission was the fact that the United States has witnessed a long record of controversy over national identity, history and social studies education standards, and the appropriate lessons for children. Those controversies swirled around race and ethnicity in the 1920s, patriotism and social class in the 1930s, multiculturalism and diversity in the 1960s and 1970s, and the attempt to establish national standards in the 1990s.

In the twenty-first century, Democrats and Republicans in Minnesota produced two separate sets of standards, policymakers in North Carolina threatened to omit history before the Civil War, and legislators in Florida banned the "interpretation" of history. Seen within this wider context, the struggle in Texas was not entirely new. But analysis of the Texas story too often repeated the same old themes already discussed endlessly in the literature on education reform: the idea of history or social studies "wars" that reflect a broader culture war, the rising influence of conservatives, their push against experts for a more "positive" history, the fight over multiculturalism and representative examples, the confusion of standards and textbooks, and the absurdity of permitting politicians to design curriculum.[4] Media stories often failed even to note that this very same SBOE had, in fact, in years previous revised standards in other subjects to teach creationism, promote abstinence, and discourage dual-language instruction. The controversy over history was not a flash in the culture war pan.

Attention to a broader context also would have helped to underscore the fact that Texas was not merely revising textbooks, but rather its entire education system—a prospect made possible by the rise of standards and testing within the past two decades. Standards serve as a master blueprint to which textbooks, curriculum, standardized tests, and educator credentials must eventually conform. The concept first came into practice in California in the 1980s as a way to reform and unify the entire education system instead of focusing on its parts. Other states followed California's systemic-reform model, including Texas in the mid-1990s.

When George W. Bush, the Texas governor who endorsed systemic reform in Texas, was elected president of the United States in 2000, he took the concept to Washington and embedded it into his No Child Left Behind program. The Obama administration perpetuated the program and further enshrined the idea of systemic reform into its own education programs, most significantly the Race to the Top. Thus, despite partisan debates over the contents of the standards, there is currently a bipartisan agreement among American politicians that standards and standardized testing should drive education reform efforts. In an education policy environment in which both sides agree on the means of reform, the Texas blueprint can easily become a de facto model for other states.

Beyond past context, the culture war narrative and media circus metaphor likewise obscured the present and future political stakes in the contest. The culture war storyline assumes two opposing factions and a backstory that underdog conservatives have "risen up" or "resurged" to compete with liberal elites. Invoking this narrative, the SBOE could cast its own actions as redemptive, the work of outraged political newcomers who were "standing up to experts" and "fixing liberal textbooks."

Yet, in reality, the conservative state board of education was simply revising the standards written by a previous conservative Texas school board. In 2010, the 15-member board hosted ten Republicans, in 1998 it held nine—and four of the members served on both occasions. The crucial difference lay not in a culture war difference between liberals and newly surging conservatives, but in a present-day intraparty difference between moderate conservatives and social conservatives. Self-described "true Christian conservatives" obtained an eight-member voting majority after 1998 and, in the twenty-first century they set out to rewrite all the state's curricula, codifying their beliefs on topics as diverse as evolutionary science and Ronald Reagan's memory. Seen in this light, the Texas social studies debate was not the latest chapter in an ongoing culture war, but rather part of a new narrative about the dilemmas of conservative governance. The tension between Christian conservatives and moderate Republicans in

Texas mirrors the nationwide fissure between fiscal and social conservatives in the former Reagan coalition. Advocates of small government in other contexts, the social-conservative Texans who obtained control of the SBOE did so in order to *use* its centralized power to enact their political agenda.[5]

Evidence of interconservative tension emerged from several corners of the contest. In March 2010, two of the board's conservative Christians—including outspoken dentist Don McLeroy—lost primary elections to moderate Republican challengers. Similar signs appeared in the board's handling of the media. Despite that fact that dozens of news organizations made errors—misidentifying the chair of the board, conflating the standards with textbooks, and misunderstanding the place of Thomas Jefferson in the standards (the board rejected a recommendation to add him to the world-history standards instead of calling for his removal from US history)—the board only corrected errors made by Fox News, the media outlet most important to its social-conservative audience.[6]

Thus to describe the battle in Texas as a culture war between liberals and conservatives was disingenuous and overblown. The Texas story does not represent another "right wing assault" on mainstream America or a mere culture war between two equally polarized factions. Using the culture war narrative to describe the struggles *between* conservatives is absurd in this case—this is less a real conflict than a manufactured one, a drama more akin to a phone company denigrating its old model to tout the new one. The conservative restoration of the 1970s and 1980s is only relevant as a prelude to the modern state of conservative governance. Conservatives in Texas are not angry "outsiders" seeking to "infiltrate" government. They are the executors of power, and they disagree with each other.[7] Thus promotion of the culture war narrative served as a sleight of hand that drew attention away from intraparty differences. It is a strategy that worked in the Texas debate and that will likely be employed again.

Finally, the Texas social studies debate emerges as a profoundly significant national development precisely because it reveals the blurred lines between politics, media, and education. Some commentators speculated about a conservative conspiracy or naively criticized the SBOE for "politicizing" the process. In reality, the state of Texas politicized the process more than half a century ago by centralizing education policy making in the hands of a publicly elected board of education. These 15 politicians of both political parties simply act like politicians—working for their reelection, making alliances with like-minded colleagues, and endorsing potential allies in races in other districts. They also drew on their political connections to carry out their duties.

Take this example: When the time came for the board to appoint expert reviewers to make recommendations for the new curriculum, it appointed one of *Time Magazine*'s top 25 most influential evangelicals, David Barton. Barton has no training in history or education but instead works as a pastor, conservative radio program host, and Republican Party activist. In this latter role he served as the vice chairman of the Texas Republican Party from 1997 to 2006, filed briefs and gave testimony in court cases, and gave hundreds of speeches on behalf of the Republican National Committee during the past two presidential campaigns. He has been praised by presidential candidates Newt Gingrich and Michele Bachmann, current Republican governors Sam Brownback (Kansas) and Bobby Jindal (Louisiana), and conservative media hosts Mike Huckabee and Glenn Beck—and he appeared regularly on the latter's now-canceled Fox News program and as part of the "faculty" of Beck University. The materials produced by Barton have been used by Pat Robertson and the Christian Coalition, James Dobson and Focus on the Family, Jerry Falwell and Liberty University, James Kennedy and Coral Ridge Ministries, and Phyllis Schlafly and her Eagle Forum. The adoption of a "Christian America" perspective and the infusion of neo-Confederate ideology into the standards represent the fruits of the Republican Party's now decades-old "Southern Strategy." Thus, far from a sudden, "simple conspiracy" of the few, the debacle in Texas illustrates one astute observer's characterization of conservatives in general as a "well-financed, well-coordinated, savvy movement."[8] Social conservatives on the SBOE acted as part of a nationwide mobilization of politicians and media to implement a systematic conservative agenda.

So why would politicians use the culture war narrative? And why would the media fall for it? For politicians, the story buries internal differences by emphasizing only the rivalry with the opposing party. Conservatives in particular have been very successful in recent decades at mobilizing voters by appealing to a sense of "outsiderness" and dissatisfaction with elites in the academy and in the halls of power.[9] For the media, sensationalism, crisis, and spectacle draw an audience—a fact that remains essential to the bottom line in an environment marked by global corporatization and economic recession. The Manichean culture war narrative both simplifies complex details and attracts consumers. Ignoring the longer history and separating a story from its context makes it "news"—something new that consumers should notice.[10] With Christian conservatives on the SBOE using the storyline, the culture war circus provided the perfect blend of politics and media by bringing about the ends desired by both.

But the culture war marriage of politicians and the media produced one more extremely significant impact on the way the revision process unfolded. Because in a culture war there are two—and only two—ideological sides to every question, ideological "balance" became enshrined as the dominant value in the process, leaving no room to talk about sound education principles or even about whether creating a list of names to memorize constitutes good education. For example, early in the process the world history review committee proposed limiting the study of religious holidays to one per world religion (choosing Easter over Christmas for Christianity), and one of the expert reviewer ministers recommended removing civil rights leader César Chávez. Though neither Christmas nor Chávez ever left the standards, the resultant media firestorm evoked protests, petitions, and warnings from across the spectrum. When Christmas was retained and those who had "opposed" civil rights joined Chávez in the standards, all sides declared victory. The media praised this culture war "compromise" for avoiding "extremes" and maintaining "balance."[11]

Christian conservatives on the SBOE, however, were the true winners. Activists on the left could now be kept in their place at any point in the future by merely reviving the possibility of removing Chávez. Meanwhile the so-called War on Christmas gave the impression that attacks were coming from all sides, strengthening the board's self-presentation as a neutral, compromising mediator best suited to rise above the culture war fray. Focusing on culture war balance, the SBOE would not have to address the really difficult problems of the state's high dropout rate, funding inadequacies, and poor education standards. The culture war circus permitted politics to hijack education, as the debate over who was on or off the laundry list substituted for informed discussion of education reform. As long as students memorized a balanced list of names—no matter its length or relevance—there would be no need for problem solving, analysis, or historical reasoning.

How the Circus Will Impact History Education

By the end of the process, it became apparent that the culture war circus will impact history education in Texas in very significant ways over the coming decade. The first problem facing teachers is the sheer size of the new standards. The eleventh-grade US history standards grew from 2,428 words to 3,963 words, 163 percent of the original size. Across the entire curriculum, only ninth-grade geography and the elective psychology courses shrunk (by 168 and 38 words, respectively). Every other course from kindergarten to twelfth grade grew, with the new standards weighing in with 5,929 more words than the 1998 edition, a net growth of 121 percent.[12] The rhetorical ideal of culture war "balance" found its real-world resolution through a formula of simply adding more [fill in the blank] to appease [fill in the blank]. For teachers who already struggle to cover everything in the curriculum while preparing for increasingly influential standardized tests, the challenge is daunting.

Teachers will also have to compensate for the fact that the culture war circus grew the standards in uneven ways. Some examples can be traced to ideological drift: the "free enterprise system" has only "benefits," while the Great Society, Title IX, and affirmative action have only "unintended consequences." These can be fixed simply by adopting language that appears in other parts of the standards that expects students to examine both costs and benefits or benefits and challenges. Other problems can be traced to the lack of editorial synthesis that resulted from board members in the ring of power passing hundreds of amendments in the last few months without an adequate system of review. The standard on World War I, for example, now lists five "technological innovations" and one battle; and the Great Depression now erroneously "immediately" follows the war.

Other issues stem from the complete lack of context brought about under the guise of ideological balance. In eighth-grade US history, Native Americans do not exist during exploration and colonization, westward expansion, or the section on people and the environment. They are precluded from consideration as an ethnic group that "settled in the United States" and earn their only mention when the Cherokee were removed under Andrew Jackson. Religion rightly influences government, impacts the "American way of life," and motivates immigration and social movements—but nowhere do students learn that religion also prompted persecution of Catholics, Mormons, Jews, and now Muslims; justified the Spanish-American War; and fueled political and cultural debates. In the standards, civil disobedience can be used to oppose taxes but not war or social issues. Twentieth-century decolonization movements appear without any mention of colonization, and the Cold War is ended by a new "Fantastic Four" composed of Ronald Reagan, Mikhail Gorbachev, Lech Walesa, and the Pope. Arab rejection of the Israeli state leads to conflict without recognition of Israeli intrusion onto Arab lands.[13] Like a fun-house mirror that emphasizes some things while minimizing others, the new curriculum presents the three Cs of American history in Texas: Christians, confederates, and conservatives. Collectively, the history sections reveal a general disconnect between a Texas vision of the past—rooted in nineteenth-century Manifest Destiny, rugged individualism, and social Darwinism—and Texas's twenty-first-century urban, multiethnic, and global present.

The most significant problem with the standards lies not in omitting one Founding Father here or a million Hispanics there, but in adopting a laundry list of names instead of holding out the expectation that students learn to read, think, solve problems, and communicate. Students who spend 13 years memorizing the list of names—whether the subjects are liberal, conservative, or whatever—will find themselves seriously unprepared for the realities of college and the workplace. A growing chorus of business leaders, educators, and parents are calling for education that teaches students to adapt old knowledge, seek new knowledge, and try (while sometimes failing) to implement new ideas.[14]

Both the 1998 and the new 2010 standards contain a "social studies skills" section with a standard addressing problem solving, but it is copied and pasted at the end of every grade from kindergarten to twelfth. Thus in terms of problem solving, analysis, and decision making, the Texas social studies standards require nothing more of seniors than they do of kindergartners. When this issue was raised at the May 2010 meeting of the SBOE, the only board member with classroom experience dismissed it, saying, in essence, "We leave that to the classroom teachers."[15] The phrase "All I really need to know I learned in kindergarten" works far better as a bumper sticker than as a governing education philosophy.

Perhaps the saddest irony in this story is that the state of Texas had already recognized that its elementary and secondary students were not being adequately prepared for college and careers. In 2006, after learning that 40 percent of Texas students require remedial college courses at a cost of $80 million per year to Texas taxpayers, the state legislature authorized the creation of College Readiness Standards. Prepared under the direction of the Texas Higher Education Coordinating Board, the standards were adopted in January 2008, one year before the social studies review committees went to work. These standards emphasize interdisciplinary training, thoughtful and responsive civic engagement, and the cognitive skills of critical reading, communication, and problem solving. When the state board of education assembled the review committees, it provided copies of the College Readiness Standards, but over a year later the board's chair confessed to not following up. Only two media stories out of the veritable flood of commentary raised the question of college readiness. As the revision process drew to a close, a new study revealed that 48 percent of community college entrants and 14 percent of incoming university freshmen required remedial courses in at least one subject. Trumpeted as "one of the first" states to adopt college readiness standards, Texas now claims the additional distinction of being one of the first states to disregard them.[16]

Sound principles of history education were left behind in the media spectacle over the culture war in Texas. After the final votes were cast, social conservatives celebrated on blogs and in an awards ceremony at Phyllis Schlafly's Eagle Forum. The matron of grassroots conservative politics thanked McLeroy for adding her to eleventh grade by presenting him with her organization's Patriot Award as David Barton looked on and Texas governor Rick Perry delivered a speech on religion.[17]

Echoes of the culture war continue to linger in the air. In December 2010, a coalition of civil rights groups for African Americans and Hispanics filed a complaint in federal court that alleged discrimination in the standards. Two months later, the conservative Thomas Fordham Institute awarded the standards a grade of D for being "a politicized distortion of history . . . unwieldy and troubling" and containing "misrepresentations at every turn." SBOE members shrugged off both charges, explaining away the liberals for being liberal and the conservative think tank for advocating for national standards. Once again, criticism from both sides of the culture war served as proof that ideological balance had been achieved. The standards are being used to craft new standardized tests—but in light of its current budget woes, the state recently moved away from statewide textbook adoptions to allow local districts to choose whatever materials they wish to help their students pass the tests.[18]

The culture war circus, embraced by politicians and the media, obscured the divisions among Texas conservatives while reshaping the state's social studies curriculum into an ideologically balanced laundry list. In the 2010 general election, one of the board members lost his seat to a challenger who called for a return to phonics as the centerpiece of public reading education. That a candidate could win while advocating only one-third of the nineteenth-century standards of "readin', 'ritin', and 'rithmetic" suggests that the culture war circus may yet return for another showing. Next time, Texans and Americans will be better served by paying less attention to the performance and more attention to context, principles of sound education, and power.

Notes

1. James Davison Hunter, *Culture Wars: The Struggle to Define America* (New York: Basic Books, 1991); Edward Tabor Linenthal and Tom Englehart, eds., *History Wars: The Enola Gay and Other Battles for the American Past* (New York: Metropolitan Books, 1996); Stephanie Simon, "The Culture Wars' New Front: U.S. History Classes in Texas," *Wall Street Journal*, July 14, 2009; April Castro, "Conservatives See Texas Social Studies Proposal as 'War' on Christianity," *Associated Press*, September 11, 2009; Bill Ames, "The Left's War on U.S. History," 3 parts, *Texas Insider*, November 9–11, 2009; Brian Thevenot, "The American History Wars," *Texas Tribune*, January 14, 2010.
2. The most informed regulars included the *Houston Chronicle*, the *Austin American-Statesman*, the *Dallas Morning News*, and the *Texas Tribune*; a digital archive of media coverage is online at TEKSWatch, *http://tekswatch.utep.edu*.
3. Gene B. Preuss, *To Get a Better School System: One Hundred Years of Education Reform in Texas* (College Station: Texas A&M University Press, 2009); Michael E. McClellan, "Permanent School Fund," *Handbook of Texas Online*, *http://www.tshaonline.org/handbook/online/articles/khp01*.
4. Ira Shor, *Culture Wars: School and Society in the Conservative Restoration, 1969–1984* (Boston: Routledge, 1986); Gary B. Nash, Charlotte Crabtree, and Ross E. Dunn, *History on Trial: Culture Wars and the Teaching of the Past* (New York: Vintage Books, 2000), 4–17; Jonathan Zimmerman, *Whose America?: Culture Wars in the Public Schools* (Boston: Harvard University Press, 2002), 107–29; Ronald W. Evans, *The Social Studies Wars: What Should We Teach the Children?* (New York: Teachers College Press, 2004), 149–74; Joseph Moreau, *Schoolbook Nation: Conflicts over American History Textbooks from the Civil War to the Present* (Ann Arbor: University of Michigan Press, 2004), 264–30; Diane Ravitch, *The Death and Life of the Great American School System: How Testing and Choice Are Undermining*

Education (New York: Basic Books, 2010), 225–26; Sara Evans and Lisa Norling, "What Happened in Minnesota?" *OAH Newsletter* (November 2004); Mary Beth Norton, "History Under Construction in Florida," *The New York Times*, July 2, 2006; Erik Robelen, "Proposed Rewrite of N.C. Social Studies Standards Draws Fire," *Education Week*, February 5, 2010.
5. Kate Alexander, "Texas Curriculum Fight Was Orchestrated over More Than a Decade," *Austin American-Statesman*, May 15, 2010; Mariah Blake, "Revisionaries: How a Group of Texas Conservatives Is Rewriting Your Kids' Textbooks," *Washington Monthly*, January/February 2010; Jim Vertuno, "New Education Board Chair Off to Rocky Start," Associated Press, July 20, 2011.
6. Texas Education Agency, "Fox Inaccurately Reporting State Board of Education Action," March 10, 2010; Terrence Stutz, "Fox News Clarifies Reports on Texas' Social Studies Curriculum, But Doesn't Apologize," *Dallas Morning News*, March 11, 2010.
7. Nash, Crabtree, and Dunn, *History on Trial*, 188–222; Barbara B. Gaddy, T. William Hall, and Robert J. Marzano, *School Wars: Resolving Our Conflicts over Religion and Values* (San Francisco: Jossey-Bass Publishers, 1996), 57–58; Ronald W. Evans, *The Tragedy of American School Reform: How Curriculum Politics and Entrenched Dilemmas Have Diverted Us from Democracy* (New York: Palgrave Macmillan, 2011).
8. Jean Hardisty, *Mobilizing Resentment: Conservative Resurgence from the John Birch Society to the Promise Keepers* (Boston: Beacon Press, 1999), 7–8; Lee Blankenship Emmert, "The Lesson Planner," *Time*, February 7, 2005; Chris Vaughn, "A Man with a Message; Self-Taught Historian's Work on Church-State Issues Rouses GOP," *Fort Worth Star-Telegram*, May 22, 2005; Erik Eckholm, "Using History to Mold Ideas on the Right," *The New York Times*, May 4, 2011; John Fea, "Should Christians Trust David Barton?" May 10, 2011, http://www.patheos.com/Resources/Additional-Resources/Should-Christians-Trust-David-Barton-John-Fea-05-11-2011.html.
9. William Martin, *With God on Our Side: The Rise of the Religious Right in America* (New York: Broadway Books, 1996); Bruce J. Schulman and Julian E. Zelizer, eds., *Rightward Bound: Making America Conservative in the 1970s* (Cambridge, MA: Harvard University Press, 2008); Clyde Wilcox and Carin Larson, eds., *Onward Christian Soldiers? The Religious Right in American Politics*, 3rd ed. (Boulder, CO: Westview Press, 2006).
10. Margaret Smith Crocco, ed., *Social Studies and the Press: Keeping the Beast at Bay?* (Greenwich, CT: Information Age Publishing, 2005), 15–23, 39–54, 109–18, 251–53.
11. Kate Alexander, "Social Studies Standards Strike Compromise: Most Controversial Expert Recommendations Left Out of Draft Standards," *Austin American-Statesman*, August 7, 2009; "So Far, State Education Board Is Finding Sweet Spot on Standards," *Dallas Morning News*, September 30, 2009.
12. This is based on words in the "knowledge and skills" section of the Texas Essential Knowledge and Skills (TEKS), which are the state standards for what students should know and be able to do (adopted August 23, 2010).

13. In TEKS (8/23/10): see free enterprise system (TEKS.10.c.18, TEKS.econ.c.6); Great Society, Title IX, and affirmative action (TEKS.11.c.17.D); costs and benefits (TEKS.11.c.15.B) and benefits and challenges (TEKS.9.c.7.D); World War I (TEKS.11.c.4) and the Great Depression (TEKS.10.c.11); Cherokee removal (TEKS.8.b.5.G); indigenous peoples omitted (TEKS.8.b.1–2, TEKS.8.b.6, TEKS.8.b.23.A); religion (TEKS.8.b.3.C, TEKS.8.b.25.A, TEKS.8.b.25.B); civil disobedience (TEKS.8.b.20.C); decolonization (TEKS.10.c.13); Cold War (TEKS.10.c.13.D); Arabs and Israelis (TEKS.10.42.c.13.F).
14. Bradley Commission, *Building a History Curriculum: Guidelines for Teaching History in Schools* (Washington, DC: Educational Excellence Network, 1995); Tony Wagner, *The Global Achievement Gap: Why Even Our Best Schools Don't Teach the New Survival Skills Our Children Need—And What We Can Do about It* (New York: Basic Books, 2010).
15. TEKS.K.b.16 and 12.c.22 (8/23/10).
16. Kate Alexander, "College Readiness Overlooked in Social Studies Fight," *Austin American-Statesman*, March 19, 2010; Holly K. Hacker, "Students Playing Catch-Up as They Hit College," *Dallas Morning News*, March 21, 2010; Texas College Readiness Standards (2008), social studies I.D.1 and page 25; "Achievement Gaps for Texas College Students Still a Challenge," *Fort Worth Star-Telegram*, August 22, 2011; Keith A. Erekson, *Bridging the Gap between K-12 and College Readiness Standards in Texas: Recommendations for U.S. History* (Arlington: Texas Faculty Collaborative for Social Studies, 2011).
17. Ken Paxton, "SBOE, Thanks for Social Studies Curriculum Update," *Texas Insider*, May 27, 2010; Jonathan Saenz, "What's in the New Social Studies Standards? Just State the Facts," *Texas Legislative Update: A Liberty Institute Blog*, May 28, 2010, http://texaslegislativeupdate.wordpress.com/2010/05/28/whats-in-texas-social-studies-just-state-the-facts/; Kelley Shackelford, "Texas Textbook Critics Just Can't Handle the Truth," June 4, 2010, http://www.foxnews.com/opinion/2010/06/04/kelly-shackelford-texas-textbook-social-studies-standards-boycott-delay/; Dan Flynn, "Liberals Incensed Because SBOE Succeeded," *Texas Insider*, June 24, 2010; Lauri Lebo, "Don McLeroy to Receive Eagle Forum Patriot Award," *Religion Dispatches*, June 2, 2010; Schlafly named in TEKS.11.c.10.E (8/23/10).
18. Steve Thompson, "Two Civil Rights Groups Claim Texas Education Discriminates against Minorities," *Dallas Morning News*, December 21, 2010; Mary Turna, "SBOE's Bradley Calls Civil Rights Groups' Accusations 'Reverse Racism,'" *American Independent*, December 22, 2010; Michelle D. Anderson, "Report Gives a Majority of States Poor Grades on History Standards," *Education Week*, February 16, 2011; Lauri Lebo, "Fundamentalist-Led Texas History Standards Get 'D' from Conservative Think Tank," *Religion Dispatches*, February 21, 2011; Bill Bumpas, "Liberals Continue to Rip Standards," *One News New*, March 1, 2011; Morgan Smith, "Texas Schools, Publishers Adjust to New Power Shift," *Texas Tribune*, September 29, 2011.

Figure 2 Cold War roots of the recent debate
The roots of the recent debate in Texas can be traced to broader cultural and political differences that took shape during the Cold War. Grassroots conservatives in Texas developed means of evaluating textbooks that were imitated in school debates throughout the nation, including in West Virginia in the 1970s (pictured) and over national standards in the 1990s.

CHAPTER 2

"As Texas Goes, So Goes the Nation"
Conservatism and Culture Wars in the Lone Star State

Gene B. Preuss

"We're in an all-out moral and spiritual civil war for the soul of America, and the record of American history is right at the heart of it," explained Reverend Peter Marshall, one of the reviewers appointed by the Texas State Board of Education (SBOE), when asked about the proposed revisions of the Texas social studies standards in the summer of 2009.[1] The battle for the hearts and souls of Texas schoolchildren would be the minister's last battle. Peter John Marshall, son of famous Christian missionaries Peter and Catherine Marshall, succumbed to a heart attack just over a year later, yet long enough to see the resolution of one of the most vigorous battles in the recent culture wars: how history will be taught in Texas public schools.

In one sense, Marshall's death soon after the SBOE adopted the proposed revisions of history standards parallels the death of William Jennings Bryan just after the close of the Scopes trial in Dayton, Tennessee, 85 years earlier. Like the Tennessee trial, the atmosphere in Austin became a media circus that drew national attention to what some perceived as a religious battle over Texas history standards. Like Bryan's role in the Scopes "Monkey Trial," in which he stood against teaching the theory of evolution in public schools, many believe that Marshall and his followers were fighting to preserve the Christian heritage that shaped the nation. Yet many educators and professional historians believe that traditionalists like Marshall clung to a mythological image of the past that ignores much of the historical scholarship of the past forty years. This chapter traces the historical antecedents of 2009–10 SBOE social studies standards controversy to the history of a larger culture war in Texas and the battle's significance to American history. In order to reach this goal, this chapter will examine how public education became seen as a safeguard for American democracy, how the struggles over civil rights and religion in schools became battlegrounds for social conservatives, and how teaching students a politicized version of American history has taken on an almost religious zeal. The implications of the decision reach beyond the media attention it received and the strong personalities that colored the news reports. The immediate impact of the standards the SBOE adopted in 2010 will shape the curriculum influencing how millions of schoolchildren will learn history as they make their way through the Lone Star State's public school system for at least a decade.

Shaping the Texas History Curriculum Battle

In Texas public schools, "social studies" designates a series of courses, including economics, government, and geography, but most especially history. Texas schoolchildren take Texas history courses in the fourth and seventh grades, and US history from the colonial period through the Civil War in eighth grade. High school students must take classes in US history since reconstruction, US government, world history, and world geography. Economics courses stressing the importance of the free enterprise system are also required of high school students. Imbedded so thoroughly across the public school curriculum, history became a convenient political battleground. Even before the revisions began, some already believed the history standards tended to stress conservative values. Some conservatives wanted the revisions to pay more attention to political heroes such as Newt Gingrich, Phyllis Schlafly, and politically conservative lobbying groups. Yet even conservative members of the SBOE warned of bias. "It is hard to believe that a majority of the writing team would approve of such wording. It's not even a representative selection of the conservative movement, and it is inappropriate," argued board member Terri Leo. Still another board conservative, Ken Mercer, said "I think, at the end of the day, we will want the young students to be able to identify what's conservative, what's their advocacy and who are the conservative groups, individuals and leaders. And what is liberal in contrast."[2] Political conservatives in Texas hoped that the 2008 presidential election would draw more religious conservative voters to the polls because the election ballot also included 7 of the 15 seats on the SBOE that year. Since the SBOE has the responsibility for selecting the textbooks that the state's public schools may assign to students, conservatives have long been concerned about controlling the board. During the Republican primary campaign earlier that year, one of Arkansas governor Mike Huckabee's Texas supporters hoped that the election of more social and political conservatives on the SBOE would protect Texas schoolchildren from liberal indoctrination.[3]

Ultimately, three concerns emerged in the Texas history curriculum battle: (1) whether the United States would be treated as a traditional or a multicultural society, (2) the role of Christianity in American society, and (3) a resurgence of the Cold War battle between capitalism and other "isms." These three threads are interwoven through Texas's history curriculum wars and the history of Texas public education since the mid-twentieth century. How did we get to this point? What forces have combined to create an environment hostile enough to nurture the type of ideological battle represented by the Texas history standards conflict? It would be easy to dismiss this confrontation as the result of the larger-than-life braggadocio of the Texan personality, but the roots of the conflict are deep and tangled. History has played a role in the culture wars of the twentieth century for many years. Certainly, the recent battle that unfolded in the Lone Star State was not the first time school history standards raised hackles on both sides. For example, in the mid-1990s, former National Endowment for the Humanities chair Lynn Cheney began a very public criticism of the National Standards for History as indicative of general waning of knowledge about American history.[4] But concerns over a decline in American historical knowledge can be traced much farther back.

In 1943, the *New York Times* reported that a survey of some seven thousand students in 36 colleges and universities across the nation revealed a shameful ignorance of the nation's past. The survey revealed that only 6 percent of college freshmen could correctly identify the original 13 colonies, just 7 percent recognized prominent railroad industrialists, and a mere 16 percent knew that Thomas Jefferson had been president of the United States, authorized the Louisiana Purchase, or wrote the Declaration of Independence. In response, Hugh Russell Fraser, chair of the Committee of American History and a US Office of Education official, complained that American historical knowledge began to decline the day in 1924 when the superintendent of schools in Denver, Colorado, replaced an American history course with one on social science.[5] The battles in the larger culture war over how history is taught in the public schools originated in World War II. Many feared that the growing power of the federal government during the New Deal represented "creeping socialism" in American society. And during World War II, some educators argued that in order to prevent the same extremist forces that overtook Europe following the worldwide economic crisis in the 1920s and 1930s from overtaking the United States, American schoolchildren should receive more instruction in American civics and history in order to prevent the encroachment of various "isms" from infiltrating American society and culture. Some worried that these dangerous ideas already had a foothold on the American republic.

The emergence of the Soviet Union as the dominant power in Europe threatened even the casual observer. In April 1949, the United States and Western European nations signed the NATO (North Atlantic Treaty Organization) alliance as result of the Berlin Blockade and Airlift crisis of 1948–49 in order to check the expansion of Soviet control over Eastern European nations. Moreover, when the Russians tested atomic weapons in August 1949, the Chinese Communists took control of their nation a few months later with the victory of Communist forces, and North Korea attacked South Korea the next year, most Americans were convinced that democracy was being threatened on a worldwide scale. Others worried that the United States' membership in the United Nations surrendered American sovereignty to a world government. In the October 1947 issue of *The School Executive*, Abel Hanson, the superintendent of schools in Elizabeth, New Jersey, suggested that schools could be used as the "front line against communism." In his article, Hanson explains that students should be properly educated about communism and its threat to the free world. He cautioned that while many confused reform with communism, they were misinformed. He advocated for a proper education about communism, saying that it would help prevent the spread of the ideology. He stated, "Let it be understood at the outset that freedom and the hope it holds for the future is well worth defending and that a spiritual and intellectual bulwark must be erected against Communism."[6] Hanson's call for better education to fight communism was not the method that prevailed in the United States or in Texas.

In February 1950, Wisconsin senator Joseph McCarthy announced to the Republican women of Wheeling, West Virginia, that avowed Communists and "fellow-travelers" infested the federal government; many Americans agreed and sought ways of eradicating them. Many Texans agreed with McCarthy's sentiments, if not his methods. Wealthy Texans were avid supporters of the anti-Communist movement, and many contributed to McCarthy's campaigns, much as they had supported Texas's own Communist hunter, Martin Dies, a few years earlier. In Houston, conservative groups, such as the local chapter of the Minute Women, were very well organized and actively sought to ferret out communism. In 1951, the Texas Communist Control Law required all state employees, including schoolteachers and other school employees, to sign a notarized oath that they were "not, and have never been a member of the Communist Party," or for the previous five years knowingly been a member of any "totalitarian, fascist, communist or subversive" organization.[7] The US Attorney General and the Texas Department of Public Safety compiled a lengthy list of suspect organizations that fit these categories.

Lawmakers also encouraged patriotism and religion as measures against communist subversion. When, in 1947, the Supreme Court ruled in *Everson v. Board of Education* that the First Amendment constituted a "wall of separation between church and state," Congress reacted by inserting the phrase "under God" in the Pledge of Allegiance and adopted "In God We Trust" as the nation's motto and ordered it to be printed on all currency. In a letter to the editor of the *Houston Chronicle*, one man argued, "The overwhelming majority of the American people all along was always in favor of religion having the right of way," with some limitations. He condemned those who sought to remove religion from schools because that was "where religion could do the greatest amount of good." He concluded, "When it comes to our public schools, they want to rule out all spiritual guidance. How unreasonable and how inconsistent such objections are!" In West Texas, conservative rancher and historian J. Evetts Haley encouraged Texas Tech University to implement a mandatory six-hour American history requirement for all students. Haley was able to parlay a generous donation by a West Texas banker into the establishment of the short-lived Institute of Americanism, which he directed. Later, he successfully lobbied the state legislature to implement a six-hour American history requirement for all Texas college students.[8]

Like Haley, most Americans believed that if the United States wanted to win the battle against communist subversion, it had to inculcate Americanism in the hearts and minds of students. In 1953, the US Senate's Committee on the Judiciary's Subcommittee to Investigate the Administration of the Internal Security Act and Other Internal Security Laws published a report titled "Subversive Influences in the Educational Process." William Jenner, the committee's chair, stated, "If a totalitarian organization such as the evidence shows to exist in our Nation's schools is allowed to flourish in our institutions of learning, unexposed and unchecked, not only will our youth be infused with seeds of their own and the Nation's destruction." To Jenner and many others, the committee hearings uncovered a vast clandestine network of communists and other subversives working within the nation's education system. Jenner warned, "World Communist leaders have made schools and colleges of the United States a target of infiltration and activity as part of their program to destroy the United States" and "Communist teachers use their positions in the classroom and in extracurricular activities to subvert students and other teachers and the public to promote the objectives of communism." The committee's report was an amazing example of circular logic, self-celebration, and self-justification. They did not uncover many communists, but they did suspect "an organized conspiracy [with] an influence far more extensive than [the number of actual communists] would indicate." The committee explained that actual communists were hard to identify because "penetration of the schools is becoming more covert, and Communist teachers are being organized into a secret underground more difficult to detect." In fact, the report stated, "Teachers, students, and educational authorities, public and private, do not today have the means to identify, unassisted, secret members of the Communist Party or to trace their conspiratorial activities." Instead, only legislative investigative panels, like Jenner's committee, could uncover these plots and give "authorities the evidence by which some hidden Communists could be removed from teaching positions." In practice, any teacher brought before such investigative boards was already suspect, and any refusal to cooperate was considered an indication of guilt. "A teacher who invokes his privilege against incrimination rather than deny membership in the Communist organization," the committee asserted, "violates his trust and forfeits his right to shape the character of our youth."[9]

Conflating Conservatism, Civil Rights, and Religion

In addition to the vast communist conspiracy, a series of threats from within the American government soon shook the very foundations of American culture. In the mid-1950s, when the Supreme Court ruled against segregation in public education in the *Brown v. Board of Education* decisions, many began to decry "activist judges." Within a few years, the African American struggle against discriminatory Jim Crow laws spread across the south. Protests, freedom rides, and sit-ins brought unwanted media attention to southern culture, often resulting in violent backlashes from whites. In Mansfield, Texas, when the school board approved integrating the high school by enrolling three black students, white protesters demonstrated, made threats, and even hung three effigies of the students. Traditionalists viewed prointegrationist views, prolabor sentiments, UN support, and government programs like the New Deal and Fair Deal as dangerous. They saw these issues and other so-called liberal sentiments as communist-inspired, or worse, communist-led.

In 1957, the Texas Tech board of regents dismissed three professors, accusing them of numerous offenses against traditional culture. One *Houston Chronicle* letter to the editor congratulated the Tech regents for "giving the 'heave ho' to the left-wing, un-American, radical, pro-integration, egg-headed teachers."[10] Not only did many applaud the removal of schoolteachers and college professors who supported these causes, but they wanted to make sure that textbooks were free of their influences. In May 1948, the State Board of Education expressed concerns over a history and geography textbook adoption because the texts opposed "our way of life in the United States." According to newspaper reports, the texts offended members of the SBOE because they "glorified Russia as one of the greatest countries in the world, as having accomplished miraculous development, as having composed racial differences and as having accomplished some of the world's most 'amazing' results in industry and manufacturing." Board member Maco Stewart of Galveston exclaimed, "I was against these adoptions at the start and now I am fully vindicated." The director of the state textbook division, Herman A. Glass, tried to explain to the members that the publisher had already made revisions to the texts, but he did not have the changes available at the board meeting. He also pointed out that the books had been written before problems had intensified between the United States and the USSR.¹¹ Almost a decade later, concern about communist influences in schools led to a confrontation in Houston, which resulted in Houston School Superintendent William Moreland's resignation. The dispute arose when conservatives wanted to remove any textbook from the classrooms that hinted at "one-worldism." In the 1957–58 school year, the school board removed world geography and history courses and replaced them with courses focusing on Houston and Texas history and geography. One school board member warned that the result would be a "bunch of little Davy Crocketts and little Daughters of the Republic" in the classrooms. In an obvious comparison to Soviet totalitarianism, the former president of the University of Houston said that the new Texas-centric curriculum signaled a "cotton curtain" was descending across the state. Defending the new policy, the new superintendent, who was a member of the White Citizens' Council, countered that the board was "just drifting back to the fundamentals."¹²

As court-ordered challenges to the traditional social order in public education continued, conservatives were poised to challenge these threats to what they considered traditional Americanism in the classroom. The most influential combatants in the Texas textbook wars in the early 1960s were Mel and Norma Gabler. The spark that led to their decades-long crusade to root out what they considered inaccuracies in textbooks occurred in 1961 when they examined their son Jim's history textbook. They believed the book ignored "individual and state rights and responsibilities." When they read Lincoln's Gettysburg address, they found the words "under God" omitted from the text. They sought advice from a group called Texans for America that focused its efforts on rooting out any communist affiliations of history textbook authors. The Gablers soon began publicizing their own efforts and the efforts of Texans for America on a Shreveport, Louisiana, radio station call-in show. They mass-mailed a twenty-page document critical of recent textbook adoptions in Texas, and in late 1962, they aired their concerns at the state textbook committee hearings. One historian noted, "The Gablers soon became the most recognized conservative voices among the petitioners." More important, the Gablers and their associates became a constant fixture at the SBOE textbook hearings for more than four decades. In addition to their persistence, "with the aid of extensive press coverage, the Gablers brought the anti-communist crusade to a new level in Texas education beginning in 1964."¹³

The Gablers were poised to challenge nontraditional family values, multiculturalism, un-Americanism, and—as the Supreme Court declared prayer and Bible reading in classrooms unconstitutional in 1962 and 1963—secular humanism. The Gablers believed that "our basic American values are being thrown out the door," and they maintained a constant vigil against what they perceived as ideological threats that attempted to influence Texas schoolchildren.¹⁴

In May 1963, Norma Gabler told an audience at the Lovett Memorial Library in Pampa, Texas, that parents and teachers shared responsibility for their children's education. She said, "Parents should not expect the schoolteachers and churches to take the full responsibility for instilling moral values, love of country, and love of home and family in their children." She displayed 16 textbooks that she felt contained material that parents should be concerned about. For example, she noted that in one history book, *Uncle Tom's Cabin* was allocated more space than Francis Scott Key or Nathan Hale. She also stated, "Socialism is preferred in most of the economics books my husband and I have examined," although she provided no explanation of how they arrived at this conclusion.[15]

Gabler denied that she or her husband were blaming the textbook selection committees, teachers, or school administrators. To the contrary, she admitted that they were all very busy people who understandably did not have time to examine all the textbooks in detail. "All we are trying to do," she said, "is to have parents, businessmen and the general public to cooperate with and have objective discussion with school boards, teachers and school administrators about textbooks used in the schools." That October, the Gablers called for the State Textbook Committee to reject five economics textbooks because the books' contents represented a "trend in textbooks to bring about an acceptance of socialism in this country."[16]

Education historian Diane Ravitch explains the tremendous influence the Gablers had on textbook companies: "Since the 1960s, any publisher that expected to win adoption of their textbooks in Texas had to anticipate that the Gablers would review the contents and values in their books and teachers' guides on a line-by-line basis." Ravitch concluded that the detailed criticism leveled by the Gablers and others resulted in publishers censoring the materials in textbooks. "The Gablers knew that their influence in the adoption process would reverberate among like-minded conservatives nationally, and they maximized their opportunities to demand and win revisions."[17]

In June 1970, in response to changes in society influenced by the civil rights movement, the Texas Education Agency (TEA) issued a position statement regarding textbook selection that reflected the multicultural nature of Texas society: "The confluence of many cultures and cultural conflict have been characteristic of American life throughout our history. They have been powerful influences in structuring our social system, enriching our national heritage and creating some of our most critical problems. Our national future will be greatly influenced by our understanding of our cultural diversity and resolution of the problems it creates."[18]

The document suggested that the public school social studies curriculum and selected textbooks "stress, wherever relevant, the contributions of individuals from many groups to our national development and the enrichment of our heritage by influences from all cultures represented in our population." The agency expected that children from the diverse ethnic and cultural groups in Texas would be able to "identify with the whole national historical and cultural pattern, with justifiable pride in the contributions made by [their] group, or individuals from it." But, the circular cautioned, it was not enough simply to emphasize cultural differences and conflicts in social studies instruction because "concentration on cultural conflict, to the exclusion of the benefits of cultural confluence, is prejudicial. It is not enough to point out the need of certain minorities for a better image. Children from these groups are entitled to the information which will make that image improvement possible. It is erroneous to identify cultural conflict solely in terms of color; it has arisen within color groups as well as between them. It is suggested that cultural conflicts is a national problem which should be of equal concern to us as Americans, rather than solely as members of a special group, and that an approach from this point of view offers the best hope for resolution."[19] The TEA document also suggested ways for schoolteachers to implement these guidelines into their daily lesson plans.

Later the agency sponsored a series of conferences to expose administrators, school board members, and counselors to the various cultures represented in the Texas population in order to change education leaders' perceptions of diverse populations and help them to "deal positively with bilingual education, racial integration, and the implementation of court orders."[20] One conference presenter, psychologist Melvin P. Sikes, further explained that "understanding other cultures is not enough," that it was only the beginning of the process. "We must not use this conference to pay cognizance to the fact that we are a multicultural society and then go on with business as usual. New curricular offerings must not say to the student, 'We are now recognizing you and adding you to the history of this country.' Rather it must say, 'You are an integral part of American history, and we have found the courage to recognize you as Americans and as having helped to make America an outstanding country.'"[21]

Sikes, a University of Texas psychologist who directed the Houston Cooperative Crime Prevention program in the late 1960s as an effort to promote better relations between the Houston police department and members of ethnic minorities in the city, stated that the conferences must "serve eventually to remove the question mark that nonwhite students place at the end of the Pledge of Allegiance to the flag."[22]

Like the TEA, the Gablers developed their own bias guidelines, but they were opposed to such cultural awareness. "They opposed stories that encouraged permissive child rearing or portrayed rules and laws as unimportant or criticized the national or traditional values," Ravitch states. Many of the Gablers' concerns about the content of textbooks were understandable. According to

Ravitch, they opposed readings in which "bad behavior went unpunished." They also objected to passages in texts that they believed emphasized conflict, uncomfortable feelings, and violence. Beyond these topics, which many might agree should be cautioned for young readers, the Gablers' protests also included more subjective content, including "behavioral techniques like 'questions with no firm answers,' role-playing and sensitivity training; nor did they favor books that taught 'humanism,' sex-education, 'one-worldism,' 'women's lib,' or the occult." But the way the Gablers identified these topics was questionable. For example, in 1982 Norma Gabler protested a paragraph in a textbook that described the benefits of insulin for diabetics because the passage "is instilling in student minds that the term *drug* refers to a beneficial product."[23]

The Gablers influence reached beyond the state's borders. In 1974, a particularly violent battle over textbooks erupted in Kanawha County, West Virginia. Alleging that some of the books the school board approved were "anti-Christian, anti-American, anti-authority, depressing, and negative," a battle over the school board's stand to uphold its decision lasted almost a year and was marked by school shutdowns, dynamiting of the school board building, firebombing of an elementary school, intimidation from the Ku Klux Klan, and parental removal of children from the schools. The conflict revealed deep divisions between members of the community, the county, and even churches. As the controversy grew in the Kanawha community, a group of ten pastors of various denominations sent the school board a statement acknowledging that "though anyone could raise an objection to one or more specific points, the whole program shows a great respect for the students of this County and their need to understand and communicate in the real world in which they live." The ministers explained, "Any treatment, especially in the schools, of questions like war and peace, racism—black and white, religion, patriotism, etc., is bound to raise disagreements and stir emotional responses. We are convinced, however, that these matters must be discussed openly if our students are to be exposed to the great variety of issues that characterize our modern society. We know of no way to stimulate the growth of our youth if we insulate them from the real issues. We feel this program will help our students to think intelligently about their lives and our society."[24] When an inquiry panel from the National Education Agency interviewed participants in the protests, however, they found that parents did not like the "textbooks' use of open-ended questions to encourage independent thought and analysis on the part of the students." More important, parents felt "that students should not be asked what they think or how they should behave; they should be told what to think and how to behave."[25]

The organizers of the Kanawha protests were influenced by the Gablers. "When I knew the book selection was coming up last spring, I got in touch with the Gablers. They told me some of the things to watch for in the books."

Indeed, by the early 1970s, the Gablers had considerable influence across the nation. As one observer noted, "They achieved hero status in the eyes of thousands of concerned parents, fundamentalist religious leaders, and conservatives of the sort now identified with the New Right." They were successful; they took a kitchen table project and created an organization, Educational Research Analysts, with a paid staff, which distributed textbook analysis materials to other concerned parents across the country. They were frequent guests on national religious and news television programs and became a significant force in the religious right. Although the Gablers should not be associated with the violence at Kanawha, it is clear that they influenced the protests.[26]

History and the Orthodoxy of the American Civil Religion

In December 2004, just two weeks before his ninetieth birthday, Mel Gabler fell and suffered a head injury. He died two days later. In the summer of 2007, Norma Gabler passed away. Although the Gablers are gone, the organization they founded, Educational Research Analysts, continues its work. The organization no longer delivers its testimony against textbooks at the SBOE hearings. Instead, it sends board members its reports through standard mail and email. The organization's newsletters and reports also influence others who do appear before the board. Educational Research Analysts understands the influence it has on the public school textbook market. On its website, it proclaims, "Our reviews have national relevance because Texas state-adopts textbooks and buys so many that publishers write them to Texas standards and sell them across the country."[27] The Gablers' influence beyond the Lone Star State helps illustrate that the controversies over textbooks and school instruction are not isolated to Texas. The 2009–10 Texas history standards war was not a solitary or enigmatic event, far removed from the concerns or understanding of Americans in general. Instead, it represents the latest incident in a long series of battles that date back to the origins of the Cold War more than seventy years ago. Neither were the confrontations between the traditionalists and iconoclasts unique to Texas; rather they were but one example of cultural battles that have raged across the nation for as many years.

In 1970, syndicated cartoonist Jules Feiffer published an illustration that captured the feelings of many who were concerned about the changing views of American history. In the drawing, a heavy-jowled man in a hard hat explains how he learned history. "When I went to school I learned George Washington never told a lie, slaves were happy on the plantation, the men who opened the West were giants, and we won every war because God was on our side." Now, however, the figure complains, his child "learns George Washington was a slave owner, slaves hated slavery, the men who opened the West committed genocide, and the wars we won were victories for U.S. imperialism." He concludes, "No wonder my kid's not an American. They're teaching him some other country's history." Although intended as a humorous commentary on how social changes were reflected and interpreted in history textbooks beginning in the 1960s and 1970s, there were probably many people who identified with the man in the hard hat. Indeed, when the television show *All in the Family* debuted in CBS in January 1971, it was more than the generational conflict facing the Bunkers and their daughter and son-in-law that viewers connected with. It was also that many Americans longed for the simpler times reflected in the song that Archie and Edith crooned in the show's opening sequence, "Those Were the Days."

But the Texas history controversy represents more than nostalgia. Although many would portray the battle over the state's history curriculum as a modern-day Scopes trial, the adversaries in textbook controversies are not simply teachers versus parents or traditionalists versus modernists. As the Gablers' involvement in the West Virginia case illustrates, the textbook battles are not merely a case of outsiders seeking to promote an agenda, but successful textbook critics assisting other demonstrators to further a similar cause. We also often ignore the political leverage that these battles can wield. Shortly after the Scopes trial, Chicago mayor "Big Bill" Thompson launched a successful campaign to oust the city school superintendent, William McAndrew. The mayor accused the superintendent of being un-American because McAndrew refused to have schoolchildren make donations to refurbish the *USS Constitution* and because he recommended "history text books which contained pro-British propaganda and which omitted the name and exploits of many . . . heroes of the American Revolutionary War." The brouhaha led Walter Lippmann to write, "There is no higher loyalty for the teacher and the scholar than loyalty to the truth." Yet when Lippmann compared the Scopes trial and the firing of Superintendent McAndrew, he observed, "This principle is under attack today in all sections of the country" by the clergy and by patriots. "The attack of the churchmen is aimed chiefly at the teaching of the biological sciences, the attack of the patriots at the teaching of history," he explained. The authors of a book on school textbook battles note, "If American history and civics textbooks have become a battleground, it is because they now serve as the prayer-books of the United States' civil religion."[28]

In 1995, the Texas legislature rewrote the Texas Education Code (TEC) in an effort to stop the intensity of the state's textbook wars. Because the SBOE could reject textbooks arbitrarily, one proposed revision was to allow local districts to select textbooks, instead of resting the power solely in the hands of the State Board of Education. In the end, the revised statutes called for placing textbooks eligible for adoption into two lists, those books that conformed to the SBOE's curricular guidelines and those that failed to meet some of the guidelines. Local districts have the option of selecting a textbook from either the conforming or nonconforming list. Furthermore, a local district can even select a book that the SBOE had rejected, but the state would only pay a portion of the cost.[29] A few months before Texas lawmakers began working on the TEC revisions, Lynn Cheney, wife of future vice president Richard Cheney and former chair of the National Endowment for the Humanities, castigated proposed national history standards as outlined by the National Standards and Improvement Council. In an editorial in the *Wall Street Journal*, Cheney asked readers to "imagine an outline for the teaching of American history in which George Washington makes only a fleeting appearance and is never described as our first president." Instead of focusing on the important events, Cheney asserted, the standards focused on promoting liberal causes "in which the foundings of the Sierra Club and the National Organization for Women are considered noteworthy events, but the first gathering of the U.S. Congress is not." Instead of focusing enough attention on what might be called traditional history, Cheney complained, "not a single one of the 31 standards mentions the Constitution," and she concluded that "the authors tend to save their unqualified admiration for people, places, and events that are politically correct." Echoing methods similar to those the Gablers used for decades, she counted references to historical events and people, complaining that McCarthyism and the Ku Klux Klan were mentioned frequently and that African American Harriet Tubman was mentioned more times than "two white males who were contemporaries of Tubman, Ulysses S. Grant and Robert E. Lee, [who] get one and zero mentions, respectively" while "Alexander Graham Bell, Thomas Edison, Albert Einstein, Jonas Salk and the Wright brothers make no appearance at all."

Cheney blamed the "politically correct" biases of the document on the efforts of professional historians in the American Historical Association, but moreover she stated the standards reflected a growing trend toward liberalism that resulted in the 1992 presidential election of William Jefferson Clinton. She claimed an unnamed member of the National Council for History Standards stated that the 1992 election "unleashed the forces of political correctness." She went on to state, again quoting the anonymous source, that the political climate allowed pressure groups, such as African Americans, minorities, and others "pursuing the revisionist agenda" to freely demonstrate "their 'great hatred for traditional history.'" In her commentary, Cheney implied that the National Standards for United States History were the result of Goals 2000, the Clinton administration's attempt to establish national standards. In fact, however, the idea for national education standards did not originate with the Clinton presidency, but were the result of a call issued by the George H. W. Bush administration in 1990 at a meeting of the National Governors Association in Charlottesville, Virginia. Nevertheless, Cheney warned readers that although the standards were presented as a suggestion, conservatives had "every reason to believe that the certification process put in place by the Clinton Administration will lead to the adoption of the proposed standards more or less intact—as official knowledge—with the result that much that is significant in our past will begin to disappear from our schools." Moreover, she also portrayed any attempt at revisions as a quixotic task that would pit concerned citizens "against an academic establishment that revels in the kind of politicized history that characterizes much of the National Standards."[30]

Beyond the political implications of the teaching of American history, the textbook wars also have a tremendous financial aspect. As the *Times* of London stated, the beliefs of the conservatives on the SBOE "would matter little" except that the board "oversees the biggest textbook-procurement programme in the United States." In 2002, the *New York Times* reported that Texas allocated $700 million to purchase social studies textbooks. The centralized selection process for textbooks made Texas the largest purchaser of school textbooks in the nation, wielding tremendous buying power in the $4.5 billion textbook market. During the hearings before the SBOE that year, the liberal *Texas Observer* repeated the old caveat, "Publishers have thus learned to tread carefully before the watchful eye of volunteer readers . . . who, with a few well-placed objections, can make the difference between a textbook's adoption or rejection, not just in Texas, but also in the rest of the nation, which tends to follow the lead of the larger markets." That year, more than 250 volunteers read for nine conservative organizations that aimed to root out controversial and inaccurate statements in history textbooks up for adoption by the SBOE. The field director of one of those organizations, Citizens for a Sound Economy, remarked to the *New York Times*, "What we adopt in Texas is what the rest of the country gets." With its tremendous buying power mandating how textbooks are written for the rest of the nation, few states can overcome the weight of Texas's influence. California, however, could challenge Texas's dominance of the textbook market, but by 2010 California was experiencing tremendous state debt, so its ability to counteract Texas's textbook demands had been stymied. A commentator for the *San Francisco Chronicle* mourned, "Alas, if California weren't so utterly broke, slashing education budgets and shutting down schools, maybe our fair state could launch a counter-attack, demand some reasonably accurate historic revisions in those selfsame texts."[31]

Self-censorship by publishers is another result of the textbook battles. Ravitch, who served in the Department of Education during the George H. W. Bush administration, wrote of how she was named to the National Assessment Governing Board (NAGB) by President Clinton in 1998. When the NAGB took control of the National Assessment of Educational Progress, a national test that evaluates how students across the nation score in a variety of subjects, she wondered why the publisher subsequently rejected several test questions the NAGB had approved. The publisher casually explained that older literature and even many classics were difficult to include because "everything written before 1970 was either gender biased or racially biased." She discovered that the textbook publishers, test makers, and other companies who provide our schools' educational materials write strict guidelines dictated by political and consumer pressures from the left and right that effectively result in censorship. Ravitch concludes, "A new status quo emerged in which the textbook industry and the major adoption states became comfortable with one another. They shared the same bias guidelines, which quieted the critics, left and right." The result was an arrangement eerily reminiscent of Aesop's fable of the old man and the boy riding a donkey through a village: in trying to please critics, the donkey drowned. "Feminists," she wrote, "ethnic and cultural minorities, people with disabilities, and the older population had no grounds for complaint, because they had won representation. Right-wingers were generally satisfied, because the topics that angered them were excluded." Unfortunately, in the end, by pleasing everyone the textbooks pleased no one because interesting topics are removed from texts altogether.[32]

Ironically, because of self-censorship by textbook publishers, modern-day textbook battles have more in common with the Scopes trial than meets the eye. Although the Tennessee Supreme Court overturned Scopes's conviction and only two states considering similar laws prohibiting evolution eventually passed those laws, in the end most biology textbooks removed the theory of evolution from their pages to avoid controversy. Despite the fact that Scopes won the battle, in the end the traditionalists triumphed because the textbook publishers wanted to avoid controversy in order to sell books.

If stories are removed from textbooks to avoid political controversies, what remains in the history texts our schoolchildren read? In 1995, sociologist James W. Loewen wrote an eye-opening analysis of American history textbooks, *Lies My Teacher Told Me*. He evaluated how 12 of the most popular history textbooks used in public schools presented the past. When he revised his analysis in 2007, however, there were only six books to consider because of publisher consolidation. After 12 years he arrived at the same conclusion: history textbooks are boring to students, and the students hate American history classes because reading history textbooks is the main activity in history classes. He argues that the books substitute trivia and minutia for substantial historical analysis. "The books are huge," Loewen writes, "so no publisher will lose an adoption because a book has left out a detail of concern to a particular geographical area or group." One textbook wanted students to learn 840 "main ideas," 310 "skill builders," 890 "terms and names," and 466 "critical thinking" questions. All of this, he argues, leads teachers to "fall back on one main idea: to memorize the terms for the test on that chapter, and forget them to clear the synapses for the next chapter. No wonder so many high school graduates cannot remember in which century the Civil War was fought!"[33]

Just as in textbooks, the detailed social studies standards finally adopted by the State Board of Education in August 2010 have been criticized for being overly detailed and far too complex to be useful in teaching American history.[34] Loewen's observation about overly detailed history textbooks and historians' concerns about Texas's overly detailed standards are self-perpetuating aspects of the same problem, however, because the history textbooks students read in public schools across America are determined by the choices made by the Texas State Board of Education, which in turn selects books that conform to the social studies standards it writes.

As Texas Goes, So Goes the Nation

Does self-censorship affect what our schoolchildren are learning in their history courses? One observer notes that because publishers do not want a book that will be rejected by Texas or California, they will take measures to ensure that a book will not be rejected again. "Thus, discrimination among textbooks by states like Texas and California based on the viewpoints expressed in those texts has the practical effect of silencing that author's viewpoint from being heard in any state or school across the nation." Although the SBOE may reject a textbook only because it contains factual errors, what constitutes a "factual error" has been questioned. In 1999, the SBOE rejected *Environmental Science: Creating a Sustainable Future*, sixth edition, a science text by Daniel Chiras. Chiras believed that the SBOE gave undue consideration to two conservative groups who brought last-minute criticism against his book the day before the board voted on his book. Chiras sued, accusing the SBOE of conspiring with the protest groups against his textbook. The district court found that the "textbook did not accurately reflect what [the SBOE] perceived to be the traditional, conservative values of most Texans" and dismissed the case.[35] When the plaintiffs appealed to the Fifth Circuit Court, the justices dismissed the case on the grounds that public school textbooks constituted government speech, and thus did not have to conform to First Amendment liberties. Based upon these broad interpretations of "factual errors," the SBOE therefore can simply reject any book that it does not agree with.

In February 2011, the conservative Thomas Fordham Institute issued a dismal appraisal of state history education standards across the United States. In the Forward to *The State of State U.S. History Standards 2011*, Chester E. Finn and Kathleen Porter-Magee write, "We have mounting evidence that American education is . . . creating a generation of students who don't understand or value our own nation's history."³⁶ Yet the reason behind the low rankings of state public school history standards was not the content in textbooks, but that most states gave only lip service to evaluating and assessing their history requirements, leading the writers to conclude that "few states and school systems take U.S. history seriously. So why should students?" In evaluating state history standards, the authors of the report state, "A majority of states' standards are mediocre-to-awful. In fact the average grade across *all* states is barely a D." In fact, although the poor rating was not because of information in the texts, Texas's ratings still dropped from a C in 2003 to a D in 2011 largely because of the battle over the state's history standards.³⁷

The report criticized the SBOE for its political biases and for its dismissal of the work of professional historians and academics in favor of political and religious pundits. Instead of trying to correct what its members perceived as left-leaning ideology in the old standards, the SBOE simply swapped one ideology for another, the report stated. The report's authors predict this will serve to extend the culture wars by playing "straight into the left-wing victim narrative, strengthening its grip in other states and threatening the progress that has been made in breaking its hold. A reinvigorated left will then further goad the right, leading to a vicious cycle of accusations and politics at the expense of education." In the end, the report states, "The chief casualties are historical comprehension, and the good of the students themselves—which is always the case when education becomes an ideological weapon." When informed about the Fordham Institute's scathing report, SBOE chair Gail Lowe replied that the low grade was "based on misinformation." She justified the decisions the board made, stating that the institute "obviously does not know that the Texas Education Code requires us to teach the free enterprise system and its benefits. That's the primary reason the free enterprise system is emphasized throughout the document, rather than just relegated to a high school economics class."³⁸

Although the history standards controversy that occupied Texans during the fall and spring of the 2009–10 school year makes for good headlines, pithy quotes, and fodder for late-night comedians, what difference does it make what Texas teaches about history? In the end, the answer is, quite a bit. One of the SBOE members said in frustration, "History is written by the majority in control."³⁹ Who owns history? Who writes history? Who decides what will be taught? The answers to these questions will continue to be quarreled over for years to come. It would be presumptuous to think that we will be able to solve these issues when people around the globe have fought over them for millennia. In the meantime, the children affected will be those who attend school in Texas as well as schoolchildren across the nation.

Notes

1. Stephanie Simon, "The Culture Wars' New Front: U.S. History Classes in Texas," *Wall Street Journal*, July 14, 2009.
2. Gary Scharrer, "History's First Draft: Newt Gingrich But No Liberals," *Houston Chronicle*, August 20, 2009.
3. Hilary Hylton, "Huckabee's Texas Evolution," *Time*, February 29, 2008.
4. Gary B. Nash, Charlotte Crabtree, and Ross E. Dunn, *History on Trial: Culture Wars and the Teaching of the Past* (New York: Vintage Books, 2000), xiii.
5. Benjamin Fine, "Ignorance of U.S. History Shown by College Freshmen," *The New York Times*, April 4, 1943; "Social Studies Extremists Blamed for Ignorance of Nation's Record," *The New York Times*, April 5, 1943.
6. Abel Hanson, "Good Schools—Front Line Against Communism," *The School Executive*, October 1947, 11.
7. Don E. Carlton, Red Scare!: Right-Wing Hysteria, Fifties Fanaticism, and Their Legacy in Texas (Austin: Texas Monthly Press, 1985), 64–100; "Non-Subversive Oath," in Chester E. Ollison to Kenyon F. Clapp, May 27, 1970, Texas Education Agency Records, 1979/237–43 (Texas State Library and Archives, Austin, TX).
8. James W. Fraser, *Between Church and State: Religion and Public Education in a Multicultural America* (New York: St. Martin's Griffin, 1999), 142–49; C. F. Schmidt, letter to the editor, *Houston Chronicle*, August 23, 1957; Anna L. Morales, "Repainting the Little Red Schoolhouse: The Texas American History Requirement and McCarthyism" (master's thesis, Texas Tech University, 1985), 57–69.
9. Senate Judiciary Committee, Subcommittee to Investigate the Administration of the Internal Security Act and Other Internal Security Acts, "Subversive Influences in the Educational Process," 83rd Cong., at 2, 27–29 (1953).
10. O. K. McCarter, letter to the editor, *Houston Chronicle*, August 1, 1957.
11. William M. Thornton, "Communist Adulation in Textbooks Blasted," *Dallas Morning News*, May 11, 1948.
12. "Education: Cotton Curtain," *Time*, August 5, 1957.
13. Keith Alan Evetts, "The Gablers: Instigators or Products of Cold War Mentality in Texas?" (master's thesis, Baylor University, 1995), 24.
14. "Education: Was Robin Just a Hood?" *Time*, December 31, 1979.
15. "Parents Urged to Take Active Interest in Textbook Content," *Pampa Daily News*, May 19, 1963.
16. "Two Protest Economics Textbooks," *El Paso Herald*, October 12, 1965.
17. Diane Ravitch, *The Language Police: How Pressure Groups Restrict What Students Learn* (New York: Alfred A. Knopf, 2003), 105.
18. L. Harland Ford, "The Concept of the Confluence of Texan Cultures in Curriculum Planning," attached to L. Harland Ford memo to School Administrator, June 10, 1970, Texas Education Agency Records, 1979/237–43.
19. *Ibid.*
20. "Texas Agency Holds Languages Conferences," *The Linguistic Reporter* 15 (May–June 1973): 5.

21. Melvin P. Sikes, "Confluence of Texan Cultures in Curriculum Planning," in Texas Education Agency, Administrators Conferences on Language and Cultural Difference, 1973, ERIC (111169), 7.
22. L. Deckle McLean, "Psychotherapy for Houston Police," *Ebony*, October 1968, 78; Sikes, "Confluence of Texan Cultures," 7.
23. Ravitch, *Language Police*, 105–6; Ellie McGrath and Sam Allis, "Education: Showdown in Texas," *Time*, August 23, 1982.
24. Teacher Rights Division, *Kanawha County, West Virginia: A Textbook Study in Cultural Conflict* (Washington, DC: National Education Association, 1975), 2, 14–15.
25. Ibid., 29.
26. Carol Mason, *Reading Appalachia from Left to Right: Conservatives and the 1975 Kanawha County Textbook Controversy* (Ithaca, NY: Cornell University Press, 2009), 103, 172; William Martin, "The Guardians Who Slumbereth Not," *Texas Monthly*, November 1982.
27. Educational Research Analysts, "Our Mission," on the web page Meet Gablers, http://www.textbookreviews.org.
28. Robert Lerner, Althea K. Nagai, and Stanley Rothman, *Molding the Good Citizen: The Politics of High School History Texts* (Westport, CT: Praeger, 1995), 1, 3; "Education: Merry McAndrew," *Time*, October 10, 1927; Walter Lippmann, *American Inquisitors* (1928; repr., New Brunswick, NJ: Transaction Publishers, 1993), 7.
29. John J. Goodson, *State Board of Education: Controversy and Change* (Austin: House Research Organization, Texas House of Representatives, 2000), 3, 7; "A Look at the Key Issues," *Austin American-Statesman*, January 8, 1995.
30. Lynn V. Cheney, "The End of History," *Wall Street Journal*, October 20, 1994.
31. Giles Whittell, "Don McLeroy, the Dentist Who Wants to Drill Pupils in Creationism," *Sunday Times*, May 7, 2010; Alexander Stille, "Textbook Publishers Learn: Avoid Messing with Texas," *The New York Times*, June 29, 2002; Goodson, *Controversy and Change*, 6; James McWilliams, "History 101: Ignorance as Power," *Texas Observer*, August 30, 2002; Mark Monford, "Dear Texas: Please Shut Up. Sincerely, History," *San Francisco Chronicle*, March 17, 2010.
32. Ravitch, *The Language Police*, 6–7, 19–20, 111; Ellie McGrath, et al., "Education: Texas Eases Up on Evolution." *Time*, April 30, 1984.
33. James W. Loewen, *Lies My Teacher Told Me: Everything Your American History Textbook Got Wrong*, 2nd ed. (New York: New Press, 2007), 5.
34. Jesús F. de la Teja, "An Almost Impossibly Large Set of Standards Produced by a Problematic Process," *History News Network*, May 5, 2010; Traci Shurley, "State Board of Education Member Wants Slimmed-Down Social Studies Standards," *Fort Worth Star-Telegram*, April 20, 2010; David Upham, "Is Texas Messing with History?" *Wall Street Journal*, April 27, 2010.
35. Rebecca Tanglen, "Comment and Casenote: Local Decisions, National Impact: Why the Public School Textbook Selection Process Should Be Viewpoint Neutral," *University of Colorado Law Review* 78 (Summer 2007): 1021, 1023–24.
36. Chester E. Finn, Jr., and Kathleen Porter-Magee, foreword to *The State of U.S. History Standards 2011*, by Sheldon M. Stern and Jeremy A. Stern (Washington, DC: Thomas B. Fordam Institute, 2011), 3.

37. Sheldon M. Stern and Jeremy A. Stern, *The State of State U.S. History Standards 2011* (Washington, DC: Thomas B. Fordham Institute, 2011), 15–16
38. Ibid.; Gary Scharrer, "State History Standards Get 'D': Conservative Think Tank Says Politicians Have Distorted Curriculum," *Houston Chronicle*, February 15, 2011.
39. Gary Scharrer, "Textbook Battle Goes Late and Loud," *San Antonio Express-News* May 21, 2010.

As members of the TEKS review committee for the high school United States history survey, we sifted through bloody battles—both literally and figuratively—to build a new curriculum that reflected how we as American citizens negotiated the concept of democracy over the last 150 years. Often times the meaning of words like "democracy" or "citizen" were lost among our fellow curriculum writers, and now among many of our State Board of Education members, who do not understand that our nation has been crafted from changing notions of freedom. Why should the children of the millennia suffer the SBOE's inability to grapple with these ideas? The SBOE's suggested edits to the new curriculum reflect their lack of historical knowledge and their failure to listen to the appointed-citizen review committees. . . .

We feel that the SBOE's biased and unfounded amendments undercut our attempt to build a strong, balanced and diverse set of standards. Texans should be outraged at the ways in which the SBOE rewrote the TEKS without regard to standard historical interpretations. They adopted antiquated and inaccurate language such as the use of the term "expansionism" in lieu of "imperialism". . . .

Now as the SBOE approaches its final curriculum decision, we have reunited as public citizens to voice our concern, our collective disgust if you will, at the distorted culmination of our work.

Figure 3 The US History Review Committee speaks out
The standards for the second half of US history drew the most media coverage and the most ire. Members of the committee appointed by the Texas State Board of Education to revise the standards spoke out against the way the politicians distorted their work.

CHAPTER 3

Hijacks and Hijinks on the US History Review Committee

Laura K. Muñoz
Julio Noboa

On May 20, 2010, the Associated Press reported a revolt on the US History II TEKS Social Studies Review Committee, the committee tasked with revising the standards for eleventh-grade US history classrooms in the state of Texas. Concurrent with the first day of testimony at the Texas State Board of Education's (SBOE) last hearing on the new social studies standards, six of the nine committee members released a collective statement for the public record to denounce the Texas Essential Knowledge and Skills (TEKS). The dissenters wrote, "Now as the SBOE approaches its final curriculum decision, we have reunited as public citizens to voice our concern, our collective disgust if you will, at the distorted culmination of our work." They joined critics, such as Benjamin Jealous, president of the NAACP, and former US Secretary of Education Rod Paige, who demanded a delayed voted and "fresh rewrite" of the standards. The six committee members expressed contempt over the SBOE's decisions to override the new curriculum. "The SBOE's biased and unfounded amendments undercut our attempt to build a strong, balanced and diverse set of standards. Texans should be outraged at the ways in which the SBOE rewrote the TEKS without regard to standard historical interpretations."[1]

The dissenters' perspective became a surprising voice in the national critique. The majority of the committee, which served from January through October 2009, had been rather silent, focused instead on completing the standards rewrite and on their primary roles as teachers and professors in the state's public schools and colleges. Throughout 2009, most committee members observed the SBOE's actions from afar, restricting their participation to the three writing retreats, to correspondence requests from the Texas Education Agency (TEA) for feedback, and to summons to appear before the board.[2] But in November 2009, committee member Bill Ames published an online series, "The Left's War on U.S. History," for TexasInsider.org detailing his interpretation of the curriculum work. A retired marketing manager and self-described activist "who served as a Minuteman on the Texas and Arizona borders," Ames proclaimed that "liberal activists hijacked Texas' social studies curriculum process." He characterized his fellow committee members as "leftists," "revisionists," "liberals," and "radical members of the education establishment." Yet he portrayed himself as a victimized conservative and as the lone "non-educator" who "objected in vain" as "the review panel, during its meetings in February, July and October, went out of their way to focus on negative aspects of history."[3] Former SBOE chairman Don McLeroy had nominated Ames to the committee and the TEA assigned him to a "citizen" position on the eleventh-grade US history committee.

Ames's unethical and inaccurate descriptions of the committee's work spurred committee members—one by one—to speak out about the TEKS and to consider the possibility of an organized response as the SBOE neared its final vote to the adopt the new standards. Lubbock high school teacher Dennis Berger posted corrections to the information at TexasInsider.org, clarifying his stance as a Republican and a 21-year veteran of the US Air Force (retired).[4] Education professor Julio Noboa formally organized the Multicultural Alliance of Social Studies Advocacy (MASSA) to recruit "faculty, teachers, and students . . . to provide oral and/or written testimony" at the spring SBOE meetings in order "to ensure that these standards are accurate, significant, relevant and culturally diverse."[5] After the SBOE's January 2010 meeting, Grand Prairie high school teacher Britine Burton emailed many committee members, asking, "Are we just going to let this be?"[6]

No one responded immediately, but after watching the TEKS maelstrom unfold in the national news throughout the spring a majority of the committee members agreed to compose a formal statement to oppose the standards. History professor Laura Muñoz drafted the statement, and emailed it to the committee members except for Ames. Noboa edited the statement, and Burton confirmed the signatures. Meanwhile, Deborah Pennington, the former social studies curriculum coordinator for Conroe Independent School District, defended the committee's work in two public debates, first at a University of Houston forum that was broadcast on public radio 88.7 KUHF and later on television for Houston PBS Channel 8.[7] With history of education scholars at the American Educational Research Association, Muñoz also proposed a resolution to oppose the standards at the association's national conference in Denver.[8] Finally, in May 2010, on the eve of the last SBOE public hearing, Muñoz disseminated the "Collective Statement on the TEKS" to Texas newspaper editors and to the SBOE so that it could be entered into the public record.[9] The six dissenting committee members had finally had enough! After two years of debate and press scrutiny, the dissenters needed the SBOE to understand that they had done their duty honorably and with the highest commitment to their professions. "We are in this together," they wrote. "Our collective experience is American history and the Texas historical standards need to reflect it all—the good, the bad and the ugly."[10]

In this chapter, two committee members—Laura Muñoz and Julio Noboa—reunite to document our perspective of the US history committee's work, to interpret our own experiences, and to reassess what took place on our committee in 2009. We are speaking for ourselves as education scholars and do not intend this to reflect the views of our fellow committee members, although many of them may agree with our interpretation. One aspect of this account is to challenge the conservative media's characterization of our committee, which was drawn wholly from Ames's perspective. More important, however, we highlight how historical consensus, not personal politics, shaped the standards. We argue that the committee actively and ethically engaged the standards writing process, working diligently to build a set of standards that met the historical criteria and pedagogical goals for eleventh-grade US history since 1877. The committee attempted at every meeting to fulfill the SBOE and TEA directives presented to us, despite the changing rules and procedures over the course of the yearlong writing process.

In this retelling, we have turned to our social studies training and have drawn upon traditional historical practices to construct our narrative. We consulted primary documents such as the TEKS, its multiple revisions over the course of our meetings, and correspondence generated by the committee, the SBOE, and the TEA. We have relied upon our experiences as "participant observers" at committee meetings held in Austin, Texas, in February, July, and October 2009; at SBOE hearings in 2009 and 2010; and at academic meetings related to the standards before and after the hearings. We have spent many years studying the Texas history standards and have dedicated our careers to researching public education in the Southwest, specifically Texas and Arizona.[11] This expertise bears on our narrative as well. We also have taken inspiration from teachers and scholars who have composed similar narratives about their experiences writing standards-based curricula across the United States.[12]

Committee Appointments

In June 2008, the SBOE met with TEA officials and established a "formal TEKS review process" that detailed a procedure and timeline for revising the state's educational curricula. According to Anita Givens, an associate commissioner for standards and programs at the TEA, social studies was "the first content area to follow the approved process from the beginning" despite the SBOE's later decision to change these rules in March 2009. Still, in that summer of 2008, the TEA followed the original rules and issued a call for the social studies review. By fall SBOE members had begun nominating potential citizens to serve on the review committees, and by November the TEA had contacted nominees to submit résumés and to designate committee preferences. SBOE members reviewed the dossiers and began appointing the final list of reviewers. The TEA contacted the nominees by email on December 19, 2008, to advise us "in the event that [we] are selected to serve on a committee" to prepare for the upcoming review meetings, scheduled for January 29–31, 2009, for kindergarten through grade 8 committees and February 5–7, 2009, for grades 9–12 committees.[13]

The TEA confirmed the committee appointments throughout January 2009. Muñoz received her official letter on January 13, 2009, and Noboa received his that same day.[14] The appointment letters did not include our committee assignments; we learned on the first day of the high school committee meetings that we both had been appointed to the Review Committee for Eleventh-Grade US History Studies Since 1877. Our names, followed by the names of our SBOE representatives, appeared on a master list presented to everyone at the meeting and published on the TEA website. Our committee was composed of the following nine individuals: Bill Ames (appointed by SBOE member McLeroy); Dennis Berger, Meadow ISD (Craig); Britine Burton, Grand Prairie ISD (Knight); Bronwen Choate, Graham ISD (Lowe); Michael Howard, Midway ISD (Miller); Laura Muñoz, Texas A&M University–Corpus Christi (Berlanga); Julio Noboa, University of Texas at El Paso (Nuñez); Deborah Pennington, Conroe ISD (Cargill); and Margaret Telford, Grapevine-Colleyville ISD (Hardy). Of the nine, six were practitioners from school districts across the state, two were university professors, and one was a "citizen."[15] By the end of the our first day, which included instructions from the TEA, an overview of the review process, and an introduction to the Texas College and Career Readiness Standards (CCRS), we had learned a lot about each other. We quickly assessed our racial and political backgrounds: seven were white; one was African American; and two were Latino (the two authors of this chapter). We split almost evenly along political party lines, with committed advocates on both sides. All but one of us taught social studies and US history; many of us belonged to professional teaching and history organizations; and most of us held advanced degrees or were working toward them. We didn't discuss religion very much, although we spoke of service responsibilities to our communities. The majority of us were married or partnered. And almost all of us were Texas educated.

We took the committee assignment very seriously and had been preparing on our own in advance of the first review meeting. Many committee members reported meeting with their state representatives and colleagues to discuss the upcoming review and potential changes. For example, Telford came to our first review meeting with the proposed changes recommended by the Texas Council for Social Studies (TCSS) and the Texas Social Studies Supervisors Association (TSSSA). She recounted how these organizations had set up special computer workstations at the annual convention so that teachers could log suggested changes to the curriculum. Muñoz and Noboa explained how they had met with SBOE members Berlanga, Agosto, and Nuñez to demonstrate ways to incorporate multiple perspectives—particularly that of the Latino experience—into the TEKS and to suggest potential revisions to the 1998 social studies standards.[16] The eleventh-grade committee as a whole and especially those members who had taught the TEKS in Texas public high schools—Berger, Burton, Choate, Howard, Pennington, and Telford—possessed very clear ideas and were very enthusiastic about rewriting the standards. Unbeknownst to us at the time, Ames also arrived with a special agenda. He had sought his appointment after participating in a 2002 social studies textbook review where he found the TEKS flawed and biased toward multiculturalism.[17] His perspective stemmed from a heated history of far right Texas politics.

Conservatives and Texas Curricula

In a lengthy exposé, the *Washington Monthly* provided a historical account of the decades-long rise of the Christian right in the arena of Texas textbooks and standards, beginning in the 1960s with the founders of the movement, Norma and Mel Gabler, "homemaker and an oil-company clerk."[18] Backed up by loud supporters for three decades, they dominated the textbook adoption hearings by intimidating the board and publishers with their provocative demands to eliminate "liberal, secular, pro-evolution bias." Their followers also targeted moderate and liberal board members and thus carved out a new arena of conservative Christian activism that gradually gained political and financial support, culminating in the 1994 election that unseated several Democrats from the SBOE. A dozen years later, by the 2006 election, the Christian conservatives gained 10 of the 15 seats on the board, including McLeroy's. They were then poised to complete the mission the Gablers had initiated nearly a half-century ago.[19]

Yet what distinguished these new conservative advocacy groups from their traditional forebears was not their ideology per se, but their increased political power, financial support, and level of sophistication.[20] This network of support included donors such as John Walton (whose father Sam Walton of Wal-Mart Stores Inc. appears in the 2010 standards) and emerging institutional think tanks such as the Texas Public Policy Foundation (TPPF), which remains heavily courted and heeded by Governor Rick Perry and other powerful Republican lawmakers, such as US Senator John Cornyn.[21] McLeroy, in fact, had participated in TPPF events since its 2001 founding.[22] The TPPF regularly makes well-publicized pronouncements advocating conservative policies not only for public school curricula but also for other areas of profound public concern, such as the state's system of higher education.[23]

McLeroy, a dentist by profession, emerged as the visible "face" and most recognizable leader of the influential conservative voting bloc in the SBOE. Elected to the board in 1998, he had long advocated perennial conservative positions that impacted the TEKS in science, health, language arts, and, most recently, social studies. This included teaching creationism as science, abstinence in sex education, phonics in language arts, and a Bible-based, conservative Christian view of Texas, US, and world histories. During his two years as chairman, from his appointment by Governor Perry in 2007 to his disconfirmation by the Texas Senate in May 2009, McLeroy forcefully and often rudely imposed his views over the objections of teachers, administrators, and academic scholars. His media notoriety exploded into the national scene during the 2010 hearings for the social studies standards; yet his very widely disseminated statements were so extreme that even moderate Republicans were embarrassed, and his own district voted him off the board in the 2010 primary election.[24] McLeroy's term ended in January 2011, but for the remainder of 2010 and through the end of the TEKS adoption process, his presence and influence left an indelible mark on the social studies standards that will be felt over the next decade.

In a handwritten memorandum, a PDF copy of which was released by the *Texas Tribune*, McLeroy urged readers to "listen very closely to Bill Ames; he speaks for a lot of Texas citizens."[25] As a Minuteman and Eagle Forum volunteer, Ames had furthered conservative causes with published opinions about "illegal immigrant aliens" and the "environmentalist agenda to destroy America."[26] In 2002, Ames took his politics to the Texas textbook review committee, where he recommended more than two hundred changes (his count) to one McGraw-Hill textbook.[27] Disgusted by errors that, as he said, "traced directly to flawed TEKS standards," he began speaking under the auspices of Texas for Standards Reform.[28] Under this banner, he cosponsored the 2004 EdWatch National Education Conference, "Education for a *Free Nation*." Ames shared billing with Republican presidential candidate, then Minnesota state senator, Michele Bachmann when she gave her now infamous speech opposing gay marriage.[29]

By the time McLeroy appointed Ames to the social studies review committee in 2009, he already thought of himself as a conservative education reformer despite his lack of teaching credentials. When we began our TEKS work together, this extreme conservatism became the only lens through which he saw history or us, his fellow committee members. That's why Ames characterized us as a "leftist majority" in his published essays and speeches and why he described himself as "the only non-educator, and the only member who consistently supported conservative principles."[30]

Committee Work

Remarkably, from the start, our committee had great rapport. We handled ourselves professionally, courteously, and amicably, even in our disagreements. The TEA assigned a staff member to our group for note taking and facilitation; it also assigned public "observers" to witness our committee discussions. As we introduced ourselves, we slowly began our discussion, and we recognized that several of the high school teachers, particularly Choate and Telford, had participated in past TEA projects such as textbook reviews. They were seasoned professionals with decades of classroom experience, and our committee leaned on their leadership. In fact, our committee quickly discerned each member's strengths and drew upon them to further our task. For example, Telford brought her laptop as did others; several of us brought history textbooks, secondary source materials, and syllabi as reference tools. Telford agreed to serve as our scribe, and Berger and Howard used their laptops with Wi-Fi access for fact-checking and backing up our work. We also connected Telford's laptop to a projector so the committee could read the TEKS simultaneously and negotiate the writing and editing together as we moved down the list. After major breaks, usually at lunch or the end of the day, Telford emailed the drafts to us or saved them to our flash drives.

Although we managed the committee logistics quite easily, we had difficulty from the beginning with Ames. He had made himself known to the TEA officials and to everyone on the first morning of the February 2009 meeting when he challenged instructions in the general session. With the consent of the TEA officials present, one review committee member, an economics professor, spoke to us about the need for consistency and alignment across the curriculum. He wanted to make sure that all the committees used the terms *capitalism* and *socialism* appropriately when discussing economic systems instead of the terms *free enterprise* and *communism*.[31] This shift reflected recent economic scholarship, but Ames rejected this idea and publically challenged the professor. His outburst affected the tenor of the meeting, and our committee quickly realized that he was on our review team. Later, in special testimony hearings in March and November 2009, the conservative TPPF challenged the SBOE to reinsert "free enterprise" over "capitalism," which it did.[32]

Once we assembled for committee work, Ames promoted American jingoism and exceptionalism and used these as a litmus test for all editorial changes to the standards throughout all three meetings. TEA rules required our committee to reach consensus on every standard. This meant that we had to agree unanimously on the TEKS language or agree to concede in order to achieve some level of parity on another standard. The TEA did not allow for majority rule, so we could not simply outvote one another, even though in the TexasInsider.org Ames wrote that he felt "outvoted 8 to 1." In fact, some committee members, including Muñoz, remember being dismayed at learning that majority rule was not allowed. Had it been an option, our committee could have easily ignored Ames. Instead, because the rules demanded consensus and because we were publically observed, our committee paid close attention to consensus. As a result, we spent the bulk of our time negotiating away Ames's demands to insert patriotism into every standard. He described our opposition to his ideas as an insistence on writing "negative history."[33] But we found rather quickly that he interpreted any criticism of the American past as political bias, invention, and revision. We were quite surprised at his perspective and at his refusal to examine social studies scholarship from a range of perspectives or to discuss it openly. His resistance, then, became entrenched, the bar by which our committee wrote the standards and one of the reasons why we have chosen to address his published recollections in this chapter. Ultimately, it became clear to us that Ames was McLeroy's deliberately appointed representative, informant, and perhaps even saboteur and that Ames's conservative agenda had been firmly established before our discussions even began.[34]

Committee members took turns negotiating with Ames on every single standard. Sometimes he was amenable and willing to defer on one issue to gain concession on another. For instance, at our first meeting, he expressed frustration with but agreed to the committee's decision to use a template created by Texas social studies teachers to begin our analysis. The committee felt that using the template would be a reasonable way to enter the discussion given that the high school teachers had already pointed out the gaps and inconsistencies in the 1998 standards. Later Ames wrote that our committee, composed of "leftists, first hijacked the standards process by using a bootlegged version of standards, created by the left-leaning [TCSS] as a starting point for revision and update." Despite this hyperbole, Ames continued through the process with us.

The TCSS/TSSSA template allowed us to consider how current teachers, as practitioners, applied the TEKS in the classroom, and we never took their ideas carte blanche. For example, teachers recommended extending the list of "turning points," or important dates in American history, beyond 1957, where the timeline stopped in the 1998 version.[35] According to the 1998 standards, the most significant dates in modern US history included only: 1898 (the Spanish-American War),[36] 1914–18 (World War I), 1929 (the stock market crash), 1941–45 (World War II), and 1957 (the year that Sputnik launched the US-Soviet space race). When the committee read this list, we wondered if anything significant happened after 1957. From our teaching experiences, we were confident that our students believed that at least three major turning points—9/11, Facebook, and the iPhone—occurred in American history after 1990 and after most of them were born. We added 1968—the military escalation in Vietnam, the emergence of a youth revolution, and the double assassinations of the Rev. Dr. Martin Luther King Jr. and presidential candidate Robert F. Kennedy. Many historians—scholars and pop historians alike—write about 1968 as a pivotal year in reshaping generational attitudes, if not the global milieu of Western civilization in the twentieth century.[37] We also added 1991 (the end of the Cold War), 2001 (the terrorists attacks on the World Trade Center and the Pentagon), and 2008 (the election of Barack Obama, our first "black president" as he is described in the standard). This is, in fact, the only reference to President Obama in the standards. The SBOE eventually approved these additions to the 2010 standards, after overturning a 2009 directive to the committee to strike the year 2008 from the standards. One SBOE member said, "Ten years from now no one will think this event [the 2008 presidential election] is important."[38]

At other times, Ames's racialized ideology led to personal resentment and frustration on all sides. At the first meeting, Ames lamented to Muñoz that all the "white men" were disappearing from the standards. Muñoz empathetically replied, "Well, now you know what it feels like to be left out of history." Berger and Howard, the only other "white men" on our committee, attempted to reconcile Ames's point of view, but he refused to listen to them or to most of the "white women" on our committee. On occasion, he engaged in conversation with Burton, Pennington, and Noboa, but by the third meeting in October, Ames left courtesy by the wayside. He told Burton, the only African American on our committee, that the problems our committee had encountered resulted only after the TEA let in "people like you."[39]

In the midst of this tension, the committee still moved toward consensus in order to complete the assigned TEA tasks. Reading through the edited version of the standards, one can sense the interpretive dilemmas we encountered as we maneuvered around Ames's emphasis on American pride. The standards are littered with overused catch phrases such as "optimism," "freedom," and "patriotism." For example, in the time period 1877–98, Ames believed that it was not enough for students to study the "social issues affecting . . . immigrants." He insisted and we deferred by consensus that students must "describe the optimism of the many immigrants who sought a better life in America." In the time period 1898–1920, the United States emerged as a world power because of "American expansionism"; the SBOE directed the committee to delete the standard historiographical term *imperialism* because of its negative implication.

We also deleted presidential candidate and American labor leader Eugene Debs from the early twentieth century. According to one member (the phrase we used to describe Ames's dissent in the annotated standards submitted to the TEA), Debs did not symbolize a "good American." This overemphasis on "positive history" throughout the standards extended to the presidents as well because one member insisted that we name as many as possible, especially Richard Nixon and Ronald Reagan, in standard 10, but not Barack Obama in standard 11.[40]

Two of the most difficult discussions our committee engaged in involved "American exceptionalism" and Celebrate Freedom Week. Ames initially proposed the addition of a special standard on Celebrate Freedom Week, which the committee rejected because it fell outside the scope of the curriculum we were tasked to review, eleventh-grade US history since 1877. Ames, however, managed to get it added to the standards (at every grade level) as a SBOE special amendment after we finished writing the drafts. The introduction to the 2010 standards, unlike the 1998 version, begins with eight overarching goals. Three of these goals are statements on the "U.S. free enterprise system" (which "may also be referenced as capitalism"), the "constitutional republic" (which is defined as "representative government" and in counter to American democracy), and "Celebrate Freedom Week." Our committee opposed the addition of Celebrate Freedom Week because it was already a separate law (section 29.907 of the Texas Education Code). Its curricular application also is much wider than the eleventh grade because it applies to students who are also in grades 3 through 10 and grade 12. Further, our committee felt that its requirements were rather weak standards for high school students. During Freedom Week, students must read the US Constitution and recite in class a portion of the Declaration of Independence, beginning with "We hold these truths to be self-evident." But the majority of the SBOE members disagreed with us and dedicated the very first standard to Celebrate Freedom Week with a special emphasis on seven founding fathers: Benjamin Rush, John Hancock, John Jay, John Witherspoon, John Peter Muhlenberg, Charles Carroll, and Jonathan Trumbull Sr.[41]

Perhaps our most in-depth and contentious discussion focused on "American exceptionalism," a concept championed by Ames and appointed "expert" David Barton and that serves as a veritable mantra and patriotic "litmus test" for conservatives in Texas and nationwide. American exceptionalism holds that, among other ideas, the United States has a divine destiny of being the role model of good government and democracy to the world. Some of us interpreted this concept as a reincarnation of Manifest Destiny applied on a global scale. All our committee members, with the exception of Ames, were united in our view that this was not a concept accepted by a consensus of historians and academic scholars and one that has instead received considerable criticism.[42] Despite this, the SBOE imposed their will and over our objections inserted an entire TEKS section requiring that each student "understands the concept of American exceptionalism."[43]

Although this American glory trope twisted standard US historical interpretation, as a committee we wrangled with it as a compromise in order to add new standards and to incorporate new scholarship and skills overlooked in 1998. Again, our committee's work was bound to consensus, so we moved on issues that we could reconcile. Our committee actually worked quite well at fleshing out historical eras and extending the standards' timeline through 2010. For example, standard 2 (formerly standard 1) is about chronology, "historical eras" and "dates" as "turning points" in American history. The 1998 standards did not include any conceptual notions of time. To promote higher thinking skills and to meet our charge to write the TEKS in conjunction with the college readiness standards (which the SBOE and the TEA required), we added a new criterion to "identify the major characteristics that define an historical era."[44] Asking high school students to think about how historians build chronologies met the readiness standard that called for "periodization and chronological reasoning."[45] We felt that students needed to learn how to ask "how" and "why" a historical era or date is significant.

Throughout the new 2010 standards, we also built a comprehensive timeline and attempted to build multiple perspectives into the curriculum. For example, we basically redesigned the last half of the twentieth century, adding separate standards on World War II, the Cold War through Vietnam, 1960s movement politics, the time period of 1970–90, and the time period of 1990–2010. We also made every possible attempt to integrate many different people into the standards. The 1998 standards reflected a black/white binary and did not recognize everyday women as historical actors. In 2010, the standards separated "women" from "minorities," and included a range of references to American Indians, Asian Americans, African Americans, and Latinos.

Our conversations about women and gender in US history also sparked fiery conversations with Ames, McLeroy, and the general public. In our committee discussion over the 1960s, Ames opposed any reference to the second wave of women's movements and deplored suggestions to add "women's liberation" or the names of leaders such as Betty Friedan and Gloria Steinem. Even references to movements before and after the second wave, such as the New Women and "flappers" of the 1920s or the Stonewall Riot that led to gay, lesbian, bisexual, transsexual, and queer (GLBTQ) movements in the late twentieth century, visibly irked him. To build consensus at the first committee meeting, Muñoz suggested that we add Phyllis Schlafly's STOP-ERA campaign, which opposed the National Organization of Women's Equal Rights Amendment in 1972. Although this strategy annoyed several members, it created space within the standards for varied women's experiences. At the SBOE's April 2009

Committee on Instruction meeting, the board encouraged the committee to add a "longer list of women" to the TEKS but also to put these women in a specific context. For example, one SBOE member said, "Minorities did not earn civil rights; it was given to them by men in Congress. Did you hear that, Mavis [B. Knight]? Men gave women the right to vote."[46]

The SBOE eventually approved the addition of Friedan and Schlafly, as well as the names of 12 more women. This was a remarkable improvement over the three women already named in the 1998 standards, but this new list of 14 women is quite short compared to the 55 names of men also included.[47] Later, Ames took public credit for arguing on Schlafly's behalf and, in an ironic twist, the Texas arm of Schlafly's Eagle Forum honored McLeroy with a 2010 "Patriot Award," its highest commendation for conservative activism.[48]

It is unfortunate that our committee spent so much energy wrangling Ames's conservative agenda. In lieu of ideology and politics, the SBOE and our committee could have reconciled curricular questions by relying on the social studies disciplines. Despite questions of interpretation, historians do adhere to basic tenets of collecting evidence and interpreting it based on an established body of work that we call "historiography." As a profession, we have crafted and continue to recraft, revise, and synthesize our understanding of the American past in order to build this "deeper and richer understanding of human experience."[49] To interpret the past, we rely on a range of theoretical and methodological approaches from the most basic notions of race, class, gender, and sexuality to complex structural, philosophical, political, and social ways of knowing.[50] As it stands now, too many of the 2010 standards contain problems that can be evaluated quite easily for their failures to meet basic historiography, professional standards, or college readiness. For these reasons, our committee denounced the new standards.

Nevertheless, despite these inherent problems, our collective disgust did not diminish our recognition of the obvious improvements we were able to impart on these standards. This includes not only the additional names of women, African Americans, and Latinos whose historical significance is unquestionable but also the appropriate integration of movements, constitutional amendments, and Supreme Court decisions that especially impacted the lives of women and ethnoracial minorities and reflected their agency and activism in the face of discrimination. Millions of students in Texas will learn about the Harlem Renaissance and the Chicano Mural Movement and about the importance of *Brown v. Board of Education* as well as *Edgewood v. Kirby*. They will be required to hear not only about Rev. Dr. Martin Luther King Jr. but also about César Chávez and Betty Friedan. These modest gains may seem inconsequential when balanced against some major problems still inherent in these standards, yet in the classrooms of dedicated teachers, these historical items could be the source of awakening, enlightenment, and self-discovery for millions of Texas students over the next decade.

Conclusion

For us, the experience of participating in the standards review process was personal and professional. A descendant of nineteenth-century Texas Mexicans called Tejanos and three generations of teachers, Muñoz grew up in Corpus Christi, attended public schools, and earned her undergraduate degree at the University of Texas at Austin. Noboa, a Puerto Rican raised in Chicago, earned his PhD at that same university, and his three children were educated in Texas public schools from early elementary school through college graduation. Both writers also teach at Texas state universities. As social studies scholars, we welcomed the call to participate in the TEKS review process and to share our professional knowledge on behalf of our state. We are committed professionally to the responsibility of contributing to the record of events that trace our historical experience as Americans. Given the diversity and breadth of our country, we espouse historical interpretation that accounts for difference and that contextualizes our individual and group experiences within a range of contexts and time periods. We believe in fundamental historical concepts such as "change over time" (the idea that there is a measurable difference between time periods) and "historical significance" (that events, individuals, or themes in history possess relevance in relation to their contexts). We expect to use different historical lenses (race, class, gender, and sexuality) as well as theoretical and methodological frameworks to build historical assessments.

In our experience on the US history committee, the absence of this emphasis on the disciplinary goals of history and of the social studies readiness standards prevented our committee from succeeding at its task to write a comprehensive eleventh-grade curriculum on US history since 1877. Ironically, our committee's inability to craft the best possible standards emerged from the unresolved conflicts of our "multiple perspectives," which is a college readiness standard.[51] Our review committee could not, to borrow a phrase from the CCRS handbook, "recognize and appreciate diverse human perspectives." We lost sight of "the goal and focus of social studies . . . to promote a deeper and richer understanding of the human experience."[52]

Stakeholders, such as the SBOE and its review committee nominees, brought different ideological and pedagogical motives to the TEKS rewriting process. Some board members emphasized Christianity; others, multiculturalism and racial diversity. One member of our committee emphasized patriotism and devotion to country over others who advocated for critical thinking and analytical skills. Some committee members relied on the suggested revisions of social studies teachers, whereas others remembered their community interests.

Our inability to reconcile these different visions of "history," including our own historical experiences, emerged in the inconsistent emphasis on certain types of themes, people, and events throughout the standards. All the people arguing over the TEKS pointed to omissions of people like themselves. Where are the Latinos, Muslims, Jews, and African Americans? What about the GLBTQ communities? Or the various groups of women ranging from the Equal Rights Amendment debaters of the 1920s or 1970s to modern-day political candidates such as Hillary Clinton and Sarah Palin? And what about the white men? Are we substituting them to include so many different perspectives? This emphasis on "who's missing" prevented us from building a set of standards that called for critical analysis and intellectual engagement. In essence, we were unable to fully develop a set of standards that reflected the college readiness goals of interdisciplinarity, diversity of experience, global interdependence, cognitive development, and effective communication. Instead of focusing on the broad goals of social studies, our committee conversations disintegrated into battles over promoting one kind of history over another rather than creating a set of standards that could allow multiple perspectives or a multifaceted history to emerge.

Nevertheless, as mentioned, our committee introduced positive, meaningful, and significant improvements over the 1998 US history standards, despite the conservative onslaught of bias, distortion, and monoculturalism reflected in the SBOE's resistance to our efforts and in its heavy-handed revisions of our work. It is our firm conviction that educators, academics, and concerned citizens should closely monitor the curricular decisions made by the SBOE and be ready to respond appropriately. The social and economic well-being of our state will be ensured only if future citizens are educated with the accurate historical knowledge and critical thinking skills required to distinguish between tyranny and democracy.

Notes

1. "Critics Tear into Study Guidelines; Conservatives on State Board Defy Complaints," *Associated Press*, May 20, 2010; Dennis Berger, Britine Burton, Bronwen Choate, Laura Muñoz, Julio Noboa, and Margaret Telford, "A Collective Statement on the TEKS by Members of the U.S. History Social Studies Review Committee," May 18, 2010, 2.
2. Committee members Deborah Pennington and Bill Ames appeared before the SBOE on April 22, 2009.
3. Bill Ames, "The Left's War on History," 3 parts, November 9–11, 2009, http://www.texasinsider.org/?p=18130; Bill Ames, "Bill Ames Biography" http://www.netarrantteaparty.com/wp-content/uploads/Bill-Ames-bio.pdf and "Social Studies

Standards: North Tarrant Tea Party Presentation," September 13, 2010, http://www.netarrantteaparty.com/wp-content/uploads/Bill-Ames-091310-presentation.pdf.
4. Dennis Berger to Bill Ames, November 9, 2009, http://www.texasinsider.org/?p=18130; Dennis Berger, email to Deborah J. Pennington, Laura Muñoz, Julio Noboa, Bill Ames, Britine Burton, Bronwen Choate, and Margaret Telford, November 12, 2009.
5. Julio Noboa, email to Laura Muñoz, Manuel Medrano, Cinthia Salinas, Nicholas Emerick, Char Ullman, Aurolyn Luykx, Josiah Heyman, Paul Edison, and David Moreno, December 30, 2009.
6. Britine Burton, email to Margaret Telford, Deborah Pennington, Bronwen Choate, Dennis Berger, and Laura Muñoz, February 3, 2010; Terrence Stutz, "Texas High-Schoolers to Learn about Conservative, but not Liberal, Groups under New Standards," *Dallas Morning News*, January 16, 2010.
7. Bill Stamps, "More Debate on Social Studies Curriculum," KUHF Public Radio, February 25, 2010; "TEKS and Textbooks," Houston PBS, April 9, 2010; Britine Burton, email to Laura Muñoz, April 13, 2010. Deborah Pennington did not sign the "Collective Statement"; Muñoz was unable to locate her after she left her position at Conroe ISD.
8. K. Graves, email to AERA_Division_F-Announce Listserv, May 10, 2010; Muñoz, email to AERA_Division_F-Announce Listserv, May 7, 2010. The American Educational Research Association Council held its quarterly meeting after the May 15, 2010, deadline to register comments with the SBOE.
9. Laura Muñoz, email to editors and reporters at the *Austin American Statesman, Corpus Christi Caller-Times, Dallas Morning News, Houston Chronicle* and *San Antonio Express-News*, May 18, 2010; Muñoz, email to the Texas Education Agency [curriculum@tea.state.tx.us] and the State Board of Education [sboesupport@tea.state.tx.us], May 18, 2010.
10. Berger *et al.*, "A Collective Statement," 2.
11. Laura K. Muñoz, "Desert Dreams: Mexican American Education in Arizona, 1870–1930" (PhD diss., Arizona State University, 2006); Julio Noboa, *Leaving Latinos Out of History: Teaching U.S. History in Texas* (New York: Routledge, 2006); Julio Noboa, "Missing Pages from the Human Story: World History according to Texas Curriculum Standards," *Journal of Latinos in Education* 11, no. 1 (January 2012).
12. "National History Standards," *OAH Magazine of History* 9, no. 3 (Spring 1995); "A Life in Public Education: Honoring Gary Nash," *The History Teacher* 42 (January 2009); Virginia Sánchez Korrol, "The Star in My Compass: Claiming Intellectual Space in the American Landscape," in *Memories and Migrations: Mapping Boricua and Chicana Histories*, ed. Vicki L. Ruiz and John R. Chávez (Chicago: University of Illinois, 2008), 196–213; Diane Ravitch, *National Standards in American Education: A Citizen's Guide* (Washington, DC: Brookings Institution Press, 1995).

13. "Committee on Instruction, Work Session on the TEKS Review Process (COI 4-22-09 Draft Notes)," meeting notes emailed by Anita Givens to TEKS committee members, April 22, 2009; Linda Gomez, email to nominees, December 19, 2008.
14. Linda Gomez for Anita Givens, email to Laura Muñoz, January 13, 2009.
15. "SBOE TEKS Review Committees, Social Studies, 9–12," Texas Education Agency, September 2009, *http://www.tea.state.tx.us/index2aspx?id=3643;* Ames, who was not an educator, is listed as "citizen."
16. Laura Muñoz, "Diversity as a Historical Theme for Teaching *Texas Essential Knowledge and Skills* for Social Studies," and Julio Noboa, "Focusing on the TEKS for U.S. History" (presentations to the three Latino SBOE members at the Humanitarians Organized for Public Education (HOPE) Conference, Corpus Christi, TX, September 7, 2007).
17. Ames, "Social Studies Standards," 2–3.
18. Mariah Blake, "Revisionaries: How a Group of Texas Conservatives Is Rewriting Your Kid's Textbooks," *Washington Monthly* (January/February 2010); Sean Cavanagh, "Reading from the Right," *Education Week* 25, no. 4 (September 21, 2005): 33–36; Edward B. Jenkinson, "Protecting Holden Caulfield and His Friends from the Censors," *English Journal* 74, no. 1 (January 1, 1985): 26–33; Barbara Parker, "Your Schools May Be the Next Battlefield in the Crusade against 'Improper' Textbooks," *American School Board Journal* 166, no. 6 (June 1, 1979): 21–26.
19. Blake, "Revisionaries."
20. Texas Freedom Network, "Who's Who in the Censorship Movement," 2011, *http://www.tfn.org/site/PageServer?pagename=issues_public_schools_who_textbook_censorship.*
21. Blake, "Revisionaries"; Texas Public Policy Foundation, "Windows to the Future: 2010 Annual Summary" (Austin, TX: Texas Public Policy Foundation, 2010).
22. "The Education Connection," TPPF Photo and Video Gallery, San Antonio, TX, November 26, 2001, *http://www.texaspolicy.com/photogallery/photo/nov2001_dinner3.html.*
23. Reeve Hamilton, "UT Dean Rejects 'Seven Solutions' in New Report," *Texas Tribune*, July 6, 2011.
24. Blake, "Revisionaries."
25. "The McLeroy Memo," *Texas Tribune*, January 12, 2010.
26. Blake, "Revisionaries."
27. Ames, "Biography," 1; Ames, "Social Studies Standards," 3; Bill Ames, "Testimony to the SBOE Committee on Instruction, April 22, 2009" (Texas State Board of Education audio cassette recordings, tape 2).
28. Ames, "Biography."
29. Michele Bachmann, "The Effects of Gay Marriage on Education" (presentation at EdWatch National Education Conference: Education for a *Free* Nation, Bloomington, MN, November 6, 2004).
30. Ames, "Social Studies Standards," 3; Ames, "The Left's War on History," I:1; Ames, "The Left's War on History," II:4.
31. The term *free enterprise* emerged as a critique of the New Deal and government oversight of Wall Street after the stock market crash of 1929. See Elizabeth A.

Fones-Wolf, *Selling Free Enterprise: The Business Assault on Labor and Liberalism, 1945–1960* (Urbana: University of Illinois Press, 1994); William E. Leuchtenburg, *Franklin D. Roosevelt and the New Deal: 1932–1940* (1963; repr., New York: Harper Perennial, 2009), 335–37; Richard S. Kirkendall, "The New Deal as Watershed: The Recent Literature," *Journal of American History* 54, no. 4 (March 1968): 840; Kim Phillips-Fein, *Invisible Hands: The Making of the Conservative Movement from the New Deal to Reagan* (New York: Norton, 2009); S. Alexander Rippa, *Education in a Free Society: An American History*, 8th ed. (New York: Merrill, 1997); and S. Alexander Rippa, "Dissemination of the Free-Enterprise Creed to American Schools," *The School Review* 67, no. 4 (Winter 1959): 409–21.

32. Brooke Dollens Terry, "Testimony Before the State Board of Education Regarding Changes to the Social Studies Curriculum," Center for Education Policy, Texas Public Policy Foundation, Austin, TX, November 18, 2009.
33. Ames, "The Left's War on History," I:1–3.
34. Blake, "Revisionaries."
35. TEKS.11.c.1.C (8/23/10).
36. Muñoz and Noboa argued to change the phrase "Spanish-American War" to "Spanish-American-Cuban-Filipino War" to reflect changes in recent historiography, but this suggestion was rejected by the committee.
37. Kelly Knauer, ed., *1968: The Year That Changed the World* (New York: Time Books, 2008); Mark Kurlansky, *1968: The Year That Rocked the World* (New York: Random House, 2005); Jeremy Suri, *The Global Revolutions of 1968* (New York: W. W. Norton, 2007).
38. Deborah Pennington, email to Dennis Berger Laura Muñoz, Julio Noboa, Bill Ames, Britine Burton, Bronwen Choate, and Margaret Telford, September 18, 2009.
39. Witnessed by Muñoz at the October 2009 meeting in Austin, TX.
40. In TEKS (8/23/10) see 11.c.3.C-D, 11.c.4.B, 11.c.5, 11.c.10A-B, 11.c.11E.
41. TEKS.11.c.1.C (8/23/10).
42. See Andrew J. Bacevich, *The Limits of Power: The End of American Exceptionalism* (New York: Macmillan, 2009); Richard Cohen, "The Myth of American Exceptionalism," *Washington Post*, May 9, 2011; Akira Iriye, "Exceptionalism Revisited," *Reviews in American History*, 16 (June 1988): 291–97; Ian Tyrrell, "AHR Forum: American Exceptionalism in an Age of International History," *American Historical Review* 96, no. 4 (October 1991), 1031–55.
43. TEKS.11.c.22 (8/23/10).
44. TEKS.11.c.2.A (8/23/10); Anita Givens, handout mailed to committee members, "Guidelines for Social Studies TEKS Review Committee Members," May 28, 2009.
45. Texas Higher Education Coordinating Board, *Texas College and Career Readiness Standards* (Austin, TX: Texas Higher Education Coordinating Board, 2008), 25.
46. Pennington, email to Dennis Berger et al., April 22, 2009; "Texas Textbook Controversy," *ABC Nightline*, March 11, 2010.
47. The only women named in TEKS.11 (1998) were Susan B. Anthony, Shirley Chisholm, and Georgia O'Keeffe; TEKS (8/23/10) dropped Chisholm and O'Keeffe, retained Anthony (11.c.5.B), and added Ida B. Wells (11.c.5.B), Rosa

Parks (11.c.9.C), Betty Friedan (11.c.9.C), Phyllis Schlafly (11.c.10.), Estée Lauder (11.c.18.A), Sandra Day O'Connor (11.c.24.B), Hillary Clinton (11.c.24.B), Frances Willard (11.c.26.D), Jane Addams (11.c.26.D), Eleanor Roosevelt (11.c.26.D), Dolores Huerta (11.c.26.D), Sonia Sotomayor (11.c.26.D), and Oprah Winfrey (11.c.26.D).
48. Ames, "The Left's War on History," II:4; "Highlights from the 2010 Patriotic Banquet," *Texas Eagle Forum*, July 29, 2010.
49. Texas Higher Education Coordinating Board, *Texas College and Career Readiness Standards*, 24.
50. Gloria Anzaldúa, *Borderlands/La Frontera: The New Mestiza*, 3rd ed. (San Francisco: Aunt Lute Books, 2007); Emma Pérez, *The Decolonial Imaginary: Writing Chicanas into History* (Bloomington: Indiana University Press, 1999); Peter Novick, *That Noble Dream: The "Objectivity Question" and the American Historical Profession* (New York: Cambridge University Press, 1988); Joan Wallach Scott, *Gender and the Politics of History* (New York: Columbia University Press, 1999), Michel-Rolph Trouillot, *Silencing the Past: Power and the Production of History* (Boston: Beacon Press, 1995).
51. Texas Higher Education Coordinating Board, *Texas College and Career Readiness Standards*, 25.
52. Texas Higher Education Coordinating Board, *Texas College and Career Readiness Standards*, 24.

Guidelines for Expert Feedback on the Social Studies TEKS

Please review the current social studies TEKS for Grades K-12 and respond to the following questions. In your feedback please indicate the specific grade level/course and student expectation number you are referring to, as appropriate.

1. Do the TEKS ensure that social studies concepts are presented in an accurate and factual manner? Do the standards promote ideological neutrality by balancing people/events from various sides of the political spectrum?
2. Is a complete and logical development of social studies concepts followed for each grade level or course?
3. Are historically significant events and people included at the appropriate grade level or subject, or are there significant omissions of important historical happenings and people?
4. Have the correct vocabulary and terminology been used?
5. Are there specific areas that need to be updated?
6. Are the social studies concept/content statements grade-level appropriate?
7. Are the Student Expectations (SEs) clear and specific? Do they focus on academic content?
8. Are the "social studies skills" statements at the end of each grade level/subject handled properly, or is there a better means to address these skills within the standards?
9. Do the standards promote an appreciation for the basic values of our state and national heritage? Are the significant aspects of our state and national heritage included at the appropriate grade levels?
10. Do the standards promote citizenship, patriotism and an understanding of the benefits of the free enterprise system?
11. Do you have any other suggestions for ways in which the social studies TEKS can be improved?
12. Is the subject area aligned horizontally and vertically?

Figure 4 Guidelines for the expert reviewers
The Texas State Board of Education posed these questions to six expert reviewers—two pastors, two historians, a geographer, and a lawyer. The answers they gave transformed them from reviewers of curriculum to witnesses of a political and cultural showdown.

CHAPTER 4

A Voice Crying in the Wilderness?
An Expert Reviewer's Experience
Jesús F. de la Teja

The Texas State Board of Education is a policy-making body composed of elected members. Consequently, it is not directly answerable to anyone but the electorate. It has been a controversial body for many years, but more so in the recent past. The ideological divisions on the board are such that its every action is suspect, scrutinized, and second-guessed. Among those actions was the decision to include a group of "expert reviewers" to look over the existing social studies standards and make recommendations for changes. As I watched the process get under way, I had no idea that I would be called upon to serve as an expert witness. In the end, although I have no regrets about agreeing to participate, I would have to think more than twice about doing it again.

In April 2009, Texas State Board of Education (SBOE) member Pat Hardy contacted me to inquire if I would be interested in serving as an expert reviewer for the Texas Essential Knowledge and Skills (TEKS) for social studies. She called on behalf of Rene Nuñez and Mary Helen Berlanga, who would actually nominate me. We had a long conversation, and she later emailed me, saying, "After having conversed with you, I am more excited than ever about the possibility of you serving." She went on to ask that I fill out the application form and return it to her, after which she would contact Nuñez regarding my willingness to serve.[1]

I never did speak with either Nuñez or Berlanga during the nomination process, but by May my paperwork had been processed and I was on board as one of six reviewers. Many people believe that the expert reviewers worked as a team or together, but that was never the case. Each of us worked independently and for varying lengths of time. As far as I know, I was among the last to be appointed and I certainly had minimal contact with the SBOE and the other reviewers. In fact, except for during the September 2009 SBOE hearing, the only other reviewer with whom I had any contact was James Kracht, and that was a very brief conversation the morning of the hearing.

How I came to accept the appointment has much to do with my work as a historian of Texas and as a contributor to and reviewer of textbooks. In the previous textbook adoption cycles, I reviewed and critiqued fourth- and seventh-grade texts. A few years ago, I was a coauthor on a high school–level US history textbook, and I was a coauthor on a college-level Texas history textbook. As a past board member and president of the Texas State Historical Association and as the inaugural State Historian, I had made clear my interest in a history curriculum that reflected the state's diversity and its twentieth-century experience.

Believing myself free of ideological determinism, I had more modest goals in mind for my role as a reviewer. I wanted to see how the US and Texas history curricula (and, to the degree that my knowledge allowed, the other social sciences) might be revised to better serve the needs of an overwhelmingly urban, increasingly minority, postindustrial Texas student population. Despite being a historian of the Spanish colonial, Mexican, and Texas Revolution and Republic periods, I was (and remain) interested in advocating for greater attention to the twentieth century because it is the context in which our K-12 students understand their environment, economy, society, and culture.

By the time the package containing the instructions and my copy of the social studies TEKS arrived in May, the craziness—that is to say, the process—was already well under way. First, of course, the SBOE had already gone through two rounds of culture war–driven review in the language arts and science TEKS. Board members on the extremes seemed not only prepared for a fight but also to actually relish the prospect. The SBOE was divided coming in and appeared to be talking past each other, except for a couple of members in the center, such as Pat Hardy (who had real-life experience as a Texas schoolteacher).

Second, the media was primed to use the battle over the revisions to drive audience share, subscriptions, and sales in general. And typically the media's understanding of the issues was a mile wide and an inch deep. They mixed up curriculum standards and textbook requirements; they misunderstood prescriptive and suggestive language; they went after the most tendentious outlooks.

Third, not only had the TEKS review committees already met before I was appointed, but board members were already critiquing some of that preliminary work and preparing to openly discuss these changes at the May meeting of the SBOE. And the board itself demonstrated that some members lacked a clear understanding between prescriptive and suggestive elements and curriculum standards and curriculum (including textbook content).

Fourth, there was (and is) a profound mistrust of traditional content experts—classroom teachers and higher education faculty. A couple of the expert reviewers and some of the review committee members did not have such background, which tended to narrow the range of issues they wanted to consider. This is part of a general societal anti-intellectual reaction, as can be seen in the positions of some politicians and policy groups touting practical or applied research over pure research, placing faith-based reasoning on the same plane as scientific explanations for natural phenomena and equating social justice and cultural change with societal breakdown.

Of course, you will note that my appointment did not happen until May, so I had some idea of what I was getting into, although not the extent to which entrenched positions and deep suspicions would make it difficult for my work to be accepted at face value. It was also clear from my perspective that the process was deeply flawed, as grade-level review committees had already been assigned and were already at work. To my way of thinking, it would have been better to undertake a thorough outside review by the experts and the board, the results of which could then be handed over to the grade-level committees to use as a working document. Nevertheless, I was determined—and remain steadfast in my determination—not to be drawn into cultural warfare and to work within the parameters established.

I undertook the review of the TEKS in early June 2009, taking vacation time from my work as chairman of the History department at Texas State in order to fully concentrate on the project. In the interest of full disclosure, I was paid an honorarium for the work in the amount of $1,500. Later, when I added up the hours I worked on assignment, I calculated that I was paid about minimum wage for my time. One additional bargain for the board stemmed from my living close enough to Austin that there were no travel expenses involved in my work.

The SBOE provided guidelines consisting of 12 points, two of which I found problematic in that they seemed to contradict each other. Part of guideline 1 asked, "Do the standards promote ideological neutrality by balancing people/events from various sides of the political spectrum?" Whereas guideline 10 asked, "Do the standards promote citizenship, patriotism and an understanding of the benefits of the free enterprise system?" Assuming that the promotion of good citizenship and love of country are beyond ideological considerations, I still find the part about "the benefits of the free enterprise system" ideologically slanted. In other words, the term *free enterprise system* is not ideologically neutral, placing the request in guideline 10 in conflict with part of the request in guideline 1.

Beyond this contradiction, the guidelines made clear that the experts' job was not to propose a new set of standards but to work within the existing ones. Number 11 clearly stated, "Do you have any other suggestions for ways in which the social studies TEKS can be improved?" Under the circumstances,

I saw my job as offering changes that would improve the coverage of Texas and US history by clarifying concepts, broadening perspectives, and replacing inadequate instructional examples with others I felt might more appropriately reflect the geographic, chronological, and cultural diversity that guideline 9 appeared to address: "Are the significant aspects of our state and national heritage included at the appropriate grade levels?"

I will admit that the most important consideration for me in attempting to work within the guidelines was to make sure that the TEKS met the needs of Texas students. Arguments made by a broad range of interested parties and the media regarding the influence of Texas standards on the rest of the nation because of the state's heft in the textbook market did not hold much water for me. In this age of electronic custom publishing, multiple adoptions, and market sector consolidation, I know that publishers don't have to work with a one-size-fits-all approach.

The result of my review was a 21-page report covering the historical aspects of the TEKS from kindergarten through high school US history.[2] As they are outside my area of expertise, I did not attempt to review the TEKS for non–US history courses such as world geography, US government, psychology, and sociology. And I had no substantive problems with the TEKS for the social studies electives, Special Topics in Social Studies and Social Studies Research Methods. Not being an expert on pedagogy, I also didn't do more than make general comments regarding the guidelines that asked, "Are the social studies concept/content statements grade-level appropriate?" (guideline 6) and "Are the 'social studies skills' statements at the end of each grade level/subject handled properly, or is there a better means to address these skills within the standards?" (guideline 8).

My more substantive general comments were reserved for guideline 4: "Have correct vocabulary and terminology been used?" Here I was driven by what I had observed in media coverage and individual comments indicating a lack of clear understanding of what was involved in the student expectations for many of the TEKS. As I explained,

> Although the vocabulary and terminology are appropriate overall, I would suggest that throughout the document the term *such as* in introducing examples be replaced with "for instance." Personally, I would prefer that in the few necessary instances where students are expected to know specific individuals and events those items be required (the way they are in the seventh grade where the term "including" is used) and that otherwise no examples be provided, but I understand that many teachers and publishers like the idea of representative examples. However, because many people fail to understand that representative examples are not specific requirements, I believe that use of "for example" might make clearer that the names are provided as suggestions for the kinds of people and

events to be considered in that item but that teachers and publishers are free to look more broadly.[3]

The main thrust of this recommendation, one that I knew I was not going to make headway on because of teacher and publisher demands, was the elimination of all unnecessary examples in student expectations. The whole controversy of the elimination of holidays, founding fathers, and prominent minorities from specific student expectations was based on terms being included in individual expectations. Attempts to redesign a standard and its correspondent student expectations through changes in the examples were bound to be scrutinized on ideological (political and religious) grounds. For instance, the whole controversy about the removal of Thomas Jefferson and Christmas from the standards was based precisely on a misunderstanding of roles of these two examples in their individual TEKS.

As I noted, since I did not expect my recommendation about the removal of all nonrequired examples from student expectations to be accepted, I proceeded with my review with an eye to providing what I considered better examples where necessary. For instance, in the first-grade TEKS, one expectation asked that students "identify historic figures such as Alexander Graham Bell and Thomas Edison who have exhibited a love of individualism and inventiveness." In my comment I pointed out that both individuals represented technology innovators, but that it would be difficult to explain how they reflected a "love of individualism." I suggested that George Washington Carver replace Bell, both because he was a prime example of inventiveness and because "as a proponent of self-help and applying science to farming, [he] represented a fusion of individualism and inventiveness."[4] The original language remains in place in the revised TEKS.

In other cases, I sought to clarify ambiguous or imprecise language or concepts and correct errors. For instance, one eighth-grade standard states that "the student understands the physical characteristics of the United States during the eighteenth and nineteenth centuries and how humans adapted to and modified the environment." My comment was that the chronological limitation imposed by referencing only the eighteenth and nineteenth centuries did not fully encompass the North American experience. If we are to understand the term *humans* to encompass all residents of the territory of North America included in what is today the United States, then the activities of the native peoples and the Spanish should also be included. Consequently, my proposed language was that "the student understands the physical characteristics of North America and how humans adapted to and modified the environment through the mid-nineteenth century." Again, no change was made.

One other type of change was to add an item where I believed it was required or to propose the elimination of those I thought redundant or unnecessary. In the former case, one example is my proposed addition of a student expectation regarding the civil rights movement in the high school US history standards. My argument was that the civil rights movement invigorated other groups in American society and that the language in that standard and the existing student expectations did not adequately account for that variety of experience. I proposed that students "identify minority rights movements spawned from the Civil Rights Movement, for example the National Organization for Women, the American Indian Movement, and the Chicano Movement." This was another instance in which no substantive change was made.

The aforementioned examples should not be understood to mean that nothing that I proposed was incorporated into the review process. To the contrary, in the give and take of discussions within the grade-level committees and even among board members, many of my recommendations were incorporated into positive changes. For instance, my concern for the outdated periodization of Texas history based on scholarship from the mid-twentieth century was revised after consultation with a number of historians to reflect our feeling that the eras of Texas history not only should more sharply reflect the most recent scholarship but also should account for our twenty-first-century vantage point on the past. Of particular concern to me was the imprecise use of the term *colonization*, which was indiscriminately used with reference to both the Spanish colonial period and the Mexican period. This confusion was cleared up both in the introduction to the seventh-grade TEKS and in specific items by replacing the term *Mexican Colonial* with the term *Mexican National*.

In fact, the periodization was made much clearer and more direct in providing guidance to teachers and publishers about just what was meant by "the full scope of Texas history." The old list, "The cultures of Native Americans living in Texas prior to European exploration and the eras of mission-building, colonization, revolution, republic, and statehood," was replaced with a more functional one: "Natural Texas and its People; Age of Contact; Spanish Colonial; Mexican National; Revolution and Republic; Early Statehood; Texas in the Civil War and Reconstruction; Cotton, Cattle, and Railroads; Age of Oil; Texas in the Great Depression and World War II; Civil Rights and Conservatism; and Contemporary Texas." If I have one quarrel with the list it is the addition of "Conservatism" to the Civil Rights era period, as if civil rights and conservatism stand in contrast to each other.

By the middle of the summer I was in the *Wall Street Journal*—my first appearance in that august periodical—as an example of an expert appointed by the moderate and liberal wing of the board. According to the *Journal*, I was on one side of the battle over creeping diversity in the standards: "The conservative

Christian reviewers, in turn, are skeptical of the professional historians' emphasis on multiculturalism, views stated most forcefully by Mr. de la Teja."[5] I also wound up in stories and editorials in the *Dallas Morning News*, the *Fort Worth Star Telegram*, and the *Houston Chronicle*. I certainly did not get the play of some of the other experts, but that was probably because I wasn't trying to get into the papers.

The next time I had to deal with the TEKS was when I was sent the revisions done by the grade-level committees during their meeting of July 28–31, 2009. This was the official first draft of the revised TEKS. Not only did I receive the revised version with instructions that I should answer the same questions that were posed in the original guidelines, but I was also given a copy of the "SBOE Broad Strokes Guidance for the Social Studies TEKS Writing Teams" that the grade-level teams had used in preparing their revisions.

This one-page set of bullet points reflects the various ideological and pedagogical concerns of board members and, consequently, in a number of instances asked for consideration of the obvious. What was the purpose of asking the writing committees to "focus on the country's founding fathers and founding principles"? Similarly, what was the intent of asking that the writing committees "address global events that are occurring right now"? At the appropriate grade levels and in the appropriate courses, both these "goals and priorities" regarding the founding fathers and America's engagement with the world have been core elements of the curriculum. Did the board think that the grade-level teams would minimize either of them?

Others of the goals and priorities certainly reflected immediate agendas. For instance, some board members had expressed concern that America's history tended to be presented negatively by "revisionist" historians, and this was reflected in asking the writing teams to "ensure the TEKS include an accurate representation of history and reflect a balanced perspective of both positive and negative." The concern of other board members that minorities are underrepresented in the curriculum was probably behind the statement "Understand the demographics of the state of Texas now and who we are educating." These concerns certainly played themselves out later on when the board did its own revisions in spring 2010.

My review of the grade-level committee work then proceeded, and I came up with the 28-page report that in columnar form tackled the revised TEKS, with particular attention to the recommendations I had made but also took into consideration changes in areas where I had not commented previously.[6] I noted, for instance, that although the term *such as* had been retained, I liked how some of the committees had adopted language that made clear what was required to be included and what was meant to be an example. I also found that the range of examples reflecting the geographic, cultural, and ethnic composition of Texas and the nation was much improved, but that further consideration was required. In general, then, the committees did a good job of revising the TEKS under the circumstances.

One example of how instances where I made recommendations were subject to committee work that actually produced improved results is the third-grade student expectation regarding the formation and expansion of communities. The original expectation stated, "Describe how individuals such as Christopher Columbus and Meriwether Lewis and William Clark have contributed to the expansion of existing communities or to the creation of new communities." I had argued that for third graders the examples failed to provide the kinds of clear-cut examples that should be included. I recommended a more concrete approach: "Describe how individuals such as Juan de Oñate and Brigham Young have contributed to the expansion of existing communities or to the creation of new communities." Although it did nothing to clarify the definition of community per se, I like the way the committee reworked the item: "Describe how individuals such as Christopher Columbus, the founding fathers, and Juan de Oñate have contributed to the expansion of existing communities or to the creation of new communities." In the end, someone on the board added Daniel Boone, but at least the new mix did something about adding an important earlier figure and broadening out the examples, through inclusion of the founding fathers, to other types of communities.

I submitted my review in August 2009, at which point I was invited to provide testimony at the next meeting of the board on September 17. It was an interesting experience. I was contacted by various groups at various points on the political spectrum. One gentleman representing a Catholic group informed me that they were very upset with me because I was being anti-Catholic. Metaphorically scratching my head, given that for 15 years I had been the managing editor of a history journal called *Catholic Southwest* and that I had received prizes from the Texas Catholic Historical Society, I inquired how so. It turned out that my sin had been to omit the word *Catholic* from a reference to mission building in Texas. I had to explain to the gentleman that I thought the word *Catholic* was unnecessary since during the Spanish colonial period the Catholic faith was the only one allowed. Consequently, all missions were Catholic missions.

September 17, 2009, was a long day. When I finally got my chance to speak—I was allowed ten minutes—I presented prepared remarks that placed the issues in terms I hoped everyone on the board could appreciate. "The Founding Fathers understood that the United States was a work in progress and they embedded that knowledge right into the first sentence of the Constitution: 'We the people of the United States, in order to form a more perfect union . . .' Indeed, the history of the United States can be seen as striving to that end."

I then went on to use the concrete example of the expanding inclusiveness of "citizenship" based on changing social, economic, and political considerations from the very restricted participation at the beginning of the nation to the Voting Rights Act of 1965. My purpose was to show that we need to teach a history that discusses this process of expanding citizenship in an honest way, otherwise it makes no sense: "Why should the nation's history not include this rich tapestry of conflict, compromise, and cooperation? Why should we deprive our schoolchildren of the possibility of finding heroes among the various and varied groups that played a role in building this more perfect union? Of understanding how they and their families came to occupy the roles they play in their communities, the state, and the nation? Of recognizing individuals like them whose contributions made the country a better place? Of taking pride in their communities' roles in the building of America?" I then proposed that since the purpose of social studies in K-12 is the teaching of civics, those lessons that should prepare children to be responsible adults, our curriculum should reflect the breadth of historical experiences making up the struggle to create a more perfect union. I concluded by stating, "Our legacy to the twenty-first century should be to educate our children by giving them the civics tools they need to understand, function in, and improve our communities, our state, and our nation. We can do this by having them understand that we have not yet reached the goal set by the Founders of a more perfect union. The Founders could not see the future, but they could and did prepare for it. We should do the same." The message didn't seem to sink in very deeply. The board continued squabbling, the media continued to harp on who and what was in or out. And the various groups involved all dissected every change as if part of some big conspiracy on the left or right. I cannot speak to the existence or nonexistence of one or more conspiracies or even to whether there was collusion or collaboration between other experts, outside groups, and the SBOE. I can say that I remained independent throughout the process and have studiously avoided taking sides.

This squabbling continued in October, when the committees came together again to work on further revisions. I spent a considerable amount of time with the fourth- and seventh-grade committees, which did seem to appreciate the need for modernizing and diversifying Texas history. And cynically I have to say that they probably had more leeway to produce better results because much of the focus was on the modern US history standards, where the big battleground issues of civil rights, the moral majority, Reaganomics, separation of church and state, and abortion underlay the discussions.

I spent some time with the high school US history committee, which was locked in ideological warfare over who should be included as examples and who should not. Most of the committee seemed to be on one side, and one member appointed by a conservative member of the SBOE was on the other. The issue of examples is one of my biggest problems with the whole process because it detracted from developing clear-cut TEKS and student expectations focused on core concepts. For instance, César Chávez is more controversial than the developing notion of fair employment practices in an age of prosperity. So if you get caught up in arguing over whether or not Chávez is a role model and should or should not be included, you don't pay enough attention to the underlying need to discuss the tensions in mid-twentieth-century America over what constitutes fair treatment of workers. We do not have any problem including Adolf Hitler in history books, and he's certainly not a good role model. In any case, I was promptly dismissed from the committee's deliberations, and I was happy to get away.

In the hallway of the hotel in central Austin where all this was taking place, I was confronted by a Dallas area grandmother, a self-professed member of the tea party, who was there to make sure the committees were not undermining or distorting American values. I do not know if my attempts to reason with her that there was little to fear from committees composed of white, middle-class, mostly suburban schoolteachers in terms of what would be in the textbooks. In fact, I tried to explain that the work of the committees was standards and not textbook content.

And that was (and is) a big part of the problem as we headed into the next round of hearings in January. The SBOE, the media, and the various interest groups all talked about textbooks and what should be in them and what should not. Of course, from my perspective much of this arguing was a waste of energy. No self-respecting textbook author would omit the role of religion, specifically Christianity, in the founding of the American colonies. In fact, it would be impossible to ignore in discussing the European colonization of the New World. Christianity played an even greater role in the Spanish American context than it did in the English colonial world. Were the Founding Fathers influenced by Christianity? No doubt, they certainly were part and parcel of the Judeo-Christian tradition. Were they trying to build a theocracy? No they were not. Somewhere in the middle, where the writing committees actually were and where the textbooks will no doubt be, is an acceptable narrative that provides the basics of history without undue ideological baggage. But as I said earlier, that's not what board members and interest groups at either extreme were interested in.

I was notified in January 2010 that my services were no longer needed now that I had provided my feedback to the original and revised TEKS and had made myself available to the writing committees in October. I was paid the balance of my fee, thanked, and dismissed. The rest of the process would be in the hands of the SBOE and those lobbying its various members. So for the rest of the process I was a spectator to the political process of compromise that continued weighing down the standards with more requirements, more examples, and more ideological baggage.

Remember that I said the original guidelines I received asked, "Do the standards promote ideological neutrality by balancing people/events from various sides of the political spectrum?" Well, that's exactly what happened. For every César Chávez we got a Phyllis Schlafly; for every NAACP we got a Moral Majority—the tit-for-tat and horse trading that accompanies the political process applied to the development of curriculum standards.

This is what I told the Mexican American Legislative Caucus (MALC) of the Texas state legislature at a hearing in April 2010, when it decided to hold informal hearings on the process. Perhaps they were expecting that I would take the approach of some of my colleagues in condemning the work of the SBOE as ideologically reactionary and worthless and racist. Instead, I focused on what has been the underlying theme of this chapter, that I do not consider a social studies curriculum that takes into consideration that we live in a postindustrial, urban, high-tech, multicultural society a bad thing. That we cannot expect students to appreciate this country and this state if they do not see themselves as part of the story.

I would like to conclude by quoting two paragraphs from my testimony before the MALC:

> Anyone who reads the latest draft of the curriculum standards, which were made public a couple of weeks ago, will note that the standards have problems, but not necessarily the ones that the media has harped upon. Thomas Jefferson has not been banished from the standards, and neither has Thurgood Marshall, César Chávez, or Dolores Huerta. In fact, the inclusion of Hector Garcia, Irma Rangel, and Henry B. Gonzalez as examples is a very positive development; so, too, is the greater attention to the events and people that shaped the advent of modern Texas during Texas's participation in the struggle for Mexican independence and during the Texas Revolution. At every grade level there is a call for understanding local communities, the roles and contributions of women and minorities, and concern for instilling a sense of political responsibility in students. Although there is certainly an effort to defend the so-called conservative resurgence of the last 20 years, there are only a couple of clear examples of overreach. By and large, the inclusion of religion is well within the bounds of what is taught in most college classrooms, and there has been no effort to force curriculum to be written that overly emphasizes the Christian roots of this nation or of Western civilization.
>
> So, what are the problems? First, in an effort to accommodate everyone's wishes, the SBOE has produced an almost impossibly large set of standards. The bloat extends to repetition and confusion. There are too many required items, which the preamble to each set of standards makes clear are those items preceded by the term *including*, and there are too many examples, those items preceded by

the term *such as*. In fact, the media wars have mostly been about these examples—the most famous ones having been the attempted removal of Thurgood Marshall, César Chávez, and Thomas Jefferson from specific places in the standards. In the end, though, the bloat means that teachers cannot get through the curriculum and that testing companies will have a significant, and unfortunately large, role to play in what actually receives emphasis in the classroom.[7]

In the time since my final public comments, I have been asked to endorse the idea of scrapping the TEKS as they were finally adopted and I have been asked to endorse the idea that the TEKS be retained. I have been asked to support the candidacy of the present chairman of the SBOE (who as of this writing has not received Senate confirmation and will automatically have to step down at the end of the spring 2011 legislative session). I have been asked to condemn the various board members. I have declined all such offers. Taking sides would compromise what I see as my ability to appeal to all parties for reason, which I am still hoping is possible as education companies, testing agencies, and social studies departments in school districts start putting curriculum together. After all, some time ago the legislature took absolute power over textbooks away from the board when it gave it authority only to approve textbooks that met a minimum percentage of TEKS objectives.

Would I agree to serve as an expert reviewer again if asked? Only if the process were better organized, more professional, and more respectful of the people who actually do the teaching. I made a number of recommendations in my testimony before the MALC that I would use in judging whether or not the process was sufficiently professional for me to again participate. First, there should be a clear indication that everyone involved (board members, legislators, even lobbyists) understands the goals and objectives of the TEKS in light of the classroom experience. The standards should not be about making political points but about providing students curricula in history, government, and economics that prepare them to be informed and conscientious citizens. Second, teachers, curriculum designers, and publishers should have enough flexibility to address the standards in ways that represent the range of geographic, demographic, and economic diversity found within the state. Cookie-cutter, one-size-fits-all approaches to curriculum are inimical to good teaching, which depends on the teacher's enthusiastic engagement and ability to respond creatively to students. Third, the legislature should clearly restrict the SBOE's curricular authority to the policy-making level. Unless the composition of the board is altered to include only professionals in the field (like, for example, the Texas Medical Board and the Texas Bar Association), its members should not be involved in the direct crafting of standards or of micromanaging curriculum or learning materials. Rather, the board should provide broad guidance on goals for K-12 education and then hold accountable those professionals actually responsible for generating and delivering curriculum.

I remain hopeful that once we have purged our present-day ideological demons we will return to making the necessary compromises to move our education system forward. Our children deserve better than the process we have in place at the moment.

Until then, it's tough being a voice crying in the wilderness.

Notes

1. The application solicited contact information, a résumé or curriculum vitae, and the disclosure of business relationships with the Texas Education Agency and the SBOE, government agencies in other states, colleges and universities, textbook publishing companies, professional associations, and lobbying entities.
2. Jesús F. de la Teja, "Review of [Current] Social Studies TEKS," June 28, 2009, http://www.tea.state.tx.us/index2.aspx?id=6184.
3. de la Teja, "Review of [Current] Social Studies TEKS," 1.
4. Ibid., 2.
5. Stephanie Simon, "The Culture Wars' New Front: U.S. History Classes in Texas," *Wall Street Journal*, July 14, 2009.
6. Jesús F. de la Teja, "Review of [First Draft] Social Studies TEKS," August 29, 2008, http://www.tea.state.tx.us/index2.aspx?id=6184.
7. Jesús F. de la Teja, "An Almost Impossibly Large Set of Standards Produced by a Problematic Process," *History News Network*, May 10, 2010.

Figure 5 Tejanos in the Battle of the Alamo
The Texas State Historical Association took a proactive approach to the revision process, working both in formal roles and behind the scenes. This strategy produced several successes in the Texas history standards, including efforts to incorporate the typically overlooked role of Tejano participation in the battle of the Alamo.

CHAPTER 5

Negotiating for Quality
Taking a Proactive Approach to Achieve a Positive Outcome

Stephen Cure

What makes a relatively sane person march knowingly into what he suspects will be a firestorm in which he will expend an enormous amount of energy attempting to improve a situation while trying to avoid getting scorched? The answer in this case, which may sound utterly cliché, is both simple and complex—duty. The prospect of revising the Texas Essential Knowledge and Skills (TEKS) for social studies arose as early as 2007, and it soon became apparent that my professional duties as the director of educational services for the Texas State Historical Association (TSHA) would propel my involvement into the process. As the process moved along, it became clear that further involvement would become more public and potentially hazardous. To take involvement to that next level would mean invoking my duties as a father of two children who would be impacted by the revised standards and as a sixth-generation Texan who cares deeply for this state and its heritage. This collection of duties coupled with experience as a former seventh-grade teacher of Texas history helped form the goals that guided me throughout the process. Those goals included ensuring that the amount of instruction on Texas history remained at least constant, that the fourth- and seventh-grade standards were as accurate and as fair and balanced as possible, and that the amount of content was feasible for teachers to cover in the time they have. To accomplish such goals involved utilizing a strategy that I think is worth reviewing and replicating in other similar circumstances. To achieve a positive outcome with the aforementioned goals, institutions with a stake in social studies education must take a proactive approach throughout the process and understand that in the end, all such processes are political and will involve negotiation.

Being Proactive Early Builds Awareness, Credibility, and Opportunities

Being proactive necessitates being informed on how such processes work and remaining involved throughout the process. The processes for setting state curriculum standards vary from state to state and may or may not include dealing with elected officials, but most begin informally, as it did in Texas. Standards are usually revised in a cyclical process, the intention of which is to keep them up-to-date. Prior to the official start of the process, there is often informal work performed by teachers' groups and others to assess what may need revising and to provide recommendations on behalf of these groups when the formal process begins. Many Texas social studies leaders knew well in advance that the process was coming, and having observed English/language arts (ELA) and science go through fairly difficult processes, they also knew that it had the potential to be difficult and highly politicized. The debate over ELA was characterized by an apparent lack of agreement within the ELA community on recommendations. The science community learned from that and saw a smoother process through a more unified approach with the exception of traditional hot-button issues like how evolution is to be taught.[1]

In light of this, as early as 2007, active discussions of how to proceed were being held by groups like the Texas Council for Social Studies (TCSS) and the Texas Social Studies Supervisors Association (TSSSA). On March 5, 2008, I organized a meeting at the Bob Bullock Texas State History Museum in Austin to discuss how various organizations that have a stake in Texas social studies education could better communicate and work more effectively together. One topic of discussion was the desire for involvement on the part of such stakeholders in the upcoming TCSS and TSSSA process and the potential positive impact of having these organizations' unified support behind their recommendations.[2] The TCSS organized a meeting of major stakeholders during its 2008 annual conference, held in San Antonio in October. Teachers, curriculum specialists, and stakeholders were all encouraged to provide feedback on the previous standards and review the group's recommendations, which were formally presented to the Texas State Board of Education (SBOE) when the process formally began in January 2009.[3] Being involved in these informal processes is essential to understanding the issues facing classroom teachers and support staff and to providing the type of expertise that organizations like the TSHA can bring to the table.

As a result of the work performed through these collaborative efforts, a number of key items were identified that would impact later efforts. First, classroom teachers stressed that the standards, as they already existed, were about as extensive as they could be given the time teachers had to teach them. This position became a guiding principle of at least the seventh-grade review committee tasked with making formal recommendations to the SBOE. Second, a healthy debate existed at that time about the use of lists of illustrative examples. The majority of classroom teachers asked for them, whereas a number of curriculum specialists felt that they were not needed. In the end, a slight majority favored the use of the lists, and their inclusion became part of the final recommendations that were used widely by the review committees. Though such lists would have minimal impact on assessment, they became the source of much discussion and action as the SBOE elevated many of them from an illustrative to a required status, thereby expanding the amount of overall material that teachers must cover. Third, the TSHA established itself as a resource for assisting leaders within the social studies community. As questions arose about the accuracy of recommendations or the best way from a historical standpoint to phrase something related to Texas history, the TSHA was called upon to either answer or locate an answer from our resources or those of our academic members. This relationship reaffirmed a credible role for our organization within the community and was later replicated when we were working with the SBOE. Finally, as an interested and active participant in the early process, I was repeatedly encouraged by members of these groups to volunteer for service on the seventh-grade review committee when the SBOE issued the call for volunteers.

In summary, making an effort to be involved early in these processes helped establish positive relationships and credible roles for stakeholders. It also kept us abreast of the issues related to instructing and assessing standards.

Heeding the Call to Professional Duty: A Must for Historical Organizations

As a result of repeated encouragement and my sense of professional duty, in October 2008 when the SBOE called for volunteers—teachers, parents, interested community members—to staff the committees that would make recommendations for changes, I submitted my application. From a professional perspective, it seemed like an appropriate role for the director of educational services of the TSHA, and furthermore, my predecessor, David DeBoe, had served on the committee that wrote the 1998 TEKS that were now being revised.[4]

To form the 17 committees organized to review the existing standards, each SBOE member was able to select for each committee a person from the district the SBOE member represented. Gail Lowe—who, prior to the July 2009 meeting, would be appointed chair of the SBOE—represented the district in which I live and where the TSHA is located. I had only briefly met and corresponded with her and didn't feel a written application was sufficient to secure an appointment, so I asked SBOE member Patricia "Pat" Hardy, with whom I was acquainted through the TCSS and the TSSSA, to pass along a personal recommendation, which I followed up with a telephone call to Lowe. Though the call provided no assurances, I felt that I had utilized all traditional channels in the effort and would just have to wait and see. On January 16, 2009, I received notification of my appointment to the seventh-grade review committee.[5]

Incidentally, in my opinion, the selection process for the review committees, coupled with the content in the revised TEKS for some courses, is partially responsible for the negative reactions of many within Texas. Most of the SBOE members made appointments to the committees, but only a few filled the majority of their allotted appointments despite the existence of a multitude of qualified applicants. Some SBOE members appointed no one to the committees, which left large parts of Houston and San Antonio without representation on the committees. Shortly after learning of their exclusion, I offered my services as a conduit for their concerns on the seventh-grade standards, during a meeting in February 2009 with social studies leaders from the Houston area and through personal contacts with those in the San Antonio area. Though they expressed appreciation for the offer and some took advantage of it, it did not assuage their anger over not having a direct voice in the process. To date, many in these areas, some of whom had been leaders in the social studies community's early efforts, harbor resentment over this exclusion.

The next step in this lengthy process was service on the seventh-grade review committee (and in light of all that transpired during the work of the committees, "service" is indeed an accurate description). Though a relatively small group, the seven members of the seventh-grade review committee worked exceedingly well together throughout the entire process. Despite some infrequent differences in professional opinion, the committee engaged in polite and frank discussions, negotiated consensus on issues, and worked efficiently, which was not always the case with other committees that shared the same space. The formal process of committee work began in Austin in January 2009 with several days of meetings. The sixth- through eighth-grade committees followed the SBOE guideline to start with the existing TEKS and the evaluation of the TEKS as it related to their correlation to the recently adopted College and Career Readiness Standards (CCRS).[6] Following a review of these items, committees began to brainstorm and draft other changes. By this time, copies of the TCSS/TSSSA recommendations presented to the SBOE were distributed by fellow committee members, and many of these were also incorporated. As a representative of the TSHA who had a relationship with numerous Texas historians, I was asked to find the answers to a variety of questions related to possible changes. At the conclusion of January meetings, Texas Education Agency (TEA) staff instructed committee members to turn in their documents on a flash drive for safekeeping even though most committees indicated that they were holding off on making substantive recommendations until the committees for K-8 and the high school courses had the opportunity to meet in April. There was still substantial work to be done, especially with vertical alignment, when the committees adjourned.

Controversy arose soon after, however, when SBOE chairman Don McLeroy asked TEA staff to provide the draft documents to the nonprofit and right-leaning Texas Public Policy Foundation. The foundation's staff reviewed the documents and reported their findings at the March 2009 meeting, which resulted in a delay in the committee work, changes in the process, and additional guidance from the SBOE. A special meeting of the SBOE's Committee on Instruction was held in April 2009, after which it recommended having the expert reviewers selected by the SBOE review the existing TEKS first and make recommendations to the review committees, which admittedly was helpful. It may be worth noting that only one of the expert reviewers, Jesús F. de la Teja from Texas State University, made substantive comments on the seventh-grade Texas history material. A few others made brief comments, and some made no comments at all. The SBOE also reiterated its guideline that the existing standards were the basis for starting, that committees must focus on the regular course of study as opposed to higher-level advanced placement courses or the like, and that all changes must be accompanied by a brief justification/explanation.

I must admit a slight lapse in judgment at this juncture in the process, triggered by what truly felt like a betrayal of trust when we were required to turn over our very incomplete drafts to a third party. In written testimony to the members of the Committee on Instruction prior to their April meeting, I described the release of information as "the equivalent, in educational terms, of assigning a class a five paragraph essay which will include stated steps of brainstorming, a first written draft, peer review of that draft, editing and revision, and the production of a final paper; collecting the brainstorming and first paragraph at the end of class on the first day with the stated intent of returning it the next day; and sending it to a teacher down the hall for grading and posting in the cafeteria."[7] Maybe that statement was a bit melodramatic, but it wasn't far from the truth of what transpired. Nevertheless, the recommendations of the Committee on Instruction were accepted with a few minor adjustments by the full board in May, and the review committees were scheduled to resume their work in July.

When the review committees reconvened, the work of the seventh-grade committee consisted of reviewing our previous efforts to ensure that they were consistent with the SBOE guidelines, documenting the explanations for changes we had already drafted, and returning to many of the questions we left unresolved at our previous meeting. It was in this unresolved questions phase of our work that I believe having someone from an organization like the TSHA was most valuable. During the extended break between meetings, I was able to reach out to respected historians at a variety of institutions around the state, both for answers to specific historical questions and for general feedback on all or part of the draft TEKS. This was extremely helpful to the committee and generated a pool of additional experts to whom we could address questions. One of the items that had been requested by teachers was a defined list of the eras of Texas history, a standard that very closely aligned with the CCRS. Have you ever tried to get seven respected historians to reach a consensus on a list of names for eras? It wasn't easy, but we managed to get it done, and through the use of email and cell phones we were able to communicate with our added pool of experts in real time to get answers to additional questions as they arose. I would also like to mention that SBOE members Pat Hardy and Mavis Knight were in attendance and played a positive role in the process by listening and answering questions. It is also important to note that there was a greater degree of vertical collaboration at this meeting—the seventh-grade committee was able to assist the fourth-grade committee through our access to outside experts. The product of these meetings was a solid first draft, which was then sent to the expert reviewers and posted for informal public feedback.[8]

Following the period of feedback and review, the committees reconvened and many pored meticulously over first the feedback of the expert reviewers and then the compiled informal feedback. Many good points were made by both groups, so changes were made. I would like to point out for future reference that we were informed prior to this meeting that the Texas Navy Association had a desire to see the Texas Navy included in the standards relating to the Texas Revolution and Republic and that they had significant support. As a result, it was added to the illustrative list of notable individuals and groups related to the Republic of Texas standard. SBOE members Hardy and Knight were present again, joined by Lowe, the SBOE chair, and each played a constructive role. For example, the seventh-grade committee wanted to include Senator Kay Bailey Hutchison in the citizenship standard on contributions of Texas leaders in order to provide both gender and ideological balance, which was lacking. We were warned by some that this might not be approved by the SBOE because of the impending Republican primary in which Senator Hutchison was facing Governor Rick Perry and that we should attempt to explain the reasoning to Lowe if given the opportunity. Lowe visited with each committee to hear questions and concerns, and we were able to explain the rationale for the addition and gain her support. The end result of this final committee meeting from the committee's perspective was a document that had remained fairly constant in the amount of content teachers were expected to cover, was clearer and better structured, contained a greater diversity of examples (in terms of race, geography, gender, and ideology) through the use of illustrative lists, was more closely aligned with the CCRS, was assessable, and addressed many of the concerns of teachers, expert reviewers, and the broader public.

Sharing Expertise Shifts to Oversight and Advocacy

At this point the process shifted into yet another phase as the draft documents were submitted to the SBOE for their review, acceptance, and additional changes. Prior to the first meeting of the SBOE on this subject, the final drafts of the committees were submitted to the expert reviewers for an additional round of feedback to be provided to the board. Additionally, each committee was asked to have one member prepare brief remarks and answer questions prior to the November 2009 SBOE meeting. Likewise, the expert reviewers were invited to appear and present their views on the committee drafts. The seventh-grade committee originally turned to me to provide this testimony, but because of previously scheduled obligations out of state, my colleague Richard Vickery, from Garland, was chosen to represent us and did an excellent job. His testimony was brief as requested, and he fielded only a few questions, which was somewhat surprising given the intense scrutiny other committee representatives were subjected to.[9] The SBOE accepted the committee recommendations and used them as the starting point for several additional meetings, which specifically addressed public feedback and changes by the SBOE and provided fodder for a media onslaught.

As time neared for the January 2010 meeting—which was to include first reading of the drafts, public testimony, and edits by the SBOE—it became apparent through informal communication that the board was unhappy with the recommendations submitted by a number of the committees and intended to make a significant number of edits as part of the process. Though it did not appear that either fourth- or seventh-grade Texas history were particular targets for major changes, the TSHA leadership decided to closely monitor the proceedings and to offer once again to serve in a resource capacity. It was decided that the best approach would be twofold: to present public testimony in which we would state our institutional support for the documents generated by the committees and to offer my services as a resource for any questions related to the Texas history courses. I specifically use "we" in this instance because although I was the one who prepared and delivered the testimony, it was reviewed by several others within the TSHA leadership, resulting in a variety of edits.[10] Furthermore, it was a multilateral agreement for the organization to serve as a resource, not a unilateral one. This is worth noting because at that point a sizable media buzz regarding the upcoming process was already beginning, ironically much of it based on old information from previous committee drafts and not the actual documents the SBOE was currently working with.[11] In January 2010, the testimony was presented orally and in writing, and thus began my personal attendance at every single board meeting until the documents were finally adopted, a fact that did not go unnoticed—on more than one occasion, members of the board referred to me as the "resident Texas history expert in the back of the room" concerning content that they had already inquired about or feedback that had been provided on various amendments.

During this meeting, several SBOE members from both political parties approached me with questions both about historical content and about advice on possible wording for various matters they felt they needed to address. This was precisely the position that we had hoped to achieve as a nonpartisan authority that could field questions regardless of ideology and could attempt to guide the changes to the best possible outcome for students and teachers. With some credibility established and lines of communication opening, it was during and between these board meetings that the majority of the negotiating took place. Through communication with a variety of SBOE members before, during, and after meetings that focused primarily on issues of factual inaccuracy or confusing terminology, it was possible to build a rapport that was for the most part apolitical. Although changes were made to the fourth- and seventh-grade documents during the first meeting, the board quickly ran out of time and failed to complete their first-reading changes, pushing what remained to the next meeting, in March 2010.

By the time the SBOE completed first reading of the drafts at its second meeting, a number of changes had been made that needed to be adjusted.[12] In consultation with TSHA leaders and members, I submitted recommendations through the official online feedback mechanism on six problem areas: (1) adding representative tribes to complete an illustrative list of American Indian tribes that lacked the accurate cultural diversity; (2) removing the assertion that Spanish explorers were in search of freedom; (3) placing a Spanish revolutionary in the appropriate time period; (4) removing a finite number of Alamo defenders and replacement with language intended to emphasize the need to cover the diversity and nature of those who were there (this may sound trivial, but among Alamo enthusiasts and academic historians, there is no agreement on the exact number of defenders); (5) removing a standard that specifically emphasized the Texas Navy over other groups related to the Republic of Texas period, ensuring balance among the groups associated with the Republic of Texas; and (6) correcting a misapplication by staff of a broad amendment related to describing our form of government as a "constitutional republic" that altered the meaning of citizenship standards utilizing the term democratic society.[13] In addition, a very specific letter detailing the nature of the problems was sent to each board member whose amendment created an issue as well as suggesting alternate language that was accurate and that achieved the result intended by the member. Furthermore, a full list of the changes was sent to Lowe, the board chair. These letters were followed up with emails, phone calls, and even office visits with some. Whether for reasons of personality or access, there were instances in which it was difficult to build the rapport necessary to discuss problem areas, but the use of the official comment mechanism ensured that the feedback was received. In those cases where I was unable to build the type of relationship necessary to effect the needed changes, others were recruited to make personal contacts.

The strategy employed was simple—the least amount of controversy is likely to arise from a member revising his or her own amendment than to identify a key ally who sets about amending the work of others. It is also important to note that the recommendations distributed to the board members were a coordinated group effort of the TSHA staff and key members. The draft documents, as well as the text of the correspondence, were circulated and feedback was sought to ensure accuracy and that the proper tone was achieved. By the end of second reading in May, all the items had been addressed, five of them by the SBOE member who had originally made the change.

One of the six items in need of amendment deserves greater scrutiny because of its complexity, the number and nature of interested outside parties, and its being one of the best examples of the type of negotiations and compromise that constituted this revision processes. As mentioned earlier, the Texas Navy Association made a request to the SBOE to have the Texas Navy moved from the illustrative list where the committee had placed it into its own separate and required student expectation, which was granted. In addition to the group's oral and written testimony before the board, the association had the support of at least one well-respected and influential statewide elected leader who contacted SBOE members on behalf of the organization. The addition of the Texas Navy to the standards in itself was not an issue, as it had already been added by the committee. The issue was actually twofold: the Texas Navy had now been moved into a separate and required capacity while the remainder of the Revolution and Republic Era groups were still together and retained their illustrative status, and it was now presented in a way contrary to the way most historians and educators would logically present the material. The latter is, of course, the most important, but as a member of the historical community, I knew that the possibility of an all-out war between the various groups associated with the Texas Revolution was no laughing matter either. Many of these groups—such as the Daughters of the Republic of Texas, the Sons of the Republic of Texas, the Texas Navy Association, the Texas Rangers Foundation, the Seguin Family Association, the Descendants of Austin's Old Three Hundred Association, and a variety of others—are devout in their belief that this period of Texas history be substantively taught, and many have significant political connections.

After meeting with the SBOE member who created the new expectation on the Texas Navy Association's behalf, it became apparent that the full support of the association's leadership as well as that of the statewide elected leader who supported the change were required before the board member would alter his amendment. Meetings were scheduled with the statewide elected leader, with whom we had other programmatic ties, and he was supportive of the changes recommended by the TSHA. He even reached out to the leaders of the Texas Navy Association and endorsed the recommended changes. Multiple emails and several phone calls were exchanged with Texas Navy Association leaders to explain how teachers were going to teach the material and how separate treatment might be negatively perceived by educators. In the end, agreement was reached with the compromise that the entire list be required, but with no separate standing.[14] This was placed in writing and sent to the appropriate board member who subsequently made the change during second reading proceedings. Though the actions associated with this one seemingly minor item took a significant amount of time, it was productive in building additional relationships and was likely the type of negotiation that only a respected historical organization like the TSHA could have executed.[15]

As the second reading and final adoption process continued, there were a number of items that came up during the May 2010 meeting and were dealt with through on-site communication. It is worth noting the irony that accompanied the final meeting from a personal perspective. Because of a delay in posting the first reading draft arising from the volume of amendments and the volume of feedback received, the May 2010 board meeting was moved back a week from its originally scheduled date. This change in schedule brought my professional duties in conflict with my parental duties as the new date now conflicted with my oldest child's fourth-grade field trip to the State Capitol and Bob Bullock Texas State History Museum, which I had previously agreed to chaperone. Reconciliation of both was managed with the aid of mobile technology, and thus I was answering technical questions about historical content and appropriate placement several blocks away from the halls of the Capitol and across the street from the museum and its exhibits. Instead of riding the bus back, my daughter joined me at the still ongoing proceedings and was with me when the product of so much time and effort was finally adopted.

It would be an absolute relief to say that it was all complete at that point, but it just would not have been consistent with the process up to that point. In reviewing the minutes from the final board meeting, some inconsistencies between them and the board proceedings were noticed. Lowe and Hardy were contacted to inquire about the procedure for technical edits prior to the release of the final TEA version. Lowe stated that she would see to it, and the changes were made. All told, the final versions of the fourth- and seventh-grade Texas history standards appear to be pretty solid according to various informal interactions with academics and veteran Texas history teachers I have encountered. Are there areas where ideology has crept in? Sure—that is inevitable in most processes involving elected officials and political appointees. Examples of such ideology included adding the positive benefits of human environmental modification by both "governmental and private entities," teaching nine-year-olds how to "hold public officials to their word," and engaging in the entire debate over the use of "constitutional republic" versus "democratic republic." Are those matters that a credible nonpartisan historical organization should engage in correcting? Not if the organization wants to retain the credibility among those in positions of authority in order to affect those priorities closest to its mission of ensuring that the content being taught is accurate and balanced. During the proceedings, many stood at the podium and railed against the machine, and many of their demands are now only archived footage of those proceedings. An approach that worked quietly both in front of and away from the cameras seemed to have a greater degree of success.

Working with the Final Product and Lessons Learned

Following a process as lengthy as the revision of the Texas social studies standards, there is a lot of work for an organization like the TSHA. Having been involved throughout the process enabled our organization to better understand which information is most in need of explanation and of additional supporting material. Moreover, our involvement placed a broader cross-section of the staff and leadership in the know about the content and the process, which should be beneficial in understanding how the organization can support teachers and students going forward. Following the adoption of the new standards, the TSHA set about planning what needed updating among its resources, including curriculum resources, its resource-finding aid (TeachingTexas.org), and any content in its state history encyclopedia, the *Handbook of Texas Online*, which needed to be updated before teachers and students began searching for it in earnest. The material most in demand was related to the significant addition of historical figures, both illustrative and required, which for the most part was pretty easy to handle (though some of the more modern figures continue to present a challenge). In addition to working on these internal matters, I was called upon in a variety of settings to explain both new content and why I felt either a committee or the board made certain changes—information the TSHA would have needed even had I not been involved throughout the entire process.

In retrospect, the opportunity to experience the standards revision process provided numerous lessons that may be of value to others in similar positions or organizations, including the value of being involved, the amount of time required, and the costs associated with involvement. Though it was my understanding that the TSHA should be involved based on the experience of my predecessor and the organization's stated goal of being the leader in Texas history education, it was indeed surprising to hear the sentiments of appreciation from a variety of participants and the inquiries from those teachers and supervisors in regions that were missing from the discussion. Our presence in the process and the significant number of new relationships that participation generated has been of great benefit to the organization and will continue to be an asset for years to come. Admittedly, the time commitment was more significant than expected. I estimate that over the three-year period from the informal conversations through the final adoption of the revised TEKS, I put in four hundred to five hundred hours or more. The monetary costs to the organization were not large enough to be a concern. The most significant cost or risk is loss of personal or organizational credibility—even a minor misstep off the path of serving as a nonpartisan resource for all can result in significant difficulties for both the individual and the organization. Fortunately, this did not occur in this case. Last but not least is a lesson that fewer and fewer people are familiar with these days, that negotiation and sometimes compromise are necessary to reach an outcome that will be received by the broadest possible audience as a success.

Though there are hazards and pitfalls, historical organizations must take a proactive approach in standards processes if they expect the history education in their respective areas to be a quality one. They should be willing to engage in the discussions and negotiations to get a quality result, and in some ways it could be said that it is their duty to do so. There are often restraints based on the type of agency a historical organization is housed in, but serving as a source of quality information and nonpartisan advice is usually acceptable. There are also a variety of other opportunities—for example, reviewing textbooks and assessments—in which those with expertise and a stake in history education are welcome and encouraged to participate. It was professional and personal duty that led me into this experience, which as an Army veteran I liken to my tour of duty in Bosnia after the Dayton Peace Accords—it is an experience of a lifetime that you are probably better off for having had, but at the same time you aren't too eager to do it again anytime soon. Time will tell how these standards and their impact are judged. For the present, at least, it appears that the fourth- and seventh-grade standards for Texas history are in pretty solid shape historically.

Notes

1. Gary Scharrer, "Texas Educators Split over Teaching English Basics," *Houston Chronicle*, April 20, 2008; James C. McKinley Jr., "In Texas, a Line in the Curriculum Revives Evolution Debate," *The New York Times*, January 21, 2009.
2. Texas Studies Stakeholders Meeting minutes, Austin, TX, March 5, 2008, compiled by the author.
3. Sharon Pope, Testimony Before the SBOE on behalf of the Texas Council for Social Studies and Texas Social Studies Supervisors Association, Austin, TX, January 22, 2009.
4. David C. DeBoe, TEKS Revision Working Papers 1997–1998, Texas State Historical Association.
5. Anita Givens, letter to Stephen Cure, January 12, 2009, in author's possession.
6. Texas State Board of Education, Social Studies Gap Analysis, July 7, 2009, in author's possession.
7. Stephen Cure, Written Testimony to SBOE Committee on Instruction, May 20, 2009, in author's possession.
8. TEKS (7/31/09).
9. Richard Vickery, Testimony Before the SBOE, November 18, 2009.
10. Stephen Cure, Testimony Before the SBOE, January 14, 2010.
11. April Castro, "Texas Board to Vote on Social Studies Standards," *Seattle Times*, January 14, 2010; Veronica Flores-Paniagua, "*Kids May Lose in Textbook Debate*," *San Antonio Express-News*, January 9, 2010.
12. TEKS (3/10).
13. Stephen Cure, letter to Gail Lowe, April 26, 2010, in author's possession.
14. Frank Richard Brown, letter to Gail Lowe and David Bradley, May 26, 2010, in author's possession.
15. In the interest of full disclosure, it is important to note that evidently the entire process and the way it was handled led the president of the Texas Navy Association to recommend to Governor Perry that I be made an admiral in the Texas Navy, which was done on November 19, 2010.

Figure 6 Protesting the new standards
Throughout 2009 and 2010, a grassroots network slowly grew into a liberal-minority coalition that extended across the state of Texas. Here members hold a demonstration outside the final public hearing of the Texas State Board of Education.

CHAPTER 6

Moving the Liberal-Minority Coalition Up the Education Pipeline

Emilio Zamora

The conservative Texas State Board of Education (SBOE) presented a formidable challenge to progressives who were seeking to influence the 2009–10 revision process of the social studies curriculum for our public schools. The outcome was predictable. The SBOE largely rejected progressive claims and recommendations and adopted highly revised standards—the Texas Essential Knowledge and Skills, commonly referred to as the TEKS—with a decidedly conservative bent. Progressives, however, were not without a victory of their own. They could take comfort in having reenergized their cause for a more just and effective curriculum while reactivating links of cooperation that make up the liberal-minority coalition in the state.[1]

Advancing the organizing capacity of the coalition does not negate the significance of the loss, especially when we consider that conservatives have maintained control over the SBOE through another election cycle and will continue to shape education in Texas for the foreseeable future. One could point to the SBOE's significant influence over the state's multimillion-dollar textbook selection process and to its responsibility for the state-mandated curriculum that holds public schools accountable through high-stakes testing. The stakes in this exchange were so high that a panel at the 2011 annual meeting of the Organization of American Historians characterized the fight between conservatives and progressives as "history wars"—a fight over how we interpret the past to our children.[2] However, the breadth and depth of the conservative victory should obscure neither the content of the critique nor the significant organizational gains made by progressives during the fight over curricular revisions.

This first-person account provides my ground-level observations on the impressive reach and dedication of the network of organizations associated with the progressive coalition and the content of its critique. My concern is that important grassroots voices not get overlooked in the larger national discourse over an accountability system of conservative standards and narrow outcome measurements in state and national settings. I also wish to point out that the conservative gaze that has previously been directed primarily at K-12 education in the form of test-based accountability has also reached Texas higher education. I conclude by noting that university faculty, in particular, need to engage policies and politics by joining the state's coalition as a matter of self-interest and survival.

The Coalition

My participation in the progressive coalition did not occur by chance. My cultural membership in the Mexican community and my long-standing association with Mexican American studies in universities throughout the country explain my interest and participation in networks of individuals and organizations that ultimately galvanized resources for the fight against the SBOE. Community involvement may have a distinct beginning in a person's memory, but it also represents a continuous process that builds over time and space among consistently committed individuals and organizations. Simply put, an ethos of, and a commitment to, community involvement inevitably brings about new opportunities for participation based on preexisting associations characterized by collaborative partnerships that enable informed and decisive collection action.[3]

My decision to join took place at a book-signing event for an anthology edited by Dr. Maggie Rivas-Rodríguez and myself.[4] Dan Arellano, head of the Tejano Genealogical Society, president of an Austin council of the League of United Latin American Citizens (LULAC), and a member of a local veterans' group, Tejanos in Action, was one of our guests that evening.[5] He invited us to participate in meetings called by a community organization, Unidos de Austin, to prepare testimony on the proposed SBOE revisions. The group included Dr. Sylvia García, a retired educator who had worked at the Texas Education Agency (an affiliate body of the SBOE) for more than twenty years and had participated in feminist and education organizations throughout Texas since the late 1960s, and Andrés Tijerina, a professor of history at Austin Community College and an award-winning author of histories on the colonial and Mexican periods in Texas history. Arellano, Tijerina, and I eventually testified before the SBOE, noting the misrepresentation and underrepresentation of Mexicans in the revised curriculum. A brief examination of their recent political biographies offers an opportunity to comment on the emerging overlapping networks in the curricular revision process.

Arellano has been a prominent figure in a network of historians and genealogical researchers associated with what I term the heritage recovery enterprise in the Mexican community of Texas. He has been relentless in bringing public attention to the battle of Medina, which occurred twenty miles south of San Antonio on August 13, 1813, and was the first major bloody clash between Spanish royalists and independence-minded insurgents. Aside from his work with the Tejano Genealogical Society and LULAC, Arellano has published a family history that addresses the battle, conducted archaeological digs at the site of the battle, spoken extensively throughout the state on the battle and colonial history, and conducted reenactments of important colonial events throughout the state.[6] He uses the vast LULAC and genealogical network in the state to promote a recovered and personal view of history that places Mexicans at center stage in the story of Texas's past.[7]

Tijerina has brought scholarly standing to the Mexican recovery enterprise with his notable publications, academic appointments, memberships in professional history associations, and formal presentations on Tejano history.[8] He exemplifies the often touted, but inconsistently practiced Mexican American studies tradition of moving between the university and the community. Tijerina has been involved in Mexican genealogical activities throughout the state for at least twenty years, playing an especially important role in convening their larger organizations to sponsor annual conferences. The latest statewide meeting, hosted by Los Bejareños Genealogical Society of San Antonio in September 2011, brought together at least nine organizations and hundreds of their enthusiasts for the thirty-second annual Texas State Hispanic Genealogical and Historical Conference.

Tijerina is also a vice president of the board of directors of the Tejano Monument, a highly regarded group that has raised the funds and acquired the needed support to erect a statue that commemorates Tejano history on the grounds of the State Capitol. The statue will become a major public point of destination by virtue of its location at the Capitol, the most popular site for tourists in the state.[9] Conferences, public talks, publications, statues, and websites sponsored by genealogical societies, the Tejano Monument, and other more broadly defined outlets such as Somos Primos make up the heritage recovery enterprise that provided Arellano and Tijerina the platform to argue before the SBOE for fairer representation.

The leadership, decision making, and public discourse that Arellano and Tijerina share in their genealogical work constitute an example of overlapping space connecting other distinct networks that they inhabit. When they joined with other like-minded individuals on the issue of the revised curriculum, they reconfigured and thickened overlapping networks and extended the reach of their critique of the revised curriculum. The addition of Dr. Rivas-Rodríguez to the circle of cooperation is a case in point. She brought other networks to the mix as the founder and director of Voces Oral History Project, a program that she has directed for the last 11 years. Voces has generated more than four hundred interviews and collected thousands of artifacts that document wartime contributions by Latino veterans and family members from across the country. Aside from the affiliations with the hundreds of narrators and their families who are themselves part of other local networks of civil rights, veterans, and community organizations, the oral history project has included hundreds of volunteer interviewers, scholars, filmmakers, museum workers, genealogists, and other students of Latino history. Newsletters, newspapers, publications, conferences, films, and other kinds of outreach activities that developed alongside the oral history project have given impetus to other community initiatives that Rivas-Rodríguez has led, especially the Defend the Honor campaign, a four-year nationwide effort that challenged a 2007 PBS documentary on World War II by Ken Burns for excluding Latino soldiers.[10]

Rivas-Rodríguez testified against the revised curriculum and used her extensive network to bring public attention to the hearings. She also made use of her connections from the oral history project and the Defend the Honor campaign to organize a teach-in in May 2010 on the controversy surrounding the SBOE's deliberations. Arellano and I participated in the teach-in, alongside other presenters associated with a Texas Native American community, LULAC, the NAACP, Los Bejareños Genealogical Society from San Antonio, and the Multicultural Alliance of Social Studies Advocacy from El Paso.[11]

The Texas Freedom Network (TFN), a progressive grassroots organization that claims affiliations with 45,000 community leaders and organizations from across the state, also played an important role in the coalition. The TFN was founded in 1969 to counter the growing public influence of the far right on a number of political and public policy issues, including education. The organization was especially helpful in coordinating the work of participating groups and organizations into a concerted effort and in bringing favorable publicity to the coalition activities. This involved planning discussions, press releases, and conferences, interviews with the press, continuous communications with their affiliates and coalition participants, primarily through their electronic newsletter, and testimony before the SBOE and legislative committees that held hearings on the curriculum revision process. Their staff also benefited from its associations in the coalition. They advanced their organization's standing as an effective and trusted progressive voice in Texas politics, especially among the Mexican American and African American organizations that participated prominently in the coalition.[12]

The TFN provided printed and electronic copies of materials critical of the SBOE that reflected many of the concerns of members of the coalition. For example, a July 2010 report titled *Culture Wars in the Classroom*" highlighted a statewide survey among 972 likely voters in Texas that criticized the SBOE's handling of the curriculum revision process. Among the report's major conclusions were that curriculum should be established by educators, not politicians; that voters who followed the revision process were more likely to oppose the standards; that nearly half of voters think religion should play a larger role in schools; and that voters opposed the politicized process that omitted core concepts and put quality education at risk.[13] The TFN's wide circulation of materials such as press releases, informational packets, and reports clearly extended the reach and influence of the coalition.

The Mexican American Legislative Caucus (MALC), a group of 44 state legislators that focuses on public policies affecting the Mexican American community, served as another important focal point in the coalition. The organization emerged in 1975, soon after Mexican Americans began to effectively translate their demographic growth into a significant improvement in their representation in the state government. Although the Voting Rights Act of 1965 contributed to this momentous change in Texas politics, the successful coalitions by Mexican American community organizations also made a lasting difference. Organizations like LULAC, the American G.I. Forum, the Raza Unida Party, and the Southwestern Voter Registration and Education Project successfully demonstrated an ability to register voters, organize campaigns, and influence the Democratic Party to support their cause for equal rights. The MALC is currently one of the most influential interest groups in the state's Republican-controlled legislature, in large part because of the demographically based potential of the Mexican American population and its close alliances with other minority interest groups, like the Senate Hispanic Caucus, the Texas Legislative Study Group, and the Texas Legislative Black Caucus, as well as national civil rights organizations such as LULAC and the NAACP.[14]

State Representative Trey Martínez Fischer, head of the MALC, leveled some of the hardest-hitting critiques at the SBOE, including the charge that the board had exceeded its statutory authority when its members excluded or minimized the opinions of curriculum experts who advised the board and/or presented testimony during its hearings. The MALC received significant public attention when it called for public hearings on the SBOE's authority and curriculum revision process.[15] The public hearings, which took place on April 28, 2010, were especially important because they helped legitimate the concerns of the coalition and gave notice that progressive minority legislators will maintain close scrutiny over the SBOE and the curriculum in the public schools—where minority children are now the majority. Although the Republican-dominated legislature would eventually block the 16 house and senate bills that were proposed, the hearings produced a coherent progressive critique in the testimony of seven witnesses. Despite differences of emphasis, the general consensus was that the SBOE disregarded scholarly evidence and basic rules of writing and analysis, misrepresented and underrepresented important historical trends and themes, overextended its conservative interpretation of the past, manipulated the process of review by disregarding protocol and the advice and recommendations from expert consultants and members of the public, and acted unprofessionally when conservative members publicly disparaged its critics.[16]

The legislative hearings were also important because they occurred during the most intense phase of public debate and public testimony, and they convened representatives from most of the groups in the coalition. The hearings, in other words, represented a high point in the effort to coalesce the progressive cause. Membership in the coalition had occurred naturally with speeches, media interviews, newspaper articles, strategy meetings, testimony before the SBOE, press conferences that often turned into rallies, marches and demonstrations by a group of students from the University of Texas, letter-writing campaigns, and conversations. The relationships and implicit understandings between individuals defined the overlapping networks that included the previously noted organizations as well as the Come Crudo Native American tribe from Central Texas, student organizations that rallied under the banner of "Save Our History," the History News Network, and others. These groups may have reached a public of tens of thousands of members and allies through their meetings, rallies, press conferences, electronic sites, letter-writing campaigns, and social media communications.

Testimony

My presentations before the SBOE—in March and May 2010—and at the April 28 public hearings did not embrace the complete critique of the coalition, although I did address three of its substantive concerns: the failure to incorporate current scholarship, the lack of representation of minorities and women, and the widespread concern over the revision process among scholars from across the country.

I first suggested that our public schools are not adequately preparing our students for university studies because the public school curriculum does not come close to fully reflecting the state of the scholarship in Texas history. I did this by pointing out that Texas historians have made significant advances since at least the early 1970s and that the public school curriculum lags far behind, especially in the history of women, Mexican Americans, African Americans, workers, and civil rights.

My second observation pointed to glaring omissions in the larger field of social studies and was based on my analysis of the list of historical figures that were being proposed at the time (May 2010) as required subjects in the curriculum.[17] Only one person from Africa, two from Asia, and two from Latin

America appeared in the proposed curriculum. Indigenous persons were limited to two Native Americans from the United States, and there were none from the rest of the Americas. Mexico, the country that has been most intimately involved in Texas history, had only one representative from the period after 1836, and he was the fully scorned Antonio Lopez de Santa Anna.

To make matters worse, references to Miguel Hidalgo y Costilla, the father of Mexico's independence movement, and one of his historic speeches were deleted. The SBOE also deleted Oscar Romero, the assassinated archbishop from El Salvador who became one of the most popular Christian figures in the Americas. According to the numerous press reports, the board voted to remove him from the curriculum because a majority did not know who he was.[18]

Such striking omissions suggested a pattern of neglect and discrimination rather than happenstance or an occasional lapse of judgment. This became more apparent when I tabulated the number of times that white, Latino, black, and others were noted. Whites (males and females) from the United States and Europe predominated, appearing 154 times, 79.4 percent of the 194 entries. The 24 Latinos that were noted represented 12.4 percent of the total, 12 blacks registered 6.2 percent, and 4 others accounted for 2.1 percent. Women fared poorly: males were mentioned 179 times (92.3 percent), whereas women appeared only 15 times.

A complementary set of data derived from the list of historical figures that the SBOE was proposing as recommended—not required—for study. White males and white females each gained twenty additional entries. Minority male figures remained constant, and their female counterparts registered small numerical and proportional increases. Although a recommended designation would not theoretically limit the teacher to the list of historical figures, the skewed data suggests continued bias by the SBOE in favor of Anglos, particularly Anglo males.

Part of the explanation for the unequal representation rests in the continued predominance of white males as major figures in history books. This view of history, however, cannot be justified solely by the emphasis that we give to topics like government, industry, and war, where males dominate. A 73.2 percent male representation in the recommended category of the proposed curriculum was inordinately high, especially if we consider that the study of history has expanded significantly since the early 1970s and provides greater depth and breadth in all areas, including Mexican American and African American history. The final draft of the standards—analyzed fully in Chapter 7—indicates that the SBOE did little to address these deficiencies.

My third contribution to the SBOE hearings emerged from the numerous expressions of concern that I received from colleagues in colleges and universities from across the country, especially regarding the intemperate and ideologically driven statements by some board members. I wrote "An Open Letter to the Texas State Board of Education" during the first week of April and, with the help of Keith Erekson of the University of Texas at El Paso and an organizing committee of history faculty from the Austin and El Paso University of Texas campuses, posted it for endorsements.[19] The national signature-soliciting campaign secured 1,200 signatures in ten days. The great majority of the endorsements came from history instructors and researchers in US colleges and universities. The letter was critical of the proposed curriculum and the SBOE, claiming that the board "has been derelict in its duty to revise the public school curriculum" and that "the integrity of the curriculum revision process has been compromised." The board disregarded the critique as well as the recommendation for a reconsideration of testimony by curriculum and content specialists and a postponement of the vote. The letter did, however, become a part of the record created by the April 28 legislative hearings and informed the subsequent report and proposed house and senate bills.

Extending the Gaze from K-12 to Higher Education

Less than a year after the progressive coalition engaged the SBOE over the K-12 social studies curriculum, conservative politicians in Texas shifted their attention to higher education. Many Americans see public schools and universities as separate sites of contestation that operate in isolation of one another. In reality, successful conservative tactics at the K-12 level are being carried over into a substantial, public attack on higher education. In this new arena, the issues of accountability and standards are taking on a new life, and the progressive coalition forged during the K-12 struggle will have to unite with university administrators, staff, and faculty who previously had not been involved.

The conservative critique emerged publicly in March 2011, with Governor Rick Perry and an Austin-based conservative think tank, the Texas Public Policy Foundation (TPPF), seeking "to boost productivity and accountability" in the state's top-tier universities, the University of Texas at Austin and Texas A&M University at College Station. The collaboration between Perry, the TPPF, and conservative members of the board of regents of both institutions began as early as 2008 and culminated in a public report titled "Seven Breakthrough Solutions" in which Perry and his allies called for major alterations in how universities teach students, evaluate learning, compensate faculty, and secure accreditation from regional and national institutions. Specific proposals would reward good teaching with one-time bonuses, would separate teaching (75 percent) and research (25 percent) tracks, would provide funding in the form of student-directed scholarships, and would create a new national accrediting agency that would reward quality predicated on "outcomes-based" testing models. In short, the proposed evaluation undervalued the research-driven model of academia at the same time that it evaluated quality instruction and faculty effectiveness on the basis of a cost-effective analysis of student satisfaction measures. The obvious goals were to weaken the universities' authority—especially faculty governance—over the measuring of teaching effectiveness and to place them under greater public scrutiny.[20]

Although some of the reforms were enacted at Perry's alma mater, Texas A&M—most notably the development of a single metric for evaluating faculty performance—other voices pushed back against Perry and the TPPF. A group of prominent supporters of higher education formed the Texas Coalition for Excellence in Higher Education. State Senator Judith Zaffirini has openly challenged the proposals, and University of Texas officials, including Chancellor Francisco G. Cigarroa, President Bill Powers, and Liberal Arts Dean Randy L. Diehl, have responded with their own measured and firm defense of the university and university studies. The University of Texas Alumni Association, the Texas Exes, issued their own early rebuttal to the charges that the universities needed added oversight. At the time of this writing, the issues are still swirling around a newly appointed Joint Oversight Committee on Higher Education Governance, Excellence, and Transparency in the Texas state legislature. Other conservative leaders—most notably in Ohio, Wisconsin, and Florida—have taken note of the new Texas model and are making moves to implement their own version of it.[21] In light of this multistate, long-term attack, colleges and universities should take community engagement initiatives as reciprocal, capacity-building opportunities.

Conclusion

In summary, the shift in attention to higher education reveals an interest among conservative reformers in Texas and the nation to use the playbook from primary and secondary education to exercise greater control over what students learn under the guise of the "efficient" expenditure of scarce public dollars. The federal No Child Left Behind Act of 2001 was designed to hold primary and secondary schools accountable for student learning—primarily by applying sanctions for failing to raise test scores—but a corollary move into higher education threatens to delegitimate historic discourses related to universal access to a baccalaureate education. The appeal of "efficiency" in our universities by public figures like Governor Perry exploits a historic moment of financial insecurity to achieve conservative ends.

In Texas, administrators, state political leaders, and alumni have proven effective thus far in publicly defending the universities before the general public. University faculty, staff, and students, however, cannot claim much credit for the win because they played a largely negligible role in the controversy. Although a lack of will or interest may explain this failing, their general absence in the coalition that challenged the SBOE minimally suggests a more significant distance from protest community networks and the experience and confidence that accompanies this kind of involvement.

This is not to say that faculty, staff, and students do not participate in off-campus communities. Many of them are active members of their churches, public schools, and other community institutions. Others are associated with university-sponsored programs that offer practical and knowledge-based services that include work with community boards, electoral campaigns, classroom teaching, and media outlets. The fight with the SBOE, however, offered an opportunity to challenge the conservative accountability cause in an advanced stage of organization that foretold an unfolding agenda that ironically has direct implications for the entire higher education enterprise.

Conservatives control much of what passes for public education in Texas. Progressives were not able to do much about the conservative SBOE in 2010, but they can maintain and even increase their organizational capacity for more effective challenges in the future. Higher education faculty, however, must abandon their ivory-tower mindsets and embrace the common cause of those who are challenging the conservative agenda across the entire education pipeline, if for no other reason than to have the wherewithal to engage in successful challenges when the conservative gaze is directed toward us. There is no need to work in a vacuum. This first-person account demonstrates the potential and fruitfulness of involvement that already inheres within the state's coalition, and through this account, I call on progressives to direct their cause up the education pipeline into our institutions of higher education.

Notes

1. George Norris Green, *The Establishment in Texas Politics: The Primitive Years, 1938–1957* (Norman: University of Oklahoma Press, 1979); Randolph B. Campbell, *Gone to Texas: A History of the Lone Star State* (New York: Oxford University Press, 2004).
2. David A. Walsh, "Highlights from the 2011 Annual Meeting of the Organization of American Historians in Houston, Texas," *History News Network*, March 22, 2011. The panel, "History Wars: The Texas Textbook Controversy," included Paul S. Boyer (University of Wisconsin) as the chair and Alan Brinkley (Columbia University), Mark A. Chancey (Southern Methodist University), Rebecca A. Goetz (Rice University), Lisa Norling (University of Minnesota), and Emilio Zamora (University of Texas at Austin) as panelists.
3. See Angela Valenzuela, ed., "Presence, Voice, and Politics in Chicana/o Studies," *International Journal of Qualitative Studies in Education* 18, no. 2 (March–April 2005, special issue).

4. Maggie Rivas-Rodríguez and Emilio Zamora, *Beyond the Latino World War Hero: The Social and Political Legacy of a Generation* (Austin: University of Texas Press, 2009). The book signing was sponsored by the Center for Mexican American Studies, University of Texas at Austin, and it took place at El Mercado Restaurant, on February 18, 2010.
5. The term *Tejano* is a self-referent that Mexican Americans use to underscore a regional identity and a long-standing autochthonous connection to Texas.
6. Dan Arellano, *Tejano Roots: A Family Legend* (Austin: privately published, 2005).
7. The work of historians like Arellano obtains deep-rooted significance from the Mexican genealogical work that mostly harkens back to a colonial and indigenous past and an identity as people of the soil. Genealogical activities are intimately tied to a land grant movement that has generated legal claims against current landowners and the Mexican and US governments by the descendants of land grantees from South Texas and their Sociedad de Reclamantes. See Robert J. Salazar, "Texas Land Grant Heirs Seek Compensation*, Agenda* 9, no. 2 (March–April 1979): 14–16; Armando C. Alonzo, "Mexican-American Land Grant Adjudication," in *En Aquel Entonce (In Years Gone): Readings in Mexican-American History,* ed. Manuel G. Gonzales and Cynthia M. Gonzales (Bloomington: Indiana University Press, 2000), 64–71. The most popular land grant movement leader in the Southwest was Reies Lopez Tijerina; see his autobiography, *They Called Me "King Tiger": My Struggle for the Land and Our Rights,* trans. and ed. José Angel Gutiérrez (Houston: Arte Público Press, 2000).
8. Andrés Tijerina, *Tejanos and Texas Under the Mexican Flag, 1821–1836* (College Station: Texas A&M University Press, 1994); Andrés Tijerina, *Tejano Empire: Life on the South Texas Ranchos* (College Station: Texas A&M University Press, 1998).
9. On the Tejano monument, see Andrés Tijerina, "Constructing Tejano History," in *Lone Star Pasts: Memory and History in Texas,* ed. Gregg Cantrell (College Station: Texas A&M University Press, 2007), 176–202.
10. See *Voces, An Oral History Project,* available at *http://www.lib.utexas.edu/voces;* Defend the Honor, available at *http://defendthehonor.org.*
11. The teach-in took place on the southern steps of the State Capitol and was attended by approximately two hundred persons; see "Campaign Update: Texas State Board of Education; Teach In, Sunday, May 2, 2010," available at *http://defendthehonor .org/?page_id=254.*
12. See John M. Bruce, "A Success Story, at Least for Now," in *God at the Grassroots, 1996: The Christian Right in the 1996 Elections,* ed. Mark J. Bozell and Clyde Wilcox (Boston: Rowman & Littlefield, 1997), 45–46; Texas Freedom Network website, http://*www.tfn.org.*
13. Texas Freedom Network Education Fund, *Culture Wars in the Classroom: Texas Voters Call for a Cease-Fire* (Austin, TX: Texas Freedom Network Education Fund, July 2010).
14. Cynthia E. Orozco, "Mexican American Legislative Caucus," *Handbook of Texas Online* (Austin, TX: Texas State Historical Association).
15. Brian Thevenot, "Minority Legislators Call Hearing on History Books," *Texas Tribune,* April 21, 2010; Gary Scharrer, "History Professors Part with State Board over Proposed Standards, *Houston Chronicle,* March 31, 2010.

16. The testimonies of Michael Soto, Jesús de la Teja, Emilio Zamora, Iliana Alanís, Keith A. Erekson, Roberto R. Calderón, and Kirsten Gardner were published as "Scholars Assess the Proposed Texas History Standards," *History News Network*, May 10, 2010. The MALC joined with the Texas Legislative Caucus (TLC) and the Texas Legislative Study Group (TLSG) to issue a report on May 17 based on the hearings, *Public Comment to the State Board of Education, Comments Regarding the Currently Proposed Social Studies Curriculum Standards*" (Austin, TX: TLC/TLSG, 2010), copy in author's possession supplied by Emanuel García, policy coordinator of the Mexican American Legislative Caucus. For summaries of the bills see Texas Freedom Network, *The State Board of Education is Failing Texas School Children*" (Austin, TX: Texas Freedom Network, n. d.), *http://www.tfn.org/site/DocServer/SBOE.pdf?docID=2403*.
17. For an analysis of the finished product, see chapter 7 in this volume.
18. Steven Schafersman, "Social Studies Standards under Attack by State Board of Education Members," *Observer*, May 10, 2010.
19. The letter, signatures, and an analysis of the standards were posted online at *http://sensiblehistory.blogspot.com/*. The letter drew national coverage and commentary; a list of media stories is online at *http://tekswatch.utep.edu*.
20. Ralph K. M. Haurwitz, "UT Uproar's Roots are in '08 Summit; Perry Cites State Research Spending," *Austin American Statesman*, April 4, 2011. Although various newspapers reported on the controversy, *the Texas Tribune* stood out for its regular reporting on the issue; see, for example, Reeve Hamilton, "AAU to Texas A&M: Resist 'Ill-Conceived' Reforms," *Texas Tribune*, March 7, 2011; Reeve Hamilton, "Seven Breakthrough Solutions Would Boost Productivity and Accountability at Public Universities," *Times of Texas*, May 31, 2011.
21. Reeve Hamilton, "Prominent UT Alum Warns of 'Degradation' at University," *Texas Tribune*, March 16, 2011; Reeve Hamilton, "Joint Higher Ed Oversight Committee Gets to Work," *Texas Tribune*, September 21, 2011; Denise Maria-Balona, "Scott Explores Changes in Higher Education," *Orlando Sentinel*, August 22, 2011; John T. McNay, "The War on Higher Education," *History News Network*, September 11, 2011; Audrey Williams June, "Florida May Be the Next Battleground over Faculty Productivity," *Chronicle of Higher Education*, September 13, 2011.

PART II

Analysis and Alternatives

Changes to the Standard on Civil Rights

Texas Essential Knowledge and Skills (1998)

The student understands the impact of the American civil rights movement. The student is expected to

a) trace the historical development of the civil rights movement in the ~~18th~~, 19th, and 20th centuries, including the 13th, 14th, 15th amendments;
b) identify significant leaders of the ~~civil~~ rights movement, including Martin Luther King Jr.;
c) ~~evaluate government efforts~~, including the Civil Rights Act of 1964, to ~~achieve equality~~ in the United States; and
d) ~~identify~~ changes in the United States that have resulted from the civil rights movement such as increased participation of minorities in the political process.

Texas Essential Knowledge and Skills (2010)

The student understands the impact of the American civil rights movement. The student is expected to:

a) trace the historical development of the civil rights movement in the 19th, 20th, and *21st* centuries, including the 13th, 14th, 15th, and *19th* amendments;
b) *describe the roles of political organizations that promoted civil rights, including ones from African American, Chicano, American Indian, women's, and other civil rights movements;*

c) identify *the roles of* significant leaders *who supported various* rights movements, including Martin Luther King Jr., *Cesar Chavez, Rosa Parks, Hector P. Garcia, and Betty Friedan*;
d) *compare and contrast the approach taken by some civil rights groups such as the Black Panthers with the nonviolent approach of Martin Luther King Jr.;*
e) *discuss the impact of the writings of Martin Luther King Jr. such as his "I Have a Dream" speech and "Letter from Birmingham Jail" on the civil rights movement*;
f) *describe presidential actions and congressional votes* to *address minority rights* in the United States, including *desegregation of the armed forces*, the Civil Rights acts *of 1957 and* 1964, *and the Voting Rights Act of 1965;*
g) *describe the role of individuals such as governors George Wallace, Orval Faubus, and Lester Maddox and groups, including the Congressional bloc of southern Democrats, that sought to maintain the status quo*;
h) *evaluate* changes *and events* in the United States that have resulted from the civil rights movement, *including* increased participation of minorities in the political process; and
i) *describe how litigation such as the landmark cases of Brown v. Board of Education, Mendez v. Westminster, Hernandez v. Texas, Delgado v. Bastrop I.S.D., Edgewood I.S.D. v. Kirby, and Sweatt v. Painter played a role in protecting the rights of the minority during the civil rights movement.*

Figure 7 Changes to the standard on civil rights
The things *added to* the state's civil rights standard reveal the dynamics of the entire process in miniature. A quick examination of the changes highlights the issues of inclusion and representation, issues that were widely noted in the media. A closer examination raises additional questions about bias and intent.

CHAPTER 7

Names, Numbers, and Narratives
A Multicultural Critique of the US History Standards
Julio Noboa

This chapter provides a focused content analysis of the new US history standards taught in eighth and eleventh grades in Texas public schools. The purpose is to assess the extent to which the Texas Essential Knowledge and Skills (TEKS) are accurate, relevant, and objective in their reflection of the diverse multicultural character of Texas and the nation, with particular attention to the representation of women, American Indians, African Americans, and especially Latinos. In those instances that the standards come up short, some recommendations for improvement and modification are made for classroom practice. The analysis also includes selected comparisons with the previous curriculum standards that were in effect for more than a decade.

The special focus on Latino representation is motivated by several realities. Latinos constitute the largest ethnic minority group in the nation and the fastest-growing in public schools. In Texas, Latino students, mostly of Mexican origin, have been the single largest ethnic group in the public schools since at least 2003–4, and they surpassed the number of white students in the 2008–9 school year by well over half a million.[1] Latinos, particularly Mexican Americans, have also made a profound contribution to the culture, history, and identity of the republic and state of Texas, the West, and the Southwest. This influence is most notably evidenced in the arenas of cuisine, music, dance, dress, and language as well as in the entire American cowboy culture based on the *norteño* vaquero ranching culture of northern Mexico.[2] Despite the Mexican American influence on some of the most pivotal events and personalities of Texas and American history, Latinos are too often ignored, marginalized, denigrated, or denied in the curriculum of the public schools.[3]

This investigation analyzes the names of individuals and groups appearing in the TEKS but also extends to include narrative elements such as eras, events, movements, concepts, and judicial cases that emerge from and resonate with the historical experiences of women and minorities. The first task of this study was to compare and contrast the names of women and minorities in these newly adopted TEKS with those used during the previous ten years for the same courses. In addition to the standards, some primary source documents, secondary historical materials, and contemporary scholarly critiques were consulted to help assess the accuracy, objectivity, and precise wording of the TEKS.[4] I also benefited from participating on the TEKS review committee for the eleventh-grade course on US history since 1877. This experience provided me with more insight into the process by which these standards were developed (see chapter three).

Relevant Background and Criticism

For decades there has been a keen interest in the teaching of history at both the state level and the national level. Just how well American students know the key historical events, dates, and personalities that define our constructed national character has been of great concern to public officials, educators, and academics. Standards, textbooks, and standardized testing have become subject to extensive analysis. The results of the periodic National Assessment of Educational Progress (NAEP)—considered by many to be the "nation's report card" and the most reliable measure for determining what students' know about any subject—is closely watched and widely commented upon by scholars and journalists. The most recent results for the US history assessment were announced, coincidentally, in 2010, and they revealed that despite some overall gains in scores since 1994, only 20 percent of fourth graders, 17 percent of eighth graders, and 12 percent of twelfth graders performed at above the Proficient level. Compared with their performance in the other three areas assessed by the NAEP—math, science, and reading—students scored the lowest in US history by very wide margins.[5]

Yet the teaching of history also raises controversial political and ideological issues that affect both academic and public discourses on pluralism, diversity, multiculturalism, and national identity. The exclusion, marginalization, and stereotyping of minorities and women, and most notably Latinos, in the history and social studies curriculum and textbooks, have been documented and challenged by multicultural educators for decades, even into the twenty-first century.[6] Part of the controversy that surrounded the revisions to the TEKS drew increased attention to the ostensibly racial and ideological battles being fought.

The debate about names—and therefore about race, ethnicity, and gender—began quite early in the process when one of the "experts" appointed by the Texas State Board of Education (SBOE), Christian fundamentalist minister Peter Marshall, suggested that neither César Chávez nor Thurgood Marshall were adequate enough role models. An immediate response in opposition to this ridiculous suggestion generated not only national media attention but also a grassroots letter-writing and email campaign by thousands of Texans.[7] Statements from and interviews with unapologetic social conservative SBOE members revealed their crude attempts to impose a narrow view of history onto the standards and evoked critical responses from educators across the political spectrum. Sue Blanchette, president of the National Council for the Social Studies (NCSS), wrote, "I was stunned and appalled at some of the changes being made to the standards, changes not based in scholarship but in partisan politics and religious fervor." After reviewing standards from all fifty states, the conservative Thomas Fordham Institute gave the TEKS an overall grade of D, noting that the "evangelical, Christian-right" board incorporated "all the familiar politically correct group categories" while "suppress[ing] less triumphal or more nuanced aspects of our past that the Board found unacceptable (slavery and segregation are all but ignored)."[8] Throughout the deliberations, discussions, and public testimony, the issue of which individual is to be included or excluded became a central focus, most especially when that individual was a woman, Latino, or other minority.

Issues of inclusion and representation, however, are only part of a range of concerns related to history and diversity in textbooks. Even a cursory view of certain key controversial issues raised by these questions, such as inclusion, accuracy, bias, and intent, reveals that many were at play in both the content of the US history TEKS and the process that created them.

Key Findings

Of the 111 individuals named in the new US history TEKS, 16 are women (14.4 percent of the total), 12 are African American (10.8 percent), and 7 are Latino (5.4 percent). Table 1 summarizes these findings (listing women separately and as part of other categories when relevant) and compares names in the new and former TEKS. The TEKS distinguish between individuals that are required to be taught (noted with an asterisk) and those that are merely suggested—only the former appear on standardized tests. Thus, despite the notable increase in the absolute number of individual women and minorities, their percentages of the total individuals required to be taught are still relatively small.

Beyond these names and numbers, I also examined narrative elements such as eras, events, and movements as well as important concepts, Supreme Court

Table 1 Women and Minority Individuals in the Eighth- and Eleventh-Grade US History Standards

	1998 TEKS	2010 TEKS
Latinos	No individuals named	Roy Benavidez César Chávez* Bernardo de Gálvez* Hector P. Garcia* Dolores Huerta Lionel Sosa Sonia Sotomayor
African Americans	Shirley Chisholm W. E. B. Du Bois Frederick Douglass Martin Luther King Jr.*	Crispus Attucks* Vernon J. Baker W. E. B. Du Bois Frederick Douglass Marcus Garvey Martin Luther King Jr.* Thurgood Marshall Barack Obama* Rosa Parks* Hiram Rhodes Revels* Ida B. Wells Oprah Winfrey
Women	Abigail Adams Susan B. Anthony Shirley Chisholm Georgia O'Keeffe Elizabeth Cady Stanton	Abigail Adams* Jane Addams Susan B. Anthony (twice) Hillary Clinton Betty Friedan* Dolores Huerta Sandra Day O'Connor Rosa Parks* Eleanor Roosevelt Phyllis Schlafly* Sonia Sotomayor Elizabeth Cady Stanton Mercy Otis Warren* Ida B. Wells Frances Willard Oprah Winfrey

* Individuals labeled with an asterisk are required to be taught.

cases, and constitutional amendments related to the experience and struggle of women and minorities in American history. Before discussing the elements specific to women, African Americans, American Indians, and Latinos, we will review the findings of items that make reference to women and/or minorities in a general sense and consider their most direct implications.

General References to Women and/or Minorities

A new item appearing in the revised TEKS requires that at every grade level each school district set aside an entire week, dubbed "Celebrate Freedom Week," to provide targeted instruction on the Declaration of Independence, the US Constitution, and the Bill of Rights. In this explicitly patriotic context, students are to relate the documents to "the rich diversity of our people as a nation of immigrants, the American Revolution, the formulation of the US Constitution, and the abolitionist movement, which led to the Emancipation Proclamation and the women's suffrage movement."[9] Clearly, the struggles of women and African Americans—and perhaps by implication, other minorities—are related to the original ideas of democracy entailed in the founding documents.

In the eighth-grade TEKS for US history up to 1877, the first standard requires that the student "understands traditional historical points of reference" and provides both dates and "major eras and events" during that period. Among these are "westward expansion, reform movements, Civil War, & Reconstruction," with students expected to "describe their causes and effects."[10] These eras by their very nature imply, though do not specify, the engagement of African Americans, American Indians, women, and people of Mexican descent in the historical narrative.

Following that, the only overtly multicultural standard for this course appears in standard 23, which states that students are to understand the relationships among various "racial, ethnic, and religious groups," explain their reasons for immigration, identify ways they resolved their conflicts, and analyze their contributions to our national identity. The expectation for this standard spans three centuries (seventeenth through nineteenth), raising the question about which of the many specific possibilities are more significant and worthy of study. Standard 24 also contains direct reference to women and minorities: students are to evaluate the impact of the major reform movements of the nineteenth century, including the abolitionist movement, the labor reform movement, and the movement for women's rights.[11]

The eleventh-grade TEKS begin with the late nineteenth century, and many of the standards make either a direct or an implied reference to women or minorities. In standard 3, students are expected to "analyze" political issues such as Indian policies, economic issues including the "growth of labor unions," and "social issues affecting women, minorities, children, immigrants." In standard 6, the student is to "analyze causes and effects of events and social issues such as immigration, Social Darwinism, eugenics, race relations, nativism, . . . and the changing role of women." Standard 7 mentions the internment of not only Japanese Americans but also German and Italian Americans during World War II. Standard 9 on "the impact of the American civil rights movement" makes arguably the most direct and extended set of references to women and minorities in the entire course. Here "Martin Luther King Jr., César Chávez, Rosa Parks, Hector P. Garcia, and Betty Friedan" are named as "significant leaders"—only King appeared in the previous version of the TEKS. Standard 9 also expects students to "evaluate changes and events in the United States that have resulted from the civil rights movement, including increased participation of minorities in the political process" as well as to "describe the roles of political organizations that promoted civil rights, including ones from African American, Chicano, American Indian, women's, and other civil rights movements." These two statements are outstanding in that they make reference to women and minorities as participants and role players in the historical narrative, moving them from the objects of history to its subjects.

Standard 10 received much attention in the media and from social conservative board members for its emphasis on the "conservative resurgence" of the 1980s and 1990s. Here students are expected to describe "the causes and key organizations and individuals" of the movement, including Phyllis Schlafly, the Heritage Foundation, and the Moral Majority. Although liberal and civil rights organizations are excluded from consideration in standard 10, standard 11 engages issues that emerged from the 1990s through the twenty-first century, expecting students to "identify significant social and political advocacy organizations, leaders, and issues across the political spectrum," thus making it clear that all political viewpoints should be considered.[12]

There are also a few additional items that make direct or implied mention of women and minorities. In standard 15, reference is made to the Chinese Exclusion Act of 1882, in the context of foreign policy issues that had an economic effect. In standard 22, the student is to understand "the concept of American exceptionalism" wherein one expectation is that students "describe U.S. citizens as people from numerous places throughout the world who hold a common bond in standing for certain self-evident truths." The final two standards for this course contain various relevant items, beginning with standard 25 describing cultural movements "in art, music and literature" and mentioning both the Harlem Renaissance and the Chicano Mural Movement, along with Tin Pan Alley, the Beat Generation, country and western music and rock and roll. This was the standard to which the review committee added hip-hop music and from which the conservative SBOE members voted to remove it with much public fanfare. Most notable is the final standard, 26, wherein the student should understand "how people from various groups contribute to our national identity" by explaining the "actions taken by people to expand economic opportunities and political rights, including those for racial, ethnic, and religious minorities as well as women" and by explaining "how the contributions of people of various racial, ethnic, gender, and religious groups shape American culture."[13]

Specific References to Women

Regarding the 16 women named, which include Latina and African American women, there is a considerable variety of roles represented, including two first ladies, eight civil rights or social reformers, two political leaders, two Supreme Court justices, an author, and an entrepreneur. Four are named in eighth-grade history—Abigail Adams, Mercy Otis Warren, Susan B. Anthony, and Elizabeth Cady Stanton. In that course, standard 22 also requires students to describe the contributions of significant female leaders. What makes this standard positively outstanding is that instead of just listing names, it also requires description of the contributions of the women—a rare narrative space in which to recognize women's agency as historical actors.[14]

Many of the references to women made in the TEKS for US history since 1877 have been mentioned above because they are embedded in the same statements as those that include African Americans, Latinos, and other minorities. However, there is a more specific reference to individual women in standard 24, wherein "significant political and social leaders" from this modern era are mentioned, and included are Sandra Day O'Connor and Hillary Clinton. The most direct reference to individual women appears in standard 26, which states that students are to "identify the political, social, and economic contributions of women such as Frances Willard, Jane Addams, Eleanor Roosevelt, Dolores Huerta, Sonia Sotomayor, and Oprah Winfrey to American society."[15]

The nineteenth amendment, which granted women the right to vote, is mentioned twice, in standard 5 in the context of the Progressive Era and in standard 9 in the context of the Civil Rights Movement.[16] In a very general way, but without clear direction, the last item in eighth-grade standard 23 asks students to identify the social, economic, and political contributions of women over three centuries, without any specific items identified. Standard 24 calls on students to evaluate the impact of the major reform movements of the nineteenth century, including the abolitionist movement, the labor reform movement, and the "women's rights movement."[17]

Specific References to African Americans

Among the 12 African Americans mentioned, 6 were either civil rights and/or abolitionist leaders; but also included were a Supreme Court justice, an entrepreneur, a military hero, the first African American senator and president, and a martyr for American independence.

The first mention appears in the eighth grade-course in standard 4, in which the Afro-Native American, Crispus Attucks, is included in a list of "significant individuals during the American Revolution." In standards 7 and 8, students are to understand the causes and events of the Civil War. In that context, the Emancipation Proclamation is mentioned, as well as the conditions of slaves and free blacks, and slavery is listed as a contributing cause to the Civil War. Nevertheless, there is no examination of slavery as an institution, its origins, its growth, and its ethical issues until standard 12, wherein the expectation is that students will "explain reasons for the development of the plantation system, the transatlantic slave trade, and the spread of slavery." Thus slavery is explained within an economic framework, confirming the popular notion, often expressed by social studies and even history teachers themselves, that slavery was simply an "economic system" without any moral, social, or political considerations. In standard 22, students are to understand the importance of effective leadership, including the contributions of Frederick Douglass. Here again, Douglass is set within a rare narrative space that recognized his agency as a historical actor.[18] Students are also expected to examine only the impact of the election of Hiram Rhodes Revels, the first black senator, who is examined more fully in Chapter 9.

The first implied references made to African Americans in the second part of US history appears in standard 2, wherein the following dates were identified as "turning points": the 1968 assassination of Martin Luther King Jr. and the 2008 election of Barack Obama. Both Ida B. Wells and W. E. B. Du Bois are mentioned in standard 5 as "muckrakers and reformers," and Marcus Garvey appears in standard 6 as a "significant individual." In standard 7, focusing on World War II, students are to consider "the bravery and contributions of the Tuskegee Airmen, the Flying Tigers, and the Navajo Code Talkers," thus recognizing the contributions of both African Americans and Native Americans to the war effort. In standard 9, students are also to contrast the nonviolent approach of Dr. King with that of the Black Panthers, and Dr. King is mentioned a third time wherein students discuss the impact of his speeches and writings. In standard 11, which covers the 1990s into the twenty-first century, students are to "discuss the historical significance of the 2008 presidential election," an obvious reference to President Obama without mentioning his name.

In standard 24, another black leader from the civil rights era survived in the TEKS, despite an attempt by the SBOE conservatives to exclude him, namely, Thurgood Marshall. Finally, the last item relevant to African Americans is found in standard 26 wherein students understand "how people from various groups contribute to our national identity." Here they are also to "discuss the importance of Congressional Medal of Honor recipients, including individuals of all races and genders such as Vernon J. Baker." He was awarded the medal in 1997 by President Clinton and was the only surviving black World War II veteran of the seven who were belatedly awarded the medal.[19]

Key historical documents related to African Americans appear in both the first and second parts of US history. The Emancipation Proclamation appears as a part of Celebrate Freedom Week (in every grade level) and in eighth grade the case of *Dred Scott v. Sandford* is named as the only example of a landmark Supreme Court decision that had an "impact on life in the United States."[20] The eleventh-grade course names the Reconstruction amendments—13, 14, and 15—that ended slavery and granted blacks the rights of citizenship and the vote. Also mentioned in standard 9 are the Civil Rights Acts of 1957 and 1964 as well as the Voting Rights Act of 1965. Appearing later in standard 23 is the Twenty-Fourth Amendment, outlawing poll taxes on voters. Finally, two pivotal court cases relevant to African Americans are also included in this same standard, among the six listed in the civil rights standard, namely *Sweatt v. Painter* and *Brown v. Board of Education*. This second case, involving issues of education equity, is also mentioned a second time, along with *Plessy v. Ferguson*, in standard 21.[21]

Specific References to American Indians

The Fordham Institute characterized the treatment of Native Americans in the US history TEKS as "almost totally missing."[22] Only one American Indian individual is mentioned in all the TEKS, from grade 1 through 12—Chief Bowles in seventh-grade Texas history, who was a tragic figure at best.[23] It may be difficult to rationalize, yet it is reflective of the political nature of the process, that Geronimo, Sequoyah, Sacagawea, and Chief Joseph are not mentioned in the standards for any other grade level or course. Also astounding is the absence of any pre-Columbian Native American society, even though they had organized into tribes, nations, confederations, and empires with a long history of cultural development and impressive civilization. To begin the history of our nation with the European "exploration and colonization" while ignoring the centuries and millennia of the Native American presence is not only dishonest history but also dehumanizes them so as to more easily justify their ultimate conquest and dispossession.

In the eighth-grade TEKS, standard 4 expects students to understand only the events following the French and Indian War—not the roots or reasons for the conflict itself. Nearly a century later, students are to "analyze the reasons for the removal and resettlement of Cherokee Indians during the Jacksonian era, including the Indian Removal Act, *Worcester v. Georgia*, and the Trail of Tears." Although there may indeed be critical thinking involved in analyzing these "reasons," nowhere are students directly encouraged to consider the Native American perspective on these policies, nor are they made aware of Native forms of resistance. What is again missing is any recognition that the Cherokees had legitimate claims to their land, had adopted many of the Georgian ways of farming and lifestyle, had developed their own alphabet, and still had to confront, resist, and finally succumb to white encroachment on their lands. In standard 6, students are introduced to the era of "westward expansion" and "Manifest Destiny," about which they are to explain and analyze the social, economic, and political roots and relationships, yet, again, there is no mention of what these movements meant for Native Americans, let alone how they asserted their will as historical actors through their resistance.[24]

In the eleventh-grade TEKS, students are required to "analyze political issues such as Indian policies" with no indication of what such analyses entail nor which specific Indian policies are to be considered. Beyond mention of the Navajo Code Talkers during World War II, the only mention of Native Americans comes in standard 23, wherein students are expected to "evaluate various means of achieving equality of political rights, including the 19th, 24th, and 26th amendments and congressional acts such as the American Indian Citizenship Act of 1924."[25] This latter act, also known as the Snyder Act, which granted US citizenship to more than 100,000 American Indians, is certainly worthy of consideration by students, but with so little perspective on Native American history throughout the TEKS, it is difficult to expect students to understand the full significance of this act.

Specific References to Latinos

It perhaps bears repeating, especially when evaluating the current TEKS, that there were no names of individual Latinos mentioned at all in the 1998 version of the US history TEKS, which was used for more than a decade. Also missing from that version was any mention of such terms as *Hispanic*, *Latino*, *Mexican American*, *Chicano*, *Puerto Rican*, *Central American*, or any other label designating Latino or Hispanic people.[26] Among the seven names of individual Latinos mentioned in the 2010 TEKS, three are civil rights leaders, two are military leaders, one is an entrepreneur, and one is the first Hispanic Supreme Court justice, Sonia Sotomayor.

The first—and only—individual Latino mentioned in the first part of US history is the Spanish General Bernardo de Gálvez, who is included in the list of "significant individuals during the American Revolution." His outstanding military victories against the British in the Gulf of Mexico helped the American revolutionary cause by preventing the British from establishing a second front. Among his soldiers were men from Mexico, Puerto Rico, and Cuba, some of whose descendants are the most numerous and influential Latino groups in the United States today. Yet there is no discussion or requirement that students know anything specific about him or his extraordinary contributions.[27] Later, in standard 6, which focuses on the "westward expansion," students are expected to explain the multiple roots of Manifest Destiny as well as the causes and effects of the Mexican American War. Yet nowhere is there any consideration of the various views, responses, and resistance of Mexicans to "westward expansion" and "Manifest Destiny," nor to the racist notions about Anglo-Saxon superiority on which they were founded. Neither is there any mention of the first Mexican Americans and the birth of their community based on the population of former Mexican citizens who decided to stay in their ancestral lands and become American citizens by choice after the signing of the Treaty of Guadalupe on February 2, 1848. This date does not appear on the list of significant "turning points," even though it both marked the acquisition of vast lands and resources and facilitated the linking of the East and West coasts.

Also absent from this first part of US history TEKS is any specific mention of Spanish exploration, settlement, and colonization. In standard 2, the topics of early "European" exploration and colonization are discussed.[28] However, left unspecified is that the Spaniards, more than any other European group, were the first to explore and colonize many areas of what is now the United States and created detailed maps of vast areas in the West, including towns, rivers, mountains, and coastlines of California as early as 1777. Spaniards and their descendants also established the first towns, ranches, farms, churches, and schools on American soil before the founding of Jamestown in 1607.[29] To diminish the role of the Spanish as the earliest explorers and colonizers denies students an understanding of seminal Hispanic contributions to the American way of life. It also obscures the origins of an entire ethos and discourse associated with the much-glorified and mythologized American cowboy, whose characteristic cultural lifestyle, from his rodeo to his lasso, was adapted from the rancheros and vaqueros of northern Mexico, who had developed their ranching legacy over the centuries.[30]

Although 1848 goes unlisted as an important year in the first part of US history, the second part of the study contains a very direct mention to another Latino-significant date—the Spanish-American War, which ended in 1898. Then in standard 4, students must understand "the emergence of the United States as a world power between 1898 and 1920" and "evaluate American expansionism, including acquisitions such as Guam, Hawaii, the Philippines, and Puerto Rico."[31] The criteria for this evaluation are not specified, but what is obviously neglected is how Puerto Ricans, Filipinos, Hawaiians, and the Chamorros of Guam "evaluated" and responded to "American expansionism." There is no indication or any recognition in this standard that there were political, cultural, and even military movements of resistance against US imperialism. These were not simply territorial acquisitions—they were "acquisitions" of entire nations and peoples with their own history, culture, and society.

Given the many military and political interventions the United States has sponsored or implemented in Latin America in the decades following the Spanish-American War, the use of the term *expansionism*—imposed by the

SBOE in place of the review committee's recommended "imperialism"—has direct implications for the millions of US Latinos whose roots are in Latin America. Most historical texts agree that the term *imperialism* is appropriately used when describing the international behavior of the United States in the late nineteenth and early twentieth centuries; moreover, even bestselling books by respected scholars contend that the concept of "empire" is still applicable to the United States' intervention and influence in the Third World, most notably in Latin America.[32]

Standard 7 on World War II mentions "the bravery and contributions" of African Americans and Native Americans while making no mention of the outstanding contributions of Mexican Americans whose bravery earned them the highest number of Congressional Medals of Honor in that conflict.[33] Nevertheless, one such Mexican American veteran is mentioned in standard 26, which states that students are to know, among others, of Congressional Medal of Honor recipient Roy Benavidez. The term *Chicano* makes its first appearance in standard 9 in the context of other civil rights movements, including the African American, women's, and American Indian movements. Beyond acknowledging the significance of the term itself, it is important that other civil rights movements beyond the African American are also recognized as significant parts of American history. The term also appears in standard 25 within the context of the "Chicano Mural Movement," mentioned along with the Harlem Renaissance and rock and roll as "examples of cultural movements in art, music, and literature." Finally, several landmark cases are listed that "played a role in protecting the rights of the minority" during the Civil Rights Movement, including four related directly to Latino issues: *Mendez v. Westminster*, *Hernandez v. Texas*, *Delgado v. Bastrop I.S.D.*, and *Edgewood I.S.D. v. Kirby*.[34]

Specific References to Other Minorities

It may reasonably be expected that given their larger numbers and/or longer historical trajectory, the four groups whose representation we have discussed would naturally receive more attention in the standards for US history. Nevertheless, the presence and influence of other racial, ethnic and social minorities, including Asian Americans, and members of the gay, lesbian, bisexual, transsexual, and queer (GLBTQ) community—who cross boundaries of race, gender, and ethnicity—deserve their rightful place in any honest and comprehensive set of standards. The TEKS for US history demonstrate little evidence of this recognition.

The only Asian Americans mentioned collectively are Japanese Americans, who are listed along with German and Italian Americans in reference to their internment during World War II, though the standard does not require students to consider the conditions and rationalizations for the internments. Chinese Americans are implied by the mention in standard 15 of the Chinese Exclusion Act of 1882, yet this is couched strictly within the context of economics and foreign policy, without any implication that racial attitudes were at all involved.[35]

Regarding the inclusion of the GLBTQ community, it is interesting to note that some specific names of widely known gays and lesbians appear in the US history standards, most notably Eleanor Roosevelt. She is mentioned in standard 26 with Jane Addams and Oprah Winfrey as one of several exemplary women for whom students are to "identify the political, social, and economic contributions" they have made to American society.[36] From an overview of terms appearing in the standards, it is sufficient to note that the terms *gay*, *lesbian*, and even *homosexual* do not even appear anywhere in their content.

Regarding persons with disabilities, the word *disabled* appears in the TEKS for the first part of US history in standard 24 within the context of evaluating the impact of reform movements during the nineteenth century, including the "care of the disabled."[37] However, the term *disabled* does not appear in the second part of US history standards, nor is there any mention of the 1973 Rehabilitation Act or of the more influential Americans with Disabilities Act passed by Congress in 1990.[38]

Assessment and Implication

When contrasted with the previous version of the US history TEKS, the current standards demonstrate clear evidence of increased inclusion of women, minorities, and specifically Latinos. The numbers themselves are telling when considering the issue of individual names, yet these were usually included over the objection of conservative SBOE members and rarely with their blessings. Without a doubt, public pressure, civil rights groups, and activist scholars all played a role in limiting, if not balancing the power of the conservative SBOE, but so also did the board-appointed writing committees who introduced these names into the standards in the first place.

It is also relevant to note several characteristics associated with the historical periods in which these selected names appear. All but one (Gálvez) of the seven Latino individuals appear in eleventh-grade US history since 1877. In terms of African Americans, only 3 of the 12 mentioned (Attucks, Douglass, and Revels) appear in the eighth-grade standards. In a somewhat similar pattern, only 4 of the 16 women appear in the first part of US history. This is perhaps a reflection of the fact that women and minorities gained much more social, economic, and political power later in our nation's history and therefore have more significant individuals mentioned after the nineteenth century.

There was also a considerable political and ideological range represented by these names, and that was an arena of intense discussion, debate, and compromise, mostly between the writing committee members and the SBOE. Thus, although there are a wide variety of important roles represented by the individual women and minorities mentioned in the TEKS for US history, a simple majority of these roles are as civil rights leaders and/or social reformers. This reflects the common struggle waged by American women and minorities to obtain equal protection, equality of opportunity, and recognition of their civil and human rights—struggles that were intensified during the latter part of our nation's history.

Yet the mere mention of these additional names, for all their symbolic value, may not ensure that students will be exposed to the lives and times of these historical figures with any sufficient depth to fully understand and appreciate their contributions and achievements. The standards do not provide a clear and consistent guide as to how these individuals should be approached beyond requiring or suggesting their coverage. This may seem trivial on the surface, but when teachers are confronted with the task of covering so much content within a specific week or month, then who or what is to be studied becomes critical, and the required names become a priority. In an atmosphere permeated with deadlines and time constraints, history teachers usually focus on information that students require for passing the high-stakes standardized test by which learner and instructor alike are assessed. Expressions such as "teaching a mile wide and an inch deep" are often repeated by educators, making reference to curriculum standards and pacing guides covering a multitude of mandated items within a designated time. Thus teachers are forced to forgo many natural opportunities for exploring in depth the meaning and relevance of history beyond the factoids. My own research, based on two separate studies consisting of personal interviews with more than two dozen history teachers in Texas, confirmed that "the pressure to cover a quantity of topics in limited time" was one of the major factors influencing their instructional effectiveness.[39] In this context, it is relevant to note that in terms of individual names, only 3 of the 7 Latinos, 5 of the 12 African Americans, and 5 of the 16 women are designated as required—less than half the names in each category.

This pattern, coupled with the SBOE's substitution of concepts such as free enterprise and expansionism for capitalism and imperialism, as well as the inclusion of American exceptionalism and the conservative resurgence, reveals an unmistakable political bias in the standards. Other concepts, such as Manifest Destiny, are presented without any hint of critical evaluation, let alone from the perspective of Native Americans and Mexicans most affected by genocidal and dispossessing policies and practices inspired and justified by Manifest Destiny. Because of that fundamental bias in these standards, students will be left with a very unhistorical and Hollywoodized, if not Christianized, version of "how the West was won."

Multicultural history relating to women and minorities poses a significant pedagogical challenge to the concept of American exceptionalism, a modernized version of Manifest Destiny. As the TEKS were being revised, the idea was especially championed by David Barton, one of the "experts" appointed by the conservative SBOE members. His many books, videos, and speeches have made him the darling pundit of the religious right for promoting a history that suits their vision of the world. For example, using citations from the Bible (mingled with GOP talking points), he claims that Jesus was against unions and for private enterprise; that immigration reform is evil because God established national boundaries; that the Democratic Party was responsible for black slavery; and that America is divinely ordained by God as an "exceptional" nation. According to Michele Bachmann, Barton is "a treasure for our nation"; Glenn Beck has declared him to be "the most important man in America"; and while calling him "America's greatest historian," Mike Huckabee suggested that Barton should be writing the curriculum for American students and that all Americans should be "forced at gunpoint" to listen to his broadcasts.[40] Barton's critics—among them historians, evangelicals, and civil rights institutions—have denounced his "shoddy, misleading, and politically motivated 'scholarship,' which misquotes and misleadingly portrays historical figures and documents."[41]

Regarding eras and movements, there is at least mention, thus some recognition of, there being civil rights movements of, by, and for women, as well as American Indians, African Americans, and even Chicanos. Cultural movements, such as the Harlem Renaissance and the Chicano Mural Movement, found their place in these standards and do have clear implication for students perceiving blacks and Chicanos as self-defining cultural creators worthy of historical mention. Nevertheless, there are numerous eras and movements in the history-related TEKS discussed in this chapter wherein American Indians, Filipinos, Puerto Ricans, Mexican Americans, and other conquered and/or dominated people have no presence, role, or voice, most notably in the context of Manifest Destiny and American expansionism.

Implications for Theory

Fundamental to interpreting the findings of this study are two theoretical perspectives that provide useful frameworks for analyzing this data and for interpreting the findings. Foremost among them is the concept of culturally responsive pedagogy, which was recently defined by Geneva Gay as "the behavioral expressions of knowledge, beliefs, and values that recognize the importance of racial and cultural diversity in learning." More directly relevant to the perspective of this study are three of the five qualities that Gay identifies as defining culturally responsive teaching and that could serve as qualitative criteria for assessing the TEKS: "It acknowledges the legitimacy of the cultural heritages of different ethnic groups . . . It teaches students to know and praise their own and one another's cultural heritages . . . It incorporates multicultural information, resources, and materials in all school taught skills and subjects."[42]

Another theoretical framework that contributed to the analysis and interpretation of this data emerges from the field of critical race theory (CRT). Although there is a considerable variety of beliefs and issues that the CRT movement encompasses, there are several tenets upon which most CRT scholars agree and that are relevant to this investigation. Among those agreements are the following: (1) racism in our society is normal, not an aberration, therefore it is difficult to cure or address; (2) our system of white-over-color ascendancy serves important material and psychic purposes; and (3) each race or ethnic group has its own origins and ever-evolving history, with the dominant society creating shifting images and stereotypes of each group over time and circumstance.[43] These tenets closely relate to this investigation because they could help explain the motivations and the mechanisms underlying the process of excluding, marginalizing, and stereotyping Latinos and other ethnoracial minorities in history standards.

Another key concept from CRT bears significant relevance to education issues in general, and specifically to our investigation, namely the concept of the master script. CRT views the "official school curriculum" as an artifact designed to "maintain a White supremacist master script." According to Swartz, "master scripting silences multiple voices and perspectives, primarily legitimizing dominant, white, upper class, male voicings as the 'standard' knowledge students need to know. All other accounts and perspectives are omitted from the master script unless they can be disempowered through misrepresentation."[44]

In the context of our investigation, I attempted to ascertain the extent to which the TEKS curriculum standards are master scripted to exclude or misrepresent women and minorities, and most particularly Latinos. That there were attempts on the part of the SBOE conservatives to impose onto these standards a master script that is hostile to the historical inclusion of women and minorities is well documented in the official Texas Education Agency recordings of the proceedings as well as in the contents of the standards themselves. Also confirmed is the CRT idea that maintains that racism, even though expressed in subtle ways like manipulated curriculum standards, is a deeply embedded element that permeates American life and is therefore difficult to eradicate.

Nevertheless, despite the overwhelming influence and editorial power of the SBOE conservatives, it is also evident that the members of the writing committees, who introduced the vast majority of the content related to women and minorities, were attempting not only to ensure historical accuracy and objectivity but also to weave into the standards content that would lend itself to a more culturally responsive pedagogy than was possible with the previous version of these TEKS. This approach to pedagogy responds to and counters the effects of master scripting and transforms both the content and methods of instruction so as to respond to the cultural milieu in which students are immersed.[45] Regarding content, support for this approach by both committee members and advocates resulted in the considerable increase in the number of women, minorities, and especially Latino individuals in the social studies TEKS, as well as the integration of related significant items, such as the Chicano Mural Movement and *Hernandez v. Texas*.

Implications for Practice

Although in actual practice classroom teachers generally rely on textbooks, established curricula, and/or even scripted guides that interpret the TEKS for instruction, they are still required to refer to specific TEKS in their lesson planning. At this point, the instructional materials for the social studies TEKS have not yet been firmly identified or widely adopted, but it is still possible to provide some concrete suggestions for classroom teachers based on the analysis in this chapter.

It is axiomatic, but essential that teachers not limit their instruction to the items mentioned in the TEKS; there are other individuals, examples, concepts, events, and movements that a knowledgeable and inspired teacher could integrate. Even working within the limits of the TEKS, the teacher could expand, for example, the life and times of Bernardo de Gálvez during the American Revolution and of Dolores Huerta, whose experience spans the turbulent times of the 1960s to the contentious times of today. To do so requires support, encouragement, and professional development for classroom teachers, who are well aware of the curricular requirements imposed by standards and testing, but are also experienced and sensitive enough to recognize the weaknesses and limitations of the official curriculum.[46] It is my hope that this investigation has in some way provided useful discoveries and legitimate critiques that will help Texas teachers deliver a more relevant, objective, and authentic history curriculum to the future citizens of our state and nation.

Conclusions and Recommendations

Several conclusions can be generated from the above analysis of the TEKS for the two year-long courses in US history. The new TEKS present some significant improvements over the previous TEKS in terms of the representation of women and minorities as evidenced by additional names and relevant topics and documents. Despite undeniable improvements, the overwhelming voting power of SBOE conservatives imprinted these standards with too many fundamental errors in misconceptions, misrepresentations, and ideological biases, which become obstacles to students' proper understanding of our nation's history.

Another rational conclusion poses that since the TEKS standards for US history cannot serve as a fully accurate or comprehensive guide, educators should be compelled to find effective ways of integrating events, concepts, and personalities that move students beyond the borders imposed by these standards. Conversely, while recognizing that significant progress has been made, educators could mine from these standards those elements that do effectively reflect the authentic and diverse narrative of our nation's history.

To that end, several recommendations naturally emerge from this investigation. Classroom teachers should expand upon the existing opportunities within the TEKS by accessing print, online, and media resources on women, minorities, and multiculturalism to enhance their instruction. In selecting these content enhancers, teachers should have some understanding of students' social and cultural background to integrate material that also reflects and relates to their experience as well as that of their communities. Not only should teacher educators seek to impart in pre-service and in-service teachers an appreciation for the social and instructional value of utilizing culturally responsive pedagogy, but they should also provide them with a variety of multicultural, anti-racist, and global resources that are reliable, credible, and effective.

Accountability for any state providing a public education based on a taxpaying citizenry goes beyond standardized test scores; it also includes the proper preparation of our students as future citizens. To the extent that effectively teaching our nation's history is fundamental to that task and that the TEKS play such a pivotal role in that effort, it is incumbent on educators to assess the extent to which the TEKS does prepare our students for a diverse and democratic society. It is hoped that this study will make an important contribution to that most necessary process of critical assessment.

Finally, it is imperative that teacher educators and academic scholars pay closer attention to the decision-making processes that produce curriculum standards generated by elected school boards in Texas and throughout the nation. These standards have the power to shape what thousands of schools teach and millions of students learn about our history and identity as a nation. As citizens and educators concerned about the perpetuation of democratic principles to the next generations, we must be ever vigilant and ready to challenge attempts to falsify our history and undermine our democracy in the very classrooms of our public schools.

Notes

1. Pew Hispanic Center, *One-in-Five and Growing Fast: A Profile of Hispanic Public School Students* (Washington, DC: Pew Hispanic Center, 2008); Pew Hispanic Center, *Statistical Portrait of Hispanics in the United States* (Washington, DC: Pew Hispanic Center, 2006), Table 1; Texas Education Agency, *Enrollment in Texas Public Schools 2008–2009* (Austin: Texas Education Agency, 2009).
2. David Dary, *Cowboy Culture: A Saga of Five Centuries* (Lawrence: University Press of Kansas, 1989); Nicolás Kanellos, *Thirty Million Strong: Reclaiming the Hispanic Image in American Culture* (Golden, CO: Fulcrum Publishing, 1998).
3. Jesus Garcia, "Hispanic Perspective: Textbooks and Other Curricular Materials," *The History Teacher* 14, no. 1 (November 1980): 105–20; Sonia Nieto and Patty Bode, *Affirming Diversity: The Sociopolitical Context of Multicultural Education*, 6th ed. (New York: Pearson 2012); Julio Noboa, *Leaving Latinos Out of History: Teaching U.S. History in Texas* (New York: Routledge, 2006); Linda K. Salvucci, "Mexico, Mexicans and Mexican Americans in Secondary-School United States History Textbooks," *The History Teacher* 24, no. 2 (February 1991): 203–22; Angela Valenzuela, *Subtractive Schooling: U.S.-Mexican Youth and the Politics of Caring* (Albany: State University of New York Press, 1999).
4. TEKS*Watch* was particularly helpful (http://tekswatch.utep.edu).
5. National Center for Education Statistics, *The Nation's Report Card: U.S. History 2010,* NCES 2011–468 (Washington, DC: Institute of Education Sciences, US Department of Education, 2011); Jason Amos, "Planting Cut Flowers, or U.S. History: American Students' Worst Subject," *Alliance for Excellent Education*, June 30, 2011.
6. B. Rigberg, "What Must Not Be Taught" *Theory and Research in Social Education* 19, no. 1 (Winter 1991): 14–44; Jesus Garcia, "The Changing Image of Ethnic Groups in Textbooks," *Phi Delta Kappan* 75, no.1 (September 1993): 29–35; James A. Banks, *Cultural Diversity and Education: Foundations, Curriculum, and Teaching* (Boston: Pearson, 2006); Geneva Gay, *A Synthesis of Scholarship in Multicultural Education* (Seattle: NCREL Urban Education Program, 1994); R. Lerner, A. K. Nagai, and S. Rothman, *Molding the Good Citizen: The Politics of High School History Texts* (Westport, CT: Praeger, 1995); James W. Loewen, *Lies My Teacher Told Me: Everything Your American History Textbook Got Wrong*, rev. ed. (1995; repr. New York: Simon & Schuster, 2007).
7. Terrence Stutz, "Conservatives Say Texas Social Studies Classes Give Too Much Credit to Civil Rights Leaders," *Dallas Morning News*, July 9, 2009; Gary Scharrer, "SBOE Members Clash over Racial Balance in History," *Houston Chronicle*, March 11, 2010; Kate Alexander, "Sideshow Takes Center Stage in Social Studies Fight," *Austin American-Statesman*, March 11, 2010; James C. McKinley Jr., "Texas Approves Curriculum Revised by Conservatives," *The New York Times*, March 12, 2010.
8. Sue Blanchette, "Education or Indoctrination? The Development of Social Studies Standards in Texas," *Social Education* 74, no. 4 (2010): 199–203; Sheldon M. Stern and Jeremy A. Stern, *The State of State U.S. History Standards 2011* (Washington, DC: Thomas P. Fordham Institute, 2011), 141–42.

9. TEKS.8.a.7.A (8/23/10).
10. TEKS.8.b.1 (8/23/10).
11. TEKS.8.b.23–24 (8/23/10).
12. TEKS.11.c.3, 6–7, 9–11 (8/23/10).
13. TEKS.11.c.15, 22, 25–26 (8/23/10).
14. TEKS.8.b.22 (8/23/10).
15. TEKS.11.c.24, 26 (8/23/10).
16. TEKS.11.c.5, 9 (8/23/10).
17. TEKS.11.c.23–24 (8/23/10).
18. TEKS.8.b.4, 7–8, 12, 22 (8/23/10).
19. TEKS.11.c.2, 5–7, 9, 11, 18, 24, 26 (8/23/10).
20. TEKS.8.b.18 (8/23/10).
21. TEKS.11.c.9, 21, 23 (8/23/10).
22. Stern and Stern, *State of State U.S. History Standards*, 15.
23. TEKS.7.b.4 (8/23/10).
24. TEKS.8.b.4–6 (8/23/10).
25. TEKS.11.c.3, 7, 23 (8/23/10).
26. TEKS (1998).
27. Robert H. Thonhoff, "Galvez, Bernardo De," *Handbook of Texas Online*, accessed January 30, 2012, http://www.tshaonline.org/handbook/online/articles/fga10; Lorenzo G. LaFarelle, *Bernardo De Gálvez: Hero of the American Revolution* (San Antonio, TX: Marion Koogler McNay Art Museum, 1992).
28. TEKS.8.b.1–2, 6 (8/23/10).
29. Nicolás Kanellos, *Hispanic Firsts: 500 Years of Extraordinary Achievement* (New York: Visible Ink, 1997).
30. Dary, *Cowboy Culture*.
31. TEKS.11.c.2, 4 (8/23/10).
32. Chalmers Johnson, *The Sorrows of Empire: Militarism, Secrecy and the End of the Republic* (New York: Metropolitan Books, 2004); J. Jones, P. H. Wood, T. Borstelmann, E. T. May, and V. L. Ruiz., *Created Equal: A Social and Political History of the United States* (New York: Pearson Longman, 2008).
33. Kanellos, *Hispanic Firsts*; Maggie Rivas-Rodríguez, ed., *Mexican Americans and World War II* (Austin: University of Texas Press, 2005).
34. TEKS.11.c.7, 9, 25–26 (8/23/10).
35. TEKS.11.c.7, 15 (8/23/10).
36. TEKS.11.c.26 (8/23/10).
37. TEKS.8.b.24 (8/23/10).
38. Kent L. Koppelman and R. Lee Goodhart, *Understanding Human Differences: Multicultural Education for a Diverse America*, 3rd ed. (Boston: Pearson, 2011): 293–94.
39. Noboa, *Leaving Latinos Out of History*; Julio Noboa, "Teaching History on the Border: Teachers Voice Their Views" (working paper under review in *International Journal of Qualitative Studies in Education, 2011).*
40. Ibid., 1, 3.
41. People for the American Way, "Meet the Religious Right Charlatan Who Teaches Tea Party America the Totally Pretend History They Want to Hear," April 20, 2011,

http://www.alternet.org/belief/150690/meet_the_religious_right_charlatan_who_teaches_tea_party_america_the_totally_pretend_history_they_want_to_hear/
42. Geneva Gay, *Culturally Responsive Teaching: Theory, Research, and Practice*, 2nd ed. (New York: Teachers College Press, 2010), 31–32.
43. R. Delgado and J. Stefancic, *Critical Race Theory: An Introduction* (New York: New York University Press, 2001), 6–9.
44. Gloria Ladson-Billings, "Just What Is Critical Race Theory, and What's It Doing in a Nice Field Like Education?" in *Race is . . . Race Isn't: Critical Race Theory and Qualitative Studies in Education*, ed. L. Parker, D. Deyle, and S. Villenas (Boulder, CO: Westview Press, 1999), 21; E. Swartz, "Emancipatory Narratives: Rewriting the Master Script in the School Curriculum," *Journal of Negro Education* 61 (1992): 341–55.
45. Gloria Ladson-Billings, "But That's Just Good Teaching! The Case for Culturally Relevant Pedagogy," *Theory into Practice* 34, no. 3 (1995): 159–65.
46. Noboa, *Leaving Latinos Out of History*.

Figure 8 Washington at prayer?
The Founding Fathers occupied a continuum of religious expression that ran from orthodox Christianity to radical Deism. Their ultimate concern, however, was for religious freedom, not to create a Christian America. So why do we think of America as a Christian nation? The answer to that question came in the nineteenth and twentieth centuries—an answer reflected in this engraving from 1866—when the Second Great Awakening, the Fundamentalist Movement, and American evangelicalism Christianized American politics and culture.

CHAPTER 8

Why Do We Think of America as a Christian Nation?

Richard T. Hughes

Early in the process of revising the social studies standards, the Texas State Board of Education (SBOE) appointed two ministers as expert historians. Both David Barton and Peter Marshall routinely promote the idea that America is a Christian nation, and in their capacity as advisors to the SBOE, both seemed chiefly concerned about emphasizing the way the Christian religion has shaped the American nation.

Barton heads WallBuilders, an Aledo, Texas-based organization that unabashedly promotes the idea of Christian America. And Barton has the full support of Texas Governor Rick Perry, who praised Barton in 2005 as "a truly national treasure" who "understands that America was founded on our Christian faith."[1]

In the Texas curriculum debate, the irony lies in the fact that Barton and Marshall recommended removing notable Americans who have best exemplified the values of Jesus himself—figures including César Chávez and Thurgood Marshall. Chávez, for example, embraced nonviolence, sought justice for the poor, and gave voice to the voiceless, often at great expense to himself, and thereby reflected the values of Jesus in significant ways. But of Chávez, Marshall writes that he is "hardly the kind of role model that ought to be held up to our children as someone worthy of emulation."[2]

Thurgood Marshall placed his legal career in the service of justice for oppressed minorities and successfully argued against racial segregation of America's schools before the Supreme Court of the United States—emphases that Jesus would no doubt have applauded. Yet Barton debated whether any Supreme Court justice could fit "within the technical definition" of a "significant political and social

---

Portions of this chapter appeared originally in *Christian American and the Kingdom of God*. Copyright 2009 by the Board of Trustees of the University of Illinois. Used with permission of the University of Illinois Press.

leader" and Peter Marshall rejected the African American leader on the grounds that he inadequately "impacted American history."[3]

So it is fair to ask several questions: What do Barton and Marshall and millions of other Americans mean when they speak of "Christian America"? Is it accurate to speak of America as a Christian nation at all? Obviously, there is a sense in which the United States is a Christian nation. After all, about 80 percent of Americans claim to be Christian. And at a mythical level, the United States *is* a Christian nation. When I use the word *myth* I don't have in mind a story that is fabricated or false; a myth may well have some basis in fact. But the defining characteristic of a myth is that it carries power and meaning for those who believe it and take it seriously. Understood from that perspective, the United States is a Christian nation precisely because the notion of Christian America is historically rooted and because so many Americans find comfort and meaning in that ideal.

How and why did the notion of Christian America develop in the first place? How and why have Christians sought to promote that notion? What purpose did that understanding serve? And how have Christians sought to link the nation with the biblical vision of the kingdom of God? Answers to these questions inevitably lead us to periods and events in Western history that predate the birth of the United States. To fully comprehend these answers, we must also examine the beliefs and actions of the Founding Fathers as well as the efforts of Americans in the nineteenth and twentieth centuries who sought to reverse the course established by the Founders. The kind of "Christian America" envisioned by Barton, Marshall, and their allies should raise serious questions both for those who cherish a biblical vision of the kingdom of God and for those who care about the history taught to American children.

Historical Roots of Christian America

The Biblical View of the Kingdom of God

Anyone who wants to push the notion that America is a Christian nation should first come to terms with the way the Bible measures the Christian character of people and nations. And any attempt to measure the Christian character of the United States would have to take seriously a phrase Jesus used time and again—and the only phrase in the biblical text that is even remotely analogous to the idea of a Christian nation—"the kingdom of God." According to Jesus, the kingdom of God relies on the power of self-giving love, whereas nations—even so-called Christian nations—rely on the power of the sword. Nations—even so-called Christian nations—inevitably go to war against their enemies, whereas the kingdom of God has no mortal enemies at all. The kingdom of

God is universal, and those who promote that kingdom care deeply for every human being in every corner of the globe, regardless of race or nationality. But earthly nations—even so-called Christian nations—embrace values that are inevitably tribal, caring especially for the welfare of those within their borders. And whereas the kingdom of God exalts the poor, the disenfranchised, and the dispossessed, earthly nations inevitably exalt the rich and powerful and hold them up as models to be emulated. In fact, in the context of earthly nations—even so-called Christian nations—the poor seldom count for much at all.[4]

The Constantinian/Theodosian Settlement

After Constantine legalized Christianity in 313 CE, the Roman Empire began to take on an increasingly Christian cast. In 391 CE, Theodosius the Great declared Christianity *the only* legal religion of the empire. If in earlier days the empire had launched sporadic persecutions against the church, now the empire persecuted those who *refused to convert* to the Christian faith. In time, emperors such as Justinian I in the sixth century would proclaim themselves both "priest and king"—the supreme head not only of the state but also of the church. These decisions required that the church would serve the state, even as the state protected the church—but only as long as the church was faithful to the imperial agenda.

Those developments created a type of Christianity that grew increasingly formal and ceremonial. After all, a church that rejected warfare and violence could hardly be useful to an empire. And a church whose chief concern was to care for the poor and the marginalized would be of no use at all to an empire committed to enlarging its power and wealth at the expense of the poor and the dispossessed.

It is hardly any wonder, then, that in this new imperial climate, ceremonial forms and liturgical rites increasingly displaced the ethical rigor of Jesus and the early church. What mattered now was not that one cared for the poor or the suffering or the dispossessed, but that one belonged to the church. What mattered now was not that one rejected violence, but that one participated in the Eucharist on a regular basis. What mattered now was not that one practiced the ethics of the kingdom of God, but that one confessed one's sins to an institutional priest in the context of an imperial church. The Roman Empire, in fact, hastened these transitions by constructing throughout its territories ornate and lavish buildings in which liturgy and ceremony could thrive. These developments help explain the rise of the monastic movement in which monks and nuns sought solitude in places like the Egyptian desert, where they believed they could practice an austere and rigorous kind of Christianity that seemed so lacking in the context of the imperial church. In time, everyone understood that those who practiced such a radical form of the Christian life answered to a higher calling that never came to ordinary men and women. In this way, the empire largely succeeded in banishing from ordinary life the ethical norms associated with the biblical vision of the kingdom of God.

To make these observations is not to suggest that ceremonial forms and liturgical rites were either useless or irrelevant to the life of the church. Nor do I wish to suggest that liturgy and ceremony, on the one hand, and ethical rigor, on the other, are mutually exclusive. One need only recall the ethical witness of the Roman Catholic tradition for most of its history or, in recent times, the ethical witness of Christians like Dorothy Day, Oscar Romero, and Dietrich Bonhoeffer—to name but a few—to know that liturgy and ethics can reinforce one another. Still and all, the trend in the fourth- and fifth-century imperial church was toward the enhancement of ceremony at the expense of the ethical life—a fact to which the early monks and nuns bear witness.

And yet, the empire—at least after Constantine and Theodosius the Great—was a Christian empire. The history of that ancient empire, like the history of the United States, is replete—as Barton and Marshall correctly point out—with official references to the Bible, Jesus, and the Christian faith. But the kind of Christianity that characterized this Christian empire had been severely compromised. In paying lip service to Christian peace, it practiced violence, exalted the rich over the poor, preferred power to humility, and placed vengeance above forgiveness, extravagance above modesty, and luxury above simplicity.

What does this history of the ancient and medieval world have to do with the United States? If the United States is a Christian nation, it resembles in striking ways the sort of Christianized culture that thrived in medieval and Reformation Europe. There are significant differences, of course. Every American schoolchild understands that the United States was the first nation in the history of the world to embrace the separation of church and state, never adopting the Christian religion in any official sense or mandating the Christian faith by force of law. Yet to the extent that America is a Christian nation, it conforms to the imperial pattern of a Christian nation in this crucial regard: it routinely drives out the ethical and moral rigor the New Testament associates with the kingdom of God. If ecclesiastical ceremonies and liturgical rites supplanted the kingdom of God in the state-church arrangement of Europe, churchgoing and personal piety supplant that vision in the United States today. In many instances, therefore, Christianity in the United States has conformed to the mandates of the culture and the prerogatives of the state.

The Calvinist Concern for the Sovereignty of God

Another way that the history of ancient, medieval, and Reformation Christianity influenced the United States as a nation derives from the fact that the majority of the early colonists in both New England and the Middle Colonies were Calvinists, informed not only by the long history of European Christianity but also by the theology of their mentor, John Calvin.

Calvin was one of two preeminent Protestant reformers during the early sixteenth century (the other was Martin Luther). Calvin never questioned the assumption that church and state should be yoked together in a common enterprise. But he did seek to reverse the nature of the church-state relationship. In the Constantinian vision, the church served the purposes of the state, but Calvin determined that the state would serve the purposes of the church. And whereas the Constantinian settlement mandated that the values of the state would shape the values of the church, thereby transforming the church into the image of the state, Calvin moved in just the opposite direction. Calvin insisted the church should shape the values of the state, thereby transforming both state and culture into the image of the kingdom of God.

Beginning in 1536, Calvin sought in every way possible to transform Geneva, Switzerland, into a model city of God by superimposing the values of the kingdom of God—as he understood the kingdom of God—on every dimension of Genevan life, from art, music, and education to family life and politics. It is true that Calvin sought to achieve these objectives not so much through external coercion as through careful teaching and preaching. Nonetheless, Calvin's Geneva became a model theocracy—a state in which the rule of God was both thorough and complete.

Many of the Europeans who settled the eastern seaboard of what would become the United States brought to this brave new world Calvin's assumptions about transforming both state and culture into the image of the kingdom of God. The earliest Calvinists to settle North American shores were the Puritans who came first to Plymouth in 1620 and then, in 1630, to Massachusetts Bay. These two settlements differed in significant ways, but like Calvin before them, both sought to create a culture and a state modeled in every way on biblical norms and precedents.[5] If measured by the external rules and regulations they erected, and even if measured by the pattern of the primitive church that they sought to restore, they succeeded remarkably well. But their failure to re-create the essence of the kingdom of God becomes apparent in their expulsion of dissenters, sometimes after excruciating torture; their practice of executing dissenters who proved especially recalcitrant; and their brutal treatment of Native Americans, whom they routinely viewed as children of the devil. Ironically, in their zeal to re-create the kingdom of God on Earth, the Puritans of New England stand at the fountainhead of the destruction of Native populations.

If Puritans dominated New England, other branches of Calvinism—especially the Presbyterians from Scotland and Northern Ireland—sought to impose the sovereignty of God over colonial life in the Middle Colonies. As it turned out, many in the Middle Colonies resisted Calvinist domination, and those colonies became, in some respects at least, a model for religious pluralism. In the South, while Anglicans (members of the Church of England) controlled both wealth and land, ordinary people of the region allied themselves in extraordinary numbers with another wing of Calvinism—the Baptists. The Baptists, however, differed in significant ways from their northern counterparts. Although they maintained their allegiance to some of Calvin's doctrines, they vehemently rejected the union of church and state. In time, the Baptists would ally themselves with America's Founders to overthrow religious establishments of every kind.

The Role of the American Founders

The Calvinists' dreams for a Christianized American culture hit a roadblock in the Founding Fathers of the United States, who resisted both the Calvinists' vision for a thoroughly Christianized culture and their desire to bring the nation under the sovereign sway of the Christian God. Some of the Founders were Christians, to be sure, but their great hope was for a nation whose citizens would be freed from religious constraints, not for a nation dominated by any one religion.[6] As a result, the nation's two seminal documents—the Declaration of Independence and the Constitution—effectively halted the possible creation of a Christian America.

The Declaration of Independence

Thomas Jefferson, the principal author of the Declaration of Independence, understood full well how divisive the Christian faith had been in Europe. Indeed, seventeenth-century Europe had witnessed numerous religious wars fought between adherents of competing factions of the Christian religion. Since those wars had erupted only a century before, how—asked Jefferson—could leaders of the new American nation prevent similar wars from ripping the republic apart a century later?

This question was all the more pressing by the late eighteenth century because, alongside the varieties of Calvinists (Puritans in New England, Presbyterians in the Middle Colonies, and Baptists in the South), Catholics, Anglicans, and a variety of other denominations were emerging—and sometimes flourishing—on America's religious landscape. How could Jefferson and other national leaders prevent these sects from repeating on these shores the religious wars of the seventeenth century?

Jefferson answered that question by attempting to ground the nation's Declaration of Independence in religion, but not in traditional Christianity. Instead, Jefferson rooted the Declaration in Deism—a rational form of religion that jettisoned the Trinity, denied the deity of Christ, and rejected miracles, along with most other claims for supernatural intervention. In their places, Deism substituted a sturdy belief in one God, often understood as benevolent providence; a firm conviction in an overarching moral order that governed the universe; and the belief that the best part of religion consisted in the good one might do for one's sisters or brothers.[7]

Deism also scuttled the Bible for several reasons. First, although Christians and Jews revered the Bible, most others in the human race did not. Therefore, the Bible lacked universality. Second, Deists argued that the Bible was a complex book, susceptible to a host of divergent interpretations. It lent itself, therefore, to religious divisions and potentially even to religious warfare, which the Founders were determined would never plague this new nation. However, Deists also believed that God had written a second book, the Book of Nature, that taught the core doctrines—those simple and universal truths—that were central to every religion. The Deists, therefore, held suspect any supposed truth of revelation that failed to square with what might be known by reason.

Benjamin Franklin illustrates well the skepticism many Founders held regarding the truth claims of the Christian faith, including the claims regarding the divinity of Jesus. "I have," he wrote, "with most of the Dissenters in England, some Doubts as to his Divinity; tho' it is a question I do not dogmatize upon, having never studied it, and think it needless to busy myself with it now, when I expect soon an Opportunity of knowing the Truth with less Trouble. I see no harm, however, in its being believed, if that Belief has the good Consequence, as probably it has, of making his Doctrines more respected and better observed."[8] In an 1813 letter addressed to Thomas Jefferson, John Adams wrote, "We can never be so certain of any Prophecy, or the fulfillment of any Prophecy; or of any miracle, or the design of any miracle as We are, from the revelation of nature i.e. nature's God."[9]

Other Founders expressed hostility toward the corruptions of organized Christianity. Thus John Adams, commenting on the creation of the American Bible Society in the early nineteenth century, complained to Jefferson, "We have now, it seems, a National Bible Society, to propagate the King James Bible, through all Nations. Would it not be better, to apply these pious Subscriptions, to purify Christendom from the Corruptions of Christianity; than to propagate their Corruptions in Europe, Asia, Africa, and America?"[10]

Though many of the Founders questioned the divinity of Jesus, Jefferson believed that Deism represented the heart of Jesus's teachings. He claimed, however, that orthodox Christianity—including many of the biblical writers—had warped those teachings beyond recognition. Indeed, he described the teachings of traditional, orthodox Christianity as "metaphysical insanities, . . . mere relapses into polytheism, differing from paganism only by being more unintelligible."[11] Throughout his life Jefferson embraced some of Jesus's most basic teachings regarding how we should treat our sisters and our brothers. In a letter to Miles King, he wrote, "I must ever believe that religion substantially good which produces an honest life." He made it clear that he had little time for doctrinal disputes or denominational differences. In his view, "Our particular principles of religion are a subject of accountability to our God alone. I inquire after no man's and trouble none with mine." He believed there was "not a Quaker, or a Baptist, or a Presbyterian or an Episcopalian, a Catholic or a Protestant in heaven; that on entering that gate, we leave those badges behind, and find ourselves united in those principles only in which God has united us all."[12]

The principles in which God has united us all, Jefferson believed, were the principles of Deism—a belief in God, an affirmation that a moral order governs the universe, and a commitment to love God and neighbor. Because these principles struck Jefferson as supremely rational—and because he believed in their unifying power—he firmly believed "that the present generation will see Unitarianism [the institutional embodiment of Deism] become the general religion of the United States."[13] For all these reasons, Jefferson grounded the Declaration of Independence in the tenets of the Deist faith.

Accordingly, Jefferson's Declaration appeals, not once, but several times to God. But nowhere in the Declaration does Jefferson refer to the "God of our Lord and Savior Jesus Christ" or the "God of Abraham, Isaac, and Jacob" or even to the "God we know in the Bible." Instead, Jefferson grounds the political principles of the Declaration in "the Laws of Nature and of Nature's God." Thus the first paragraph of the Declaration reads like this: "When in the Course of human events, it becomes necessary for one people to dissolve the political bands which have connected them with another, and to assume among the Powers of the earth, the separate and equal station to which *the Laws of Nature and of Nature's God* entitle them, a decent respect to the opinions of mankind requires that they should declare the causes which impel them to the separation" (italics added).

One finds, therefore, in the Declaration of Independence the very first principle of the Deist creed—an appeal to one God, knowable not from scripture but from God's second book, the Book of Nature. This appeal was not a particular appeal that only Christians could understand and appreciate, but a universal appeal that could be understood by all humankind.

The second principle of the Deist creed—an affirmation of the moral order that governs the universe—found its way into the second paragraph of the Declaration, where Jefferson wrote these words: "We hold these truths to be self-evident, that all men are created equal, that they are endowed by their Creator with certain unalienable Rights, that among these are Life, Liberty and the pursuit of Happiness." These truths, Jefferson believed, were self-evident precisely because they were grounded in the very "Laws of Nature and of Nature's God." And nature, for Jefferson, was a far stronger guarantor of moral truths than all the texts of all the world's scriptures combined.

In the very words of the Declaration, therefore, Jefferson demonstrated that he had no interest in superimposing on the nation a Christian vision of the kingdom of God. Because in 1776, virtually everyone in the nation supported the cause of independence and freedom, it took some time for the Calvinists—and other orthodox Christians as well—to discern the fundamental differences between themselves and the author of the Declaration. But when they did, they were none too happy with Jefferson's adamant refusal to support their Christian agenda for the nation.

The gulf between Jefferson and the orthodox Christians widened over the years such that when Jefferson ran for the presidency of the United States in 1800, some Christians attacked him unmercifully. Though Jefferson was profoundly religious and believed strongly in the existence and providence of God, he rejected an exclusively Christian understanding of that God. Some Christians accused him, therefore, of rank infidelity and saddled him with the label "infidel." One clergyman even argued that Jefferson had preached both "atheism" and "the morality of devils."[14] Those events transpired in the earliest years of the nineteenth century. In a short time, the gulf between Jefferson and the Christian community would grow into a much wider gulf between evangelical Christians and the Deist Founders.[15] But the realization on the part of some Christians that Thomas Jefferson and his Declaration of Independence had betrayed their cause was but a prelude to a far greater disaster for orthodox, establishment-oriented Christians in the United States—their realization that the Constitution had done the very same thing.

The Constitution

The Constitution betrayed the agenda that many Christians promoted for one simple reason: it failed to create a Christian establishment. In the first ten words of Article I of the Bill of Rights we read that "Congress shall make no law respecting an establishment of religion." And then, in the next six words, the Constitution denied to government the right to prohibit the free exercise of religion on the part of any citizen. Clearly, the Constitution had rendered null and void any hopes anyone might have had for a Christian nation enforced by law. Put another way, it failed to require by law that Christianity would become the official religion of the United States of America.

For many Christians, that failure was catastrophic because—as we have seen already—the only way they knew to create a Christian nation was to create a Christian establishment. In addition, many Calvinists still nurtured dreams of transforming the United States into a model kingdom of God. Compounding the dilemma of these establishment-oriented Christians, Article VI of the Constitution stipulated that "no religious Test shall ever be required as a Qualification to any Office or public Trust under the United States." But perhaps most detrimental to the agenda many Christians embraced was the fact that the Constitution never once mentioned God. According to one report, when Alexander Hamilton was confronted with that omission, he responded, "We forgot."[16]

What about the Founders?

The Constitution, in a word, is a fundamentally secular document. But that fact has not prevented Christians in later years from claiming that the Founders were just like them—orthodox, Bible-believing Christians whose real intent was to create a Christian nation. Pat Robertson, head of the Christian Coalition, complained in 1991 about the "emergence of a New Age world religion" that, in his judgment, aimed to replace the "biblically based . . . Christian order" authored by America's Founders.[17]

Two years earlier, future "expert" reviewer David Barton had founded Wall-Builders, an organization dedicated to rebuilding America on what Barton viewed as its original Christian foundation. Indeed, his 1989 book, *The Myth of Separation*, flatly rejected the doctrine of the separation of church and state as a fraud, designed to undermine the nation's Christian origins.[18] The Texas Republican Party elected Barton as its vice chairman in 1997, and the 2004 platform of the Texas GOP also rejected church-state separation and affirmed the United States as a Christian nation. Governor Perry praised Barton in 2005 as "a truly national treasure" who "understands that America was founded on our Christian faith."[19] Over the years, Barton's influence has extended far beyond Texas. Salaried for a time by the Republican National Committee, his materials have been used by Pat Robertson's Christian Coalition, James Dobson's Focus on the Family, Phyllis Schlafly's Eagle Forum, and D. James Kennedy's Coral Ridge Ministries.[20] In a book published in 2003 with the intriguing title *What If America Were a Christian Nation Again?*, Kennedy made the uncompromising claim that "America was a nation founded upon Christ and His Word."[21]

If Robertson, Kennedy, Barton, and others who have carried the banner of Christian America meant to suggest that the Founders were Christians, they were partly right. Some were Christians, though the most influential among the Founders were Deists. And even the Deists thought themselves committed to the core principles of Jesus Christ, as the case of Thomas Jefferson demonstrates. But even for those Founders who embraced the Christian faith, that stance sometimes made very little difference in the way they envisioned the religious life of the nation. John Witherspoon—newly added to the Texas standards as part of the annual celebration of Freedom Week—is a case in point. Witherspoon, a Presbyterian, was the president of the College of New Jersey—the forerunner of Princeton University—and perhaps the most well-known clergyman during the revolutionary generation. While still in his native Scotland, he defended orthodox Christian theology against its Enlightenment detractors and was a principal leader in the evangelical party of the Presbyterian Church, earning him the historical assessment of being "the most self-consciously evangelical of the founding fathers." Strangely, however, once he arrived in the American colonies, Witherspoon failed to translate his Christian convictions into political theory. Like the Deists who were his peers, he argued that reason and experience should guide politics, not revelation. Witherspoon was not alone. Though many of the Founders read the Bible, they rarely brought biblical texts into political debates.[22]

On the other hand, James Wilson—one of only six Founders to sign both the Declaration and the Constitution—relied quite specifically on the Christian natural law tradition to shape his political philosophy. Wilson, like Witherspoon, also had a background in the Scottish Presbyterian tradition and became an active Episcopalian later in life.[23]

Thus the Founders occupied a continuum that ran from orthodox Christianity to radical Deism. All of them—even the most radical of the Deists— were children of biblical faith, since American Deism is incomprehensible apart from Jewish and Christian biblical teachings about God. But many of the Founders—and especially the most influential of that group—also embraced, to one degree or another, a Deist perspective, and that is the difference that made all the difference.

Regardless of their religious dispositions, the Founders' ultimate concern was for religious freedom, not to create a Christian America. Following their study of the Founders' religious beliefs, Nathan O. Hatch, Mark A. Noll, and George M. Marsden bear out this conclusion when they write, "No matter how favorable toward Christianity some of the founders may have been, their goal was pluralism, rather than the preferment of one religion to all others . . . So long as religion supported political harmony, few of them were all that concerned with *what* a person believed."[24]

We must address one other aspect of the way some Christians in later years— especially since the 1970s—have interpreted the Founders. Those who argue that the Founders sought to create a Christian nation often base that claim on the simple fact that the Founders were religious and believed in God. But there are many varieties of religion, and almost all religions advocate belief in a deity. Put another way, the fact that one may believe in God—or may advocate for belief in God—hardly makes one a Christian.

An example of the way many apologists for Christian America nonetheless confuse the broad category of religion with a particular religious tradition—the Christian faith—can be found in an American history text published in 1989 and designed for home schooling or for use in Christian schools. That text claims that when the Founders used the term religion, they really "meant Christianity." When they spoke of morality, they really "meant Christian character." And when they referred to knowledge, they really "meant a Biblical worldview."[25]

Regardless of the claims Christians have made for more than two hundred years that the Founders sought to create a Christian nation, the Constitution stands as the supreme rebuttal to that contention. Indeed, the Constitution stands as written. It makes no mention of God, it prohibits the creation of a religious establishment, and it outlaws any religious test for public office. No matter how orthodox and devout certain Founders may have been in their personal religious beliefs, they refused to translate those beliefs into even the mildest constitutional requirement that the nation embrace the Christian faith.

The Battle for Christian America

In spite of the Constitution and the Founders' intentions, however, there have always been Christians who have sought to transform the nation into a Christian republic. Although their work has been constant and unremitting over the course of the nation's history, two great movements—the Second Great Awakening in the early nineteenth century and the Fundamentalist Movement in the early twentieth century—have defined the battle for Christian America.

The Second Great Awakening

Periodically, great Christian revivals have erupted in the United States, transforming America's cultural landscape in significant ways. We know the first of those revivals as the Great Awakening—a religious conflagration that swept up and down the eastern seaboard from 1739 to 1743, transforming the colonies into Christian centers of piety, zeal, and learning. The Great Awakening also paved the way for the American Revolution inasmuch as it united 13 very independent colonies into a common self-understanding, which was, for all intents and purposes, a Christian self-understanding. No one contributed to that self-understanding more than Jonathan Edwards, one of the principal leaders of the revival. In 1742, Edwards claimed that the Great Awakening would usher in the final reign of God over all the earth. In fact, Edwards believed that "this new world is probably now discovered, that the new and most glorious state of God's church on earth might commence there."[26]

By the time the Revolutionary War commenced in 1776, understandings like these allowed many colonists to interpret the Revolution as a Christian undertaking and political freedom as a Christian virtue. Abraham Keteltas, for example, argued that the Revolution was the "cause for which the Son of God came down from his celestial throne and expired on a cross."[27] Another clergyman, Samuel Sherwood, viewed the Revolution both as a Christian undertaking and as an event that would usher in the rule of the kingdom of God. Sherwood was among the first to link the new nation to the kingdom of God, but he would by no means be the last. "God almighty, with all the powers of heaven, is on our side. Great numbers of angels, no doubt, are encamping round our coast for our defense and protection. Michael stands ready, with all the artillery of heaven, to encounter the dragon, and to vanquish this black host."[28] It is revealing to compare the militaristic and nationalistic content of Sherwood's statement with the biblical vision of the kingdom of God that counseled peace, humility, and concern for the poor.

The effects of the Great Awakening, however, were short-lived because the Christian faith fell on hard times following the Revolution. Martin E. Marty has suggested that at no time in American history "were religious institutions so weak as they were in the first quarter-century after independence." Marty adds, "It is difficult to establish reliable statistics, but the best guesses suggest that from four to seven percent of the people were formally church members."[29] Add to that estimate the growing popularity of Deism, rationalism, and skepticism, and one has some measure of the crisis that faced American churches in the aftermath of the Revolution. That crisis suggests that the Christian golden age of the American founding—the age to which Christian America advocates wish the nation to return—simply never existed. It also helps to explain the rise of the Second Great Awakening in approximately 1801.

The Second Great Awakening emerged, at least in part, in response to the lifeless nature of American Christianity in the post-Revolutionary period. But it also emerged in response to the Constitution's rejection of a legally established church. As we have seen, many American Christians of that time were Calvinists who longed to bring the nation under the sovereign control of Almighty God. And almost all Christians of that time, whether Calvinist or not, knew only one way to infuse the culture with Christian influence and morals—through the power of an established church. And now that option was gone. Their only hope, therefore, for creating a Christian culture was through the power of persuasion, and the only way to persuade significant numbers of people was through a massive revival.

Stirrings of what would become the Second Great Awakening occurred as early as the 1790s, but historians generally place the birth of that awakening in 1801. In that year, significant revivals began in opposite ends of the country. A revival at Cane Ridge, Kentucky, attracted thousands to an ecumenical, backwoods, spiritual extravaganza where sinners were slain in the spirit, danced, barked, jerked, and fell to the ground under the influence of the Holy Ghost.

Also in 1801—this time in Connecticut, at the other end of the country—an altogether different sort of revival broke out among students at Yale University in response to the preaching of Yale's president, Timothy Dwight. Dwight lamented the Deism—he called it "infidelity"—that had become so popular in the nation, largely through the influence of American Founders like Jefferson. Though the Second Great Awakening grew from relatively small beginnings at opposite ends of the country, it quickly cascaded into a national revival that lasted some thirty years. This revival, however, did not rely upon preaching alone. Revivalists sought to ban the delivery of Sunday mails and restrict the consumption of liquor. They launched innumerable efforts to evangelize both the nation and the larger world. They created the American Bible Society to distribute Bibles, the American Tract Society to distribute Christian literature, and the American Education Society to promote Christian education at the outposts of the American frontier. Indeed, they established church-related colleges throughout the nation at such a rapid pace that by 1860 the number of these colleges had reached 173, up from only 9 in 1780.[30]

For much of the Second Great Awakening, the man who coordinated that revival and kept it alive was Charles G. Finney. Finney traveled from town to town and city to city all over the United States, proclaiming the good news of salvation but also proclaiming that America could and should become an outpost of the kingdom of God. Finney's work, however, represented an entirely different vision of the kingdom of God than that promoted by many other revival preachers. Finney was far less concerned that Christianity dominate American culture and far more concerned to bring his program into line with the *biblical vision* of the kingdom of God. Finney understood that vision as well as any preacher in American history. He knew what Jesus had said about Himself—that He had come to liberate prisoners, heal the sick, and bring sight to the blind. So Finney sought to translate that vision into categories appropriate for his day and age. He told his converts—and they were many—that they must seek to transform society in some meaningful way. He urged some to take up prison reform and others the banner of temperance. But most of all, he encouraged his converts to do all in their power to abolish the evil of slavery. Harriet Beecher Stowe and her antislavery novel, *Uncle Tom's Cabin*, stand as a prime example of the kind of work the Second Great Awakening promoted on behalf of slaves and their liberation. Indeed, apart from the Second Great Awakening, slavery might not have ended when it did.

Finally, we should note that the Second Great Awakening was in many respects an attempt to save the nation from the threat Protestants perceived in the rapid growth of Roman Catholicism on America's shores. By the beginning of the nineteenth century, Catholics had grown from some 20,000 during the colonial period to 40,000, and by 1850, that number would swell to 1,606,000.[31] Because Protestants felt that the Catholic Church was, in principle, inimical to the cause of liberty, the Second Great Awakening was not so much an effort to Christianize the nation as to Protestantize it.

By 1830, when the revival had run its course, the United States had become, in many respects, a Christian nation—even a Protestant nation. It was neither Protestant nor Christian, however, in any legal sense. Nor was it Christian in a biblical sense. But it was profoundly Christian insofar as many Americans now employed Christian categories to describe and interpret the cultural life of the nation. In his book *Righteous Empire*, Martin Marty reported that numerous "geographies, spellers, and readers from 1804, 1806, 1817, 1835, and 1846 included charts delineating the religions of the nations of the world. The United States was always listed as Protestant." But Marty puzzled over that fact. Only a minority of Americans belonged to Protestant churches, and the government was officially neutral toward religion. Still, Americans "had come to call their territory Protestant."[32]

Francis Wayland—preacher, economist, and president of Brown University from 1827 to 1855—made the point well. "Popular institutions," he wrote, "are inseparably connected with Protestant Christianity." Many other observers, both American and European, shared Wayland's perspective. Philip Schaff, the historian of Christianity from Mercersburg, Pennsylvania, commented in 1855, "I doubt whether the moral influence of Christianity and of Protestantism has more deeply and widely affected any nation, than it has the Anglo-Saxon." And the great French observer Alexis de Tocqueville thought that "there was no country in the world where the Christian religion retained a greater influence over the souls of men than in America."[33]

Fundamentalism in the Twentieth Century

Thanks to the success of the Second Great Awakening, evangelicals did, in fact, control American culture for most of the nineteenth century. But as the twentieth century dawned, a variety of factors—urbanization, an extraordinarily sizable influx of Catholic and Jewish immigrants, the influential rise of Darwinian evolution, the emergence of biblical criticism, and the growing popularity of new schools of psychology (e.g., Freud) that rejected God out of hand—began to undermine the evangelical Protestant dominance of American life and culture.

The Fundamentalist Movement—a belligerent wing of the evangelical tradition—emerged in the early twentieth century to battle against these modern trends, especially evolution, and to reclaim America as an outpost of their understanding of the kingdom of God.[34] But the fundamentalists differed profoundly from those early evangelicals who had launched the Second Great Awakening. Most notably, they embraced scarcely a remnant of the nineteenth-century commitment to the *biblical vision* of the kingdom of God. If the Second Great Awakening had fought for the abolition of slavery, fundamentalists fought for a nation free from Darwin's theory of evolution. If the Second Great Awakening had fought for prison reform, fundamentalists fought to defend an inerrant Bible. And if the Second Great Awakening had fought for the creation of common schools throughout the nation, fundamentalists fought to free those schools from scientific theories that failed to conform to a literal reading of the biblical text.

But there were still other differences that divided twentieth-century fundamentalism from the Second Great Awakening a hundred years before. The Second Great Awakening followed hard on the heels of the nation's birth. Leaders of that movement knew they had an opportunity to create something fresh and new. For that reason, the Second Great Awakening was a creative movement, optimistic, forward looking, and always on the offensive. Leaders of that movement waged their battles, to be sure—battles against Deism and skepticism, for example—but on the whole, that revival spread like a mighty torrent that baptized the youthful nation into Protestant versions of morality and righteousness.

On the other hand, when the Fundamentalist Movement emerged in the early twentieth century, its task was not to create something new and fresh and vibrant. Instead, its task was to defend the gains of the past against the onslaughts of modernism. That difference is crucial, for if the Second Great Awakening had been forward looking, the Fundamentalist Movement consistently looked backward—backward to a nineteenth-century golden age when the nation seemed so thoroughly Christian. If the Second Great Awakening had been optimistic about the future, leaders of the Fundamentalist Movement were often pessimistic. And well they should have been, for pluralism, on the one hand, and scientific assumptions inimical to their understanding of Christian America, on the other, now swept the nation. And if the Second Great Awakening consistently assumed an offensive posture, leaders of the Fundamentalist Movement almost always found themselves on the defense. They had enemies on every hand, and their enemies helped define the very nature of their movement. Indeed, one might well argue that apart from its enemies, fundamentalism could not exist.

Try as they might to restore the golden age of Christian America, the fundamentalists met with limited success, and at the Scopes Monkey Trial in Dayton, Tennessee, in 1925, they suffered a resounding defeat. Having lost the culture wars of their time, they retreated from the public square and took refuge in their churches, and there they remained, largely invisible to the broader public for the next fifty years. But still they longed for a "Christian America," controlled and dominated by Protestant Christianity.

In the meantime, the more moderate evangelicals who sought to put distance between themselves and the fundamentalists remained quite visible to the public eye, thanks in large part to the revivalist preaching of Billy Graham and the creation of the National Association of Evangelicals in 1942. But like the fundamentalists, they, too, sought to recover the Christian America that had been so dominant in the nineteenth century. Their work on behalf of that vision morphed into a crusade in the late 1940s and 1950s when America stood toe-to-toe against Soviet communism.

By the 1970s, in the aftermath of the cultural revolutions that dominated the 1960s, fundamentalism and evangelicalism were growing increasingly indistinguishable. Many fundamentalist and evangelical Christians were deeply troubled by the antiwar movement that rejected America's military venture in Vietnam and by the civil rights movement that threatened white dominance of American culture.

And so in 1979, Jerry Falwell summoned the fundamentalists out of their churches—the cultural silos in which they had resided for the previous fifty years—and launched his Moral Majority, a religio-political organization aimed at restoring what evangelicals and fundamentalists alike commonly viewed as traditional (i.e., pre-1960s) Christian and American values. From their perspective, this was not a vision that would define a struggling Christian minority, but a vision that should define the nation, and over the next several years, they would do everything in their power to make sure Americans embraced their vision of a godly Christian state. Other organizations similar to the Moral Majority quickly followed suit, most notably James Dobson's Family Research Council in 1981 and Pat Robertson's Christian Coalition in 1989.

All these organizations shared the traditional evangelical penchant to control American culture. But they differed from the Second Great Awakening of the early nineteenth century and the Fundamentalist Movement of the early twentieth century in one crucial way. If the Second Great Awakening had sought to exercise control through preaching and persuasion, these more recent fundamentalist and evangelical organizations sought to control the country through political manipulation and legal coercion.

Since the 1980s, for example, they have actively supported political candidates—local, state, and national—who would pass laws in sync with their vision for a "Christian America." In addition, they drew up "report cards" on candidates and office holders alike, grading them on their compliance with a host of measures they wished to see enacted into law.

Their success can be measured by the fact that by 2004, this fundamentalist/evangelical power bloc effectively controlled the Republican Party, the House of Representatives, and the Senate. That reality became evident in the report cards—technically called Congressional Scorecards—issued by the leading fundamentalist/evangelical advocacy group, the Christian Coalition.

Those report cards graded members of the House on 13 issues and members of the Senate on 6. Forty-two members of the Senate earned an A+ (a 100 percent score on all 6 issues on which they were graded), and 163 members of the House earned an A– (a 90 percent score on all 13 issues on which they were graded). And the Christian Coalition gave 45 senators and 186 members of Congress a rating of 80 percent or better. Those numbers suggest that the political organizing on which fundamentalist/evangelical Christians embarked in 1979 had paid off handsomely. Indeed, by 2004, they were well on their way toward transforming the United States into their version of Christian America and right-wing Protestantism into an informal American version of the historic state-church.

This is the twentieth-century background we must keep in mind if we wish to understand the efforts in Texas to redefine the American story in social studies texts used in Texas and throughout the nation. But to understand those efforts even more fully, we must also keep in mind the cataclysmic events that shaped the United States in the earliest years of the twenty-first century, especially during the administration of George W. Bush.

American messianism reached an apex following the terror attack on the Pentagon and the World Trade Center on September 11, 2001. Not only was the United States wholly unprepared for that attack in terms of military intelligence; the United States was also unprepared both psychologically and spiritually. Indeed, seldom has the United States more fully betrayed the claim that it functions as a Christian nation than in the aftermath of those attacks. Instead of asking the question, "Why do they hate us?" and listening carefully to the highly complex answers to that question that our enemies might have offered; instead of seizing the opportunity to create an entirely new world order by sowing seeds of friendship instead of seeds of hate; instead of building alliances and forging bonds of reconciliation; instead of using its vast wealth to alleviate hunger, poverty, suffering, and disease around the world—instead of doing all those things one might expect a Christian nation to do, America sought vengeance and retribution and went to war—and did so almost unilaterally. In that way, it perpetuated the age-old politics of violence and embraced the never-ending spiral of an eye for an eye and a tooth for a tooth. Through the instrumentality of war, America sought to export democracy and capitalism, to suppress global pluralism, and to redeem the world for American values. In all these ways, it lived out its messianic self-understanding, but in the process raised serious questions about its status as a Christian nation. The American response to 9/11 was driven by a fundamentalist vision of the world that has little in common with the historic Christian faith.

And the same can be said for the work of the Texas State Board of Education with respect to many of the standards it adopted for social studies texts. In the aftermath of 9/11, the work of that board was driven to a very large extent by its embrace of the contemporary myth of Christian America. Often disconnected from the Founders' intentions, that myth has even less to do with the biblical text and the Bible's vision of the kingdom of God. As a result, the work of the board promotes bad history, a skewed understanding of the Christian religion, and an impoverished sense of ethical norms. And that is hardly a legacy fit for America's children.

Notes

1. Chris Vaughn, "A Man with a Message; Self-Taught Historian's Work on Church-State Issues Rouses GOP," *Fort Worth Star-Telegram*, May 22, 2005.
2. Peter Marshall, "Feedback on the Current K-12 TEKS," *Texas Education Agency: Social Studies Experts*, last modified April 25, 2010, http://www.tea.state.tx.us/index2.aspx?id=6184.
3. David Barton, "Social Studies TEKS, Second Review," *Texas Education Agency: Social Studies Experts*, last modified April 25, 2010, http://www.tea.state.tx.us/index2.aspx?id=6184; Marshall, "Feedback on the Current K-12 TEKS," 8.
4. For more, see Richard T. Hughes, *Christian America and the Kingdom of God* (Urbana: University of Illinois Press, 2009), chaps. 2 and 3.
5. Theodore Dwight Bozeman, *To Live Ancient Lives: The Primitivist Impulse in Puritanism* (Chapel Hill: University of North Carolina Press, 1988).
6. See David L. Holmes, *The Faiths of the Founding Fathers* (Oxford: Oxford University Press, 2006); Jon Meacham, *American Gospel: God, the Founding Fathers, and the Making of a Nation* (New York: Random House, 2006); Edwin S. Gaustad, *Faith of the Founders: Religion and the New Nation 1776–1826* (Waco, TX: Baylor University Press, 2004); Frank Lambert, *The Founding Fathers and the Place of Religion in America* (Princeton, NJ: Princeton University Press, 2003); Daniel L. Dreisbach, Mark D. Hall, and Jeffry H. Morrison, eds., *The Founders on God and Government* (New York: Rowman and Littlefield, 2004).
7. See Thomas Jefferson, letter to Benjamin Waterhouse, June 26, 1822, in Norman Cousins, ed., *"In God We Trust": The Religious Beliefs and Ideas of the American Founding Fathers* (New York: Harper, 1958), 160–61.

8. Benjamin Franklin, letter to Ezra Stiles, March 9, 1790, in Cousins, *"In God We Trust,"* 42.
9. John Adams, letter to Thomas Jefferson, September 14, 1813, in Lester J. Cappon, ed., *The Adams-Jefferson Letters* (New York: Simon and Schuster, 1971), 373.
10. Cited in Henry F. May, *The Enlightenment in America* (Oxford: Oxford University Press, 1976), 335.
11. Thomas Jefferson, letter to Jared Sparks, November 4, 1820, in Cousins, *"In God We Trust,"* 156.
12. Thomas Jefferson, letter to Miles King, September 26, 1814, in Cousins, *"In God We Trust,"* 144–45.
13. Thomas Jefferson, letter to James Smith, December 8, 1822, in Cousins, *"In God We Trust,"* 159.
14. John M. Mason, *The Voice of Warning, to Christians, on the Ensuing Election of a President of the United States* (New York, 1800), 20, cited in G. Adolf Kock, *Religion of the American Enlightenment* (New York: Thomas Y. Crowell, 1968), 271.
15. Sidney E. Mead, *The Lively Experiment: The Shaping of Christianity in America* (New York: Harper and Row, 1963), 38–54; Martin E. Marty, *The Infidel: Free Thought and American Religion* (New York: World, 1961).
16. George Duffield Jr., "The God of Our Fathers, an Historical Sermon," January 4, 1861 (Philadelphia, 1861), 15.
17. Pat Robertson, *The New World Order* (Dallas: Word Publishing, 1991), 246.
18. David Barton, *The Myth of Separation: What Is the Correct Relationship Between Church and State?* (Aledo, TX: WallBuilder Press, 1989); Deborah Caldwell, "David Barton and the 'Myth' of Church-State Separation," *BeliefNet*, 2004: http://www.beliefnet.com/News/Politics/2004/10/David-Barton-The-Myth-Of-Church-State-Separation.aspx.
19. Vaughn, "A Man With a Message."
20. See "David Barton," http://www.speroforum.com/forum/wiki.asp?id=DavidBarton.
21. D. James Kennedy with Jerry Newcombe, *What If America Were a Christian Nation Again?* (Nashville: Thomas Nelson Publishers, 2003), 4.
22. Mark A. Noll, Nathan O. Hatch, and George M. Marsden, *The Search for Christian America* (Colorado Springs: Helmers and Howard, 1989), 81, 88–93.
23. Mark D. Hall, "James Wilson: Presbyterian, Anglican, Thomist, or Deist? Does It Matter?" in *The Founders on God and Government*, ed. Dreisbach, Hall, and Morrison, 181–205.
24. Noll, Hatch, and Marsden, *The Search for Christian America*, 133–34, 107 (italics in original).
25. Mark A. Beliles and Stephen K. McDowell, *America's Providential History* (Charlottesville, VA: Providence Foundation, 1989), 178.
26. Jonathan Edwards, "Some Thoughts Concerning the Present Revival of Religion in New England" (New York: S. Converse, 1830), 128–33.
27. Abraham Keteltas, "God Arising and Pleading His People's Cause . . . , a sermon preached October 5, 1777 in . . . Newburyport" (Newburyport, MA., 1777), in Winthrop Hudson, ed., *Nationalism and Religion in America: Concepts of American Identity and Mission* (New York: Harper and Row, 1970), 49, 52–53.

28. Samuel Sherwood, *The Church's Flight into the Wilderness* (New York, 1776), 39–49.
29. Martin E. Marty, *Righteous Empire: The Protestant Experience in America* (New York: Dial Press, 1970), 38.
30. For a succinct description of these efforts, see Thomas Askew and Richard Pierard, *The American Church Experience* (Grand Rapids: Baker, 2004), 86–90.
31. Marty, *Righteous Empire*, 127ff.
32. Ibid., 15.
33. Ibid., 89, 15, 90.
34. Martin E. Marty and R. Scott Appleby, eds., *Fundamentalisms Observed (The Fundamentalism Project)* (Chicago: University of Chicago Press, 2004); George M. Marsden, *Fundamentalism and American Culture: The Shaping of Twentieth Century Evangelicalism, 1870–1925* (New York: Oxford University Press, 1980).

Figure 9 A new victory for the Lost Cause
The new Texas history standards bring Lost Cause ideology into the mainstream school curriculum. Rebel leader Jefferson Davis (top left) is elevated to peer status with Abraham Lincoln; slaveholder Thomas J. "Stonewall" Jackson (top right) is venerated as a pious, conservative friend of blacks; and Hiram Revels (bottom), celebrated as the first African American elected to the US Senate, actually supported the cause of white supremacy.

CHAPTER 9

Neo-Confederate Ideology in the Texas History Standards

Edward H. Sebesta

The term *Lost Cause* is used by historians to refer to a historical narrative that has been advocated by partisans of the Confederacy over generations since the Civil War. The historical narrative argues that the slave states seceded for reasons other than slavery, that the Confederacy did not fight for slavery, and that slaves were contented or at least not treated badly. The term first appeared as the title of a book by A. E. Pollard published shortly after the Civil War in 1866. The Lost Cause viewpoint achieved national acceptance during the 1920s and 1930s and has had widespread acceptance since then. These interpretations of history are incorporated into the neo-Confederate ideology now advanced by a variety of white supremacist, anti-immigration, and "heritage" groups. The new Texas Essential Knowledge and Skills (TEKS) attempt to mainstream the Lost Cause ideology and neo-Confederacy history. These new standards will instill in the minds of Texas children a neo-Confederate consciousness that will greatly enable and assist the neo-Confederate movement.

The recent injection of neo-Confederate ideology into the standards adopted in 2010 by the Texas State Board of Education (SBOE) stands in striking contrast to the standards adopted by the SBOE in 1998. For example, "states' rights" as a cause of the Civil War was mentioned once in the 1998 middle school standards but is now mentioned once in the elementary school standards and three more times in the middle school standards. Tariffs, mentioned once in 1998, are now mentioned twice, and the Nullification Crisis of 1832–1833 is cast explicitly as an issue of states' rights. The 2010 standards also require middle school students to compare the inaugural addresses of Abraham Lincoln and Confederate President Jefferson Davis. Seventh-grade students will now also study Confederate Texas Governor Francis Lubbock and Confederate military officers John Bell Hood, John H. Reagan, John

Magruder, and Thomas Green. And finally in the 2010 standards, Confederate General Thomas J. Jackson (known as "Stonewall" to Lost Cause believers) is recommended as a significant figure for study.

The neo-Confederate additions did not come without controversy. Davis's inaugural address and Jackson were added on January 14, 2010, in individual and separate motions by SBOE member Barbara Cargill (R-Woodlands) and passed by the board. The minutes for these votes indicate only that it passed. On May 21, 2010, Rick Agosto (D-San Antonio) attempted to remove the reference to Davis's inaugural address but was defeated 10 to 4. The Texas Confederate figures were added on May 20, 2010, by a motion of SBOE member David Bradley (R-Beaumont) and passed by the board 8 to 7. An attempt to remove these figures on May 21, 2010, by Rick Agosto was defeated 8 to 6. The additional reference to the tariff and two of the additional references to states' rights were added by the TEKS review committees and appear in the initial July 31, 2009, draft. The final new reference to states' rights was added May 20, 2010, upon the motion of Lawrence A. Allen Jr. (D-Houston), and passed, but the votes were not recorded in the minutes. The additional reference to the tariff was added by the TEKS reviewer and appears in the July 31, 2009, draft from the reviewers.[1]

Taken collectively, the changes represent a significant mainstreaming of a troubling neo-Confederate ideology into the Texas teaching standards. At its core, neo-Confederate ideology is reactionary and antimodernist, built around a historical narrative of events leading up to, during, and after the Civil War. In this narrative, John C. Calhoun and other Southern antebellum proslavery and conservative leaders of the Confederacy as well as those who overthrew Reconstruction are held out as espousing a superior belief system in opposition to what they perceive as the historical villains—those who supported abolition, won the Civil War, and later supported civil rights for African Americans during Reconstruction and beyond. In addition to opposing civil rights and endorsing racism, neo-Confederates hold a particular hostility to Unitarians and to democracy itself as they support a hierarchal and antidemocratic society. According to this viewpoint, the Civil War was really a theological war enacted by a heretical North versus an orthodox Christian South. The problems of modern society, they believe, find their root in the triumph of the abolitionist movement, the defeat of the Confederacy, and the beginning of the decline of an orthodox Christian society. Twenty-first-century neo-Confederates therefore look to nineteenth-century proslavery theologians R. L. Dabney, James H. Thornwell, and Benjamin Palmer for guidance in religion and politics.[2] The new Texas history standards create nothing short of "A Confederate Youth's Primer" by celebrating Confederate heroes, holding up white supremacists as role models, and creating an entryway through which neo-Confederate groups can achieve the goal of Lost Cause revisionism for which they have worked for generations.

States' Rights and Tariffs

Texas students in elementary and middle school will encounter the neo-Confederate assertions concerning states' rights in their study of the causes of the Civil War. In both fifth- and eighth-grade US history, students must identify and explain "the causes of the Civil War, including sectionalism, states' rights, and slavery." In seventh-grade Texas history they will "explain reasons for the involvement of Texas in the Civil War such as states' rights, slavery, sectionalism, and tariffs." In eighth grade, they will "explain constitutional issues arising over the issue of states' rights, including the Nullification Crisis and the Civil War."[3]

The belief that the slave states seceded over tariffs and states' rights has been advocated by the Lost Cause view of the Civil War for generations. It is popular even among schoolteachers and persons interested in nineteenth-century American history. As recently as 2007, historian and public speaker James Loewen would poll his audiences as to the causes of the Civil War and was surprised to find that states' rights was given as the cause by the overwhelming majority, even with an audience of African American schoolteachers.[4]

Despite its popularity and its new emphasis in the Texas standards, states' rights were not a cause of the Civil War, as illustrated by the case of Texas. In February 1861, Texans passed "a declaration of the causes which impel the State of Texas to secede from the Federal Union" in which they outlined their reasons for secession clearly and explicitly. Texans complained of federal opposition to the expansion of slavery, of an abolitionist movement that endorsed "the debasing doctrine of equality of all men, irrespective of race or color." In the words of those Texans who seceded from the Union, slavery and white supremacy were prescribed by "Divine Law." They closed their statement by declaring that "all white men are and of right ought to be entitled to equal civil and political rights; that the servitude of the African race, as existing in these States, is mutually beneficial to both bond and free, and is abundantly authorized and justified by the experience of mankind, and the revealed will of the Almighty Creator, as recognized by all Christian nations."

Not only are states' rights and tariffs *not* mentioned, but Texans advocated *increased* federal intervention in upholding the Fugitive Slave Act and the clauses in the Constitution for the return of escaped slaves to their owners. "When we advert to the course of individual non-slave-holding States, and that a majority of their citizens, our grievances assume far greater magnitude," Texans declared. "The States of Maine, Vermont, New Hampshire, Connecticut, Rhode Island,

Massachusetts, New York, Pennsylvania, Ohio, Wisconsin, Michigan and Iowa, by solemn legislative enactments, have deliberately, directly or indirectly violated the 3rd clause of the 2nd section of the 4th article of the federal constitution, and laws passed in pursuance thereof [requiring the return of escaped slaves]; thereby annulling a material provision of the compact, designed by its framers to perpetuate amity between the members of the confederacy and to secure the rights of the slave-holding States in their domestic institutions."[5] Texans of 1861 thus opposed those northern states that expressed the closest contemporary articulation of "states' rights" in their rejection of the fugitive slave protections in the Constitution and federal laws. Therefore, to cite states' rights as a cause of Texas secession is not only unhistorical but also actually the opposite of Texas's espoused view of federalism. This highly informative document is not referenced anywhere in the Texas standards—but the obscure and very unimportant battle of Palmito Ranch is recommended.

Texans were not alone among Confederates uninterested in states' rights and tariffs. The declaration of causes and the resolutions of Arkansas, Louisiana, Mississippi, Alabama, Georgia, South Carolina, Florida, and Virginia don't mention either topic. Mississippi, Alabama, Georgia, South Carolina, and Virginia joined Texas in complaining about the refusal of northern states to return fugitive slaves. In the Georgia secession debates, Confederate Vice President Alexander H. Stephens dismissed complaints over tariffs by some proponents of secession as being without basis. Stephens briefly reviewed the history of tariffs in his speech and pointed out that the tariffs had been greatly reduced and that the current tariffs were supported and voted for by representatives from southern states, including South Carolina.[6]

Though not found in the historical records documenting the South's secession in 1860 and 1861, the issues of tariffs and states' rights would surface later in the writings of Lost Cause advocates. The arguments about tariffs and states' rights were set forth in E. A. Pollard's *The Lost Cause: A New Southern History of the War of the Confederates* (1866) and former Confederate Vice President Stephens emphasized states' rights as a reason for secession in his widely read *A Constitutional View of the Late War between the States* (1868).[7] By the early twentieth century, the arguments became standard fare in the publications of neo-Confederate organizations such as the United Daughters of the Confederacy (UDC) and the Sons of Confederate Veterans (SCV).[8] Later, in *Facts the Historians Leave Out: A Confederate Youth's Primer* (1951), John S. Tilley provided a comprehensive summary of Lost Cause arguments in which slavery is denied as the reason the slave states seceded. It presents the chapter "What Are States Rights?" followed by the chapter "Northern Violation of States Rights." The chapter "Some Reasons Why the South Seceded" specifically discusses tariffs as a cause of division between the North and South.[9] By adopting neo-Confederate portrayals of history and ignoring the documents prepared by the Texans who seceded in 1861, the Texas State Board of Education will make the state's textbooks a new "Confederate Youth's Primer."

Jefferson Davis and Abraham Lincoln

The 2010 TEKS require eighth-grade students to "analyze Abraham Lincoln's ideas about liberty, equality, union, and government as contained in his first and second inaugural addresses and the Gettysburg Address and contrast them with the ideas contained in Jefferson Davis's inaugural address."[10] Although this comparison may seem like a reasonable attempt to present their opposing views on the topic of "liberty, equality, union, and government," Davis's address is a poor choice for doing so.

In his February 1861 address, Davis discusses why he thinks states have a right to secede, but he also obfuscates the reasons the slave states and he would want to do so. For example, he announces,

> The declared purpose of the compact of Union from which we have withdrawn was 'to establish justice, insure domestic tranquillity, provide for the common defense, promote the general welfare, and secure the blessing of liberty to ourselves and our posterity;' and when, in the judgment of the sovereign States now composing this Confederacy, it had been perverted from the purposes for which it was ordained, and had ceased to answer the ends for which it was established, a peaceful appeal to the ballot-box declared that so far as they were concerned, the government created by that compact should cease to exist.

Exactly how or what "had been perverted from the purposes for which it was ordained, and had ceased to answer the ends for which it was established" isn't explained. Another section is similarly cryptic: "Through many years of controversy with our late associates, the Northern States, we have vainly endeavored to secure tranquillity, and to obtain respect for the rights to which we were entitled. As a necessity, not a choice, we have resorted to the remedy of separation." What controversy had there been? Which rights were not respected? Davis does not clearly say. Finally, Davis states,

> With a Constitution differing only from that of our fathers in so far as it is explanatory of their well-known intent, freed from the sectional conflicts which have interfered with the pursuit of the general welfare, it is not unreasonable to expect that States from which we have recently parted may seek to unite their fortunes with ours under the government which we have instituted . . . To increase the power, develop the resources, and promote the happiness of a confederacy, it is requisite that there should be so much of homogeneity that the welfare of every

portion shall be the aim of the whole. Where this does not exist, antagonisms are engendered which must and should result in separation.

How is this Constitution "freed from the sectional conflicts"? What is the "homogeneity" for the seceding states that will preclude "antagonisms"? The answers to these questions are obscured. The fact that the Confederate Constitution explicitly guarantees slavery is not clear from Davis's address. Historians who already know that Davis was talking about slavery will understand that Davis is explaining that the Confederate Constitution protects slavery and that the "homogeneity" he refers to is that all states in the Confederacy would need to be slave states. The only thing clearly stated in the speech is Davis's argument that states have a right to secede. Davis in this speech seeks to focus on a claimed right to secede but obscures why the slave states might want to secede. To successfully analyze this document would require an in-depth understanding of the nineteenth century and secession not likely to be achieved in an eighth-grade history class.[11]

Other documents far better explain Davis's reasons to support secession. One is his April 1861 address "To the Confederate Congress," in which he gives a lengthy history of the controversy over slavery and the rise of the abolitionist movement, which he calls "ultra fanaticism," stating, "Finally a great party was organized for the purpose of obtaining the administration of the Government, with the avowed object of using its power for the total exclusion of the slave States from all participation in the benefits of the public domain acquired by all the States in common, whether by conquest or purchase; of surrounding them entirely by States in which slavery should be prohibited; of thus rendering the property in slaves so insecure as to be comparatively worthless, and thereby annihilating in effect property worth thousands of millions of dollars." This address also illuminates how slavery was based on paternalism and white supremacy. Slave owners had shown "increasing care and attention for the well-being and comfort of the laboring class," Davis argued. The slave population had grown from six hundred thousand to four million and "in moral and social condition they had been elevated from brutal savages into docile, intelligent, and civilized agricultural laborers, and supplied not only with bodily comforts but with careful religious instruction. Under the supervision of a superior race their labor had been so directed as not only to allow a gradual and marked amelioration of their own condition, but to convert hundreds of thousands of square miles of the wilderness into cultivated lands covered with a prosperous people." Davis further explained, "The production of the South in cotton, rice, sugar, and tobacco, for the full development and continuance of which the labor of African slaves was and is indispensable [and] had swollen to an amount which formed nearly three-fourths of the exports of the whole United

States." Davis explains that it was the Republican threat to slavery that "menaced" the South and provoked an "alarming crisis in their history."[12] Delivered two months after his inaugural address, Davis's message to the Confederate congress decodes the earlier obfuscations and euphemisms. In other speeches, Davis made it clear that the possibility of the abolition of slavery was a reason for secession. In a speech Jefferson Davis made to the Mississippi legislature on November 16, 1858, a little more than two years prior to the start of the Civil War, he argues that the election of an abolitionist president will make secession a necessity and that the state of Mississippi should start stockpiling arms to be ready.[13] When Lincoln issued the Emancipation Proclamation, Davis explained at length that it vindicated those who advocated secession to escape the threat of the abolition of slavery.[14]

Choosing Davis's inaugural address not only obscures the reasons for secession; it also advances Lost Cause arguments. Silence about slavery opens the door for discussion of tariffs and states' rights as causes for the Civil War. Another consequence of pairing the inaugural speeches of Lincoln and Davis is to present them as peers, which has been a goal of Lost Cause advocates for generations. Here again, the effort to rewrite history is shoddy: Lincoln actually ran for office and won a presidential election, whereas Davis was elected by the provisional Confederate Congress and never stood for a presidential election. The incongruence of the comparison has not hampered neo-Confederate revisionism, which operates by pairing praise of Davis with criticism of Lincoln.

One of the earliest and most influential advocates of the comparison was Mildred Rutherford, Historian General of the UDC, later Historian General of the Confederate Southern Memorial Associations, and independent publisher of pro-Confederate materials. In the periodical *Miss Rutherford's Scrapbook, she published an article* expressing outrage that students see Lincoln as a hero and don't know who Davis is. Reporting on a visit to one school, she complains, "In that school building Lincoln's picture was in every room, Robert E. Lee in two rooms, not a picture of Jefferson Davis or of Stonewall Jackson was to be found." Her primary complaint was that the schools don't portray Lincoln as a villain.[15] In a speech to the 1914 national convention of the UDC, Rutherford noted that "when Southern young men say 'The South as well as the North is ready to admit that Lincoln is the greatest of all Americans,' it is full time to call halt." She further explained, "Nor am I willing to place Lincoln ahead of our Jefferson Davis. Our Davis never stood for coarse jokes, never violated the Constitution, never stood for retaliation—Lincoln stood for all these."[16] Rutherford also published *Miss Rutherford's Historical Notes*, with one issue titled "Contrasted Lives of Jefferson Davis and Abraham Lincoln: The Wise Politician and Statesman, the Shrewd Politician and Statesman" as well as other works and did a similar comparison in her book *The Truths of History*.[17]

Another early and very prominent example of the UDC's pointed criticism of Lincoln is explained by John Barr in his forthcoming book, "Loathing Lincoln." It is the Arlington Confederate memorial erected by the UDC and dedicated in 1914 with the inscription "*Victrix causea Diis placuit, sed victa Catoni*." The inscription, a quotation of the Roman Cato, implies that Lincoln was a despot and Cato would have supported the Confederacy as the side for freedom.[18]

When the UDC heard of the early twentieth-century Lincoln highway project in the North, they immediately decided to promote a Jefferson Davis Highway in competition to the Lincoln highway, a project that they pursue to this day.[19] Today there is a Jefferson Davis Presidential Library built and supported by the state of Mississippi even though Davis was never an American president. In a 1958 article in the *United Daughters of the Confederacy Magazine* about the Jefferson Davis Park at his birthplace in Fairview, Kentucky, the author reports a call for parity with Lincoln: "'It's high time the Jefferson Davis Memorial Park here had facilities equal to the Abraham Lincoln park near Hodgeville,' the superintendent of the Davis park said yesterday." The rest of the article focuses on why the park isn't as good as the Lincoln birthplace and how they plan to remedy the inequality.[20] In a 1966 article, the UDC was pleased to report that an Abraham Lincoln school was closed and the students sent to a Jefferson Davis school in Lexington, Kentucky.[21] The issues of the *United Daughters of the Confederacy Magazine* have been devoted to praising Jefferson Davis and criticizing Lincoln since it began publication in 1944. The new Texas standards will help the UDC and other neo-Confederate groups achieve a goal for which they have worked for generations.

Texas Confederate Leaders and Texas Civil War Battles

The new standards for studying Texas history in seventh grade turn the topic of the Civil War into nothing short of a "Texas Confederate Heroes Day." Teachers are to help students "identify significant individuals and events concerning Texas and the Civil War," such as Confederate General John Bell Hood in command of what was known as Hood's Texas Brigade, which has been argued to be "perhaps one of the finest brigade of Robert E. Lee's Army"; John H. Reagan, postmaster of the Confederacy; Francis Lubbock, Confederate governor of Texas and later a Confederate general; Thomas Green, a Confederate officer who rose to general and who was part of Confederate victories to prevent the Union armies from bringing Texas back into the Union; Confederate General John Magruder, famous for his recapture of Galveston; and the Battle of Galveston, the battle of Sabine Pass, and the battle of Palmito Ranch.[22] After the surrender of the Confederacy, Magruder offered his sword to puppet emperor

Maximilian of Mexico and vowed to continue fighting against the United States. As noted earlier, the battle of Palmito Ranch is truly not important to the Civil War, having occurred after Robert E. Lee's surrender at Appomattox, but it is presented as an example of enduring Confederate will. The battles are Confederate victories where Union forces were turned back. This list serves to instruct students to celebrate Confederates as heroes, to celebrate American defeats and Confederate victories, to identify themselves with the Confederacy, to identify Texas as a Confederate state, and to see the American government as an invader. No doubt this list will provide numerous occasions for the UDC and the SCV to visit classrooms.

The most atrocious aspect about this standard is what it obscures and omits. For example, it neglects the important fact in Texas Civil War history that there was significant dissent against the Confederacy in the state and that the dissenters were murdered en masse. At the Great Hanging in Gainesville, at least forty or more suspected Unionists were hanged, and at the infamous Nueces Massacre, German American dissenters were killed while trying to escape Texas and the Confederacy. Likewise omitted is the story of how Union soldiers had to occupy all of Texas to enforce the Emancipation Proclamation and the accounts of attacks on African Americans after the war who were celebrating their new freedom. Historian Randolph B. Campbell in his excellent book *An Empire for Slavery* describes the negative white reaction to African American freedom in Texas after emancipation: "A celebration at Huntsville ended when a sword-wielding man on horseback cut a Negro woman nearly in half on the street. According to Dave Byrd, the 'patter rollers' whipped one hundred celebrants in Crockett."[23] The standard could have considered the history of slavery in Texas, the way slave owners moved their slaves to Texas during the war because they feared losing them during the conflict, or the stated policy of Confederate officer Edmund Kirby Smith to put to death captured African American troops.[24] Hispanic students and others might be interested to know of the anti-Confederate origins of Cinco de Mayo and of the relations of the Confederacy and ex-Confederates with the empire of Maximilian, a French puppet ruling Mexico.[25] Advocates of the Lost Cause have won a decisive victory in the defining of the history of Texas and the Civil War.

Stonewall Jackson and Confederate Christianity

One particular Confederate hero is given greater emphasis than the others in the new standards. Thomas Jonathan Jackson is known to advocates of the Lost Cause by the nickname "Stonewall," which was allegedly given by General Lee who at the battle of Bull Run purportedly said, "Look! Yonder is Jackson standing like a stone wall!" The best source for this statement is a newspaper account, but the story may be more a matter of mythology than historical fact.[26] Thus when the new Texas standards recommend "Stonewall Jackson" instead of Thomas J. Jackson to eighth graders as an example of "effective leadership in a constitutional republic," they adopt Thomas J. Jackson not just as a Confederate general, but as a Confederate hero.[27] Jackson rose to prominence only in the Confederacy, so it has to be asked to which constitutional republic the SBOE is referring. To understand the importance of including Jackson in the standards in this manner, some background information needs to be provided on the neo-Confederate Christian movement, Christian Reconstructionism and the Civil War, Jackson in the Lost Cause, and conservative Christian publications concerning Jackson.

The historical memory of Jackson has been shaped and changed by multiple overlapping agendas. In an 1866 biography, proslavery theologian R. L. Dabney depicted Jackson as a pious Christian Confederate general.[28] Christian Reconstructionists expand Dabney's Lost Cause Jackson into an example of the entire Confederate army being a Christian army. A modern neo-Confederate understanding of the Civil War casts Jackson and the Confederates in a holy war between a heretical North and an orthodox Christian South.[29]

All these views continue to reverberate in neo-Confederate publications in which neo-Confederate writers use the Civil War as a gateway for making commentary about twenty-first-century America. In the November/December 2010 issue of *Confederate Veteran*, official publication of the Sons of Confederate Veterans (SCV), the chaplain-in-chief of the SCV, Mark W. Evans, outlined the theological war hypothesis in a column titled "Battle for Truth." He argues that the South remained an orthodox Christian region and that beginning in the US Northeast, "one wave of heretical teaching followed another, striking at the vitals of orthodox Christianity." Evans condemned abolitionists, whose "godless enthusiasm reached a pinnacle when they demanded the immediate elimination of slavery." Citing the conclusion of an 1850 speech by James Henly Thornwell, one of the South's most distinguished theologians, Evans quotes him, "The parties in this conflict are not merely abolitionists and slave holders—they are atheists, socialists, communists, red republicans, Jacobins on the one side and the friends of order and regulated freedom on the other. In one word, the world is the battleground—Christianity and atheism the combatants and the progress of humanity is at stake." Returning from the Civil War past to the twenty-first-century present, Evans concludes that "ungodly thinking has taken our land to the brink of destruction" and urges the readers to have faith in Christianity.[30]

The late Christian Reconstructionist leader R. J. Rushdoony advocated for the formation of a biblical republic run by Calvinistic Christians, and his Chalcedon Foundation published the *Chalcedon Report*. Interestingly, the magazine once ran an article opposing the idea that Earth revolves around the Sun.[31] One issue in particular was devoted to the idea of the Civil War being a theological conflict with the cover theme "The Civil War Revived: Secularism Versus the South," with the articles "Christianity, the South, and the Culture War," by Steve Wilkins; "He Still Haunts: Contemporary Southern Writers and Biblical Faith," by Suzanne U. Clark; "The Continuing Virtues of the Southern Heritage," by Douglas Kelley; and "The Rage of the Abolitionists," by Rev. Ben House. Wilkins, one of the founders of and former board member of the League of the South, argues that the Civil War was between a heretical and unorthodox North and an orthodox Christian South, which made it a culture war. He focuses on denigrating "Northerners" and argues that their religion is without spirit and they are less honest.[32] House argues that abolitionists, "like the monster Grendel from the Beowulf saga, delighted in the gore" of war and were "extremists, radicals, and terrorists."[33] Kelley explains that the Civil War began a long process of secularization and centralization attributable to "the soulless materialism of the amoral Yankee capitalist spirit." He sees Southern heritage as an antidote to the growth of the federal government, international trade agreements, and the United Nations.[34]

Christian Reconstructionist interpretations of the Civil War as a theological war and Lost Cause portrayals of Stonewall Jackson as a pious Confederate conservative have also seeped into popular culture. The movie *God and Generals* (2003), directed by Ronald F. Maxwell, popularized the idea of Jackson as a Christian leader, and critics widely condemned it as a neo-Confederate movie. *New York Times*' reviewer Stephen Holden pointed out, "The religiosity of the rhetoric may be authentic, but its relentlessness portrays the Confederate cause as a holy war. At the same time, the movie's undiluted adulation of Lee's and Jackson's machismo appears to put it on the Confederate side. 'Gods and Generals' goes out of its way to follow the example of 'Gone with the Wind' in sanitizing the South's treatment of African-Americans. Its one-sided vision shows freed and about-to-be-freed slaves cleaving to their benign white masters and loyally serving the Confederate army."[35] The film's promoters produced an accompanying book, *Faith in God and Generals*, a collection of essays including two by neo-Confederate authors Wilkins and John J. Dwyer, the former an avowed proslavery apologist.[36] The neo-Confederate *Southern Partisan* magazine carried interviews with producer Ron Maxwell, Steve Lang who played Jackson, and Kali Rocha who played Jackson's wife, Anna. Maxwell, in particular, displays his view of the Civil War and his Lost Cause obfuscations of the issues of race and slavery leading to the Civil War.[37]

Smaller video producers and distributors also depict the Confederate army as a Christian army. New Liberty Videos in Kansas offers *Warriors of Honor: The Faith and Legacies of Robert E. Lee and Stonewall Jackson*, which tells the audience that "most Americans believe that Southerners fought to preserve slavery; however a much deeper divide existed between the North and South" and that Lee and Jackson were "above all, faithful Christians," and it largely avoids the issue of slavery. Franklin Springs Family Media produced *Still Standing: The Stonewall Jackson Story*, which portrays Jackson as the pious Christian hero who was a "champion of the enslaved African Americans." The video argues that Virginia did not secede over slavery, and in the video, James I. Robertson, well-known biographer of Jackson, claims that Jackson, a slaveholder, did not fight for slavery because he had taught Sunday school to African American slaves.[38]

One of the interesting inversions of history comes in the reinvention of Jackson as an antislavery man. In *Stonewall Jackson: The Black Man's Friend*, Richard G. Williams Jr. quotes R. L. Dabney as saying that Jackson "was indeed the black man's friend." Dabney held a hysterical racist aversion to African Americans, and Williams's book is a largely laughable mixture of Lost Cause arguments and rationalizations about the historical record. One particularly revealing example is Williams's explanation of what he sees as the good side of the Atlantic slave trade: "Many of the Africans brought to this country in bondage experienced spiritual freedom in Christ: 'For coming to the white man's country as a slave, was the means of making me free in Christ Jesus,' exhorted 'Uncle Jack,' a Virginia slave preacher." After quoting an African American poet who expressed the same sentiments, Williams further explains, "This does not excuse the sin of man-stealing and the subsequent evils of slavery, yet God often uses apparent injustices to providentially bless His people." Williams can't seem to make up his mind whether slavery is evil or an "apparent" injustice. This book has a forward by Robertson, the aforementioned biographer of Jackson.[39]

Given the quantity of fringe writing about Jackson, it would be hoped that academic and mainstream publishers could provide factual historical work to dispel Lost Cause mythologies and neo-Confederate agendas. However, here again, the portrayal of Jackson in the literature is dominated by neo-Confederate portrayals, notably Frank E. Vandiver's *Mighty Stonewall* (1957) published by McGraw Hill and Robertson's 1997 biography, *Stonewall Jackson: The Man, the Soldier, the Legend*, published by Macmillan.

Vandiver has a long history of advocating the Lost Cause interpretation of the Civil War. For example, his book *Their Tattered Flags: The Epic of the Confederacy* explained how slaves were loyal during the Civil War. In a speech in Grimes County in 2001, Vandiver informed the audience, "It is fashionable in some parts of the nation to stereotype Rebels as fighting for slavery" and warned the audience that African American opposition to the Confederate flag would lead to a race war.[40] Robertson has been extensively involved with neo-Confederate activities over the years, attending functions of the UDC and the SCV. As noted earlier, he is involved in the production of videos about Jackson as a Christian leader. In addition, he wrote a letter to the neo-Confederate magazine *Southern Partisan* in which he said that he admired the magazine. He later consented to an interview in the magazine.[41]

Vandiver's biography has been seen by historians as a conscientiously uncritical history of the Lost Cause. Robertson asserts that Jackson was probably against slavery with no more documentation or argumentation than an uncritical recitation of Jackson's support for a Sunday school for African Americans.[42] All who seek to make Jackson a friend of African Americans overlook the antebellum debate over religious instruction for slaves. Although there was some opposition to the practice, there was also support from influential members of slave state society, such as Thornwell. In a famous 1850 sermon titled "The Rights and Duties of Masters: A Sermon Preached at a Dedication of a Church Erected in South Carolina, SC, for the Benefit of the Coloured Population," Thornwell holds that religious instruction of slaves supports and defends the system of slavery.[43]

Because every published biography of Jackson advocates either the Lost Cause or neo-Confederate ideas, to name Jackson as a subject for instruction in the public schools in Texas is to open an uncontrollable entryway for their mythologies, their unsubstantiated assertions, and a Christian Reconstructionist strategy to utilize popular identifications with the Confederacy to advance their agenda.

Reconstruction and African American Leaders

If the standards adopt a neo-Confederate distortion of slavery by singling out Stonewall Jackson, they further err in their treatment of Reconstruction. At the last adoption meeting, board member Ken Mercer (R–San Antonio) moved to add the charge that students "evaluate the impact of the election of Hiram Rhodes Revels."[44] As the first African American to be a US senator—and having been elected by the Mississippi legislature in 1870 to fill the seat formerly held by Jefferson Davis—Revels was certainly a prominent figure in Reconstruction. The election of African Americans to office was certainly representative of the civil rights revolution of Reconstruction. However, the standards do not propose to study African American congressmen as a class, instead they single out Revels as if he were the archetypical representation of African American office holders in Reconstruction.

Revels, it turns out, is a very poor choice as representative of African Americans or civil rights. At the end of his career, Revels sided with the white supremacists who overthrew Reconstruction in Mississippi with violence and terror. Revels testified before the US Senate in 1876 that the election had been held without violent intimidation of African American voters. He also wrote a long letter to President Ulysses S. Grant justifying the takeover of the state and the overthrow of Reconstruction. In language typical of white supremacist and neo-Confederate descriptions of Reconstruction, Revels portrayed African American voters as being deluded, explained falsely that whites in Mississippi "accept as fact that all men are born free and equal," and elided the fact that the purpose of the "Revolution in Mississippi" was to restore white supremacy. Revels's actions were condemned by national civil rights advocates and Mississippi African Americans, but the letter is a favorite source for white supremacist histories, such as James Garner's *Reconstruction in Mississippi* (1901) and Robert Selph Henry's *The Story of Reconstruction* (1938).[45] Revels's biographer, Julius Eric Thompson, explained that instead of leading African Americans to overcome the legacy of slavery, Revels "was comfortable with a conservative and accommodationist perspective because this viewpoint offered him the best chance of securing the favor of whites and the security which he felt was important for a good life." Furthermore, "his life serves as an example of the road which black leaders should never take if, in the final analysis, black people are to realize political, social, and economic justice in America." As for Revels's celebrated efforts to integrate schools in Washington, DC, Thompson points out that although Revels "stressed educational issues during his term in the Senate and encouraged an end to segregated schools while in Washington, D.C.; a safe distance from Mississippi . . . he never demanded full equality between whites and blacks." Thompson concludes that Revels can be seen as a hero because he was a first in history, but not for what he accomplished because he basically "betrayed his own people."[46]

In making Revels an archetype of an African American leader, the Texas history standards could easily serve as a vehicle for placing a white supremacist view of Reconstruction history in the mouth of a historical African American. In the 1950s, the White Citizens Council constantly referred to this view of Reconstruction to oppose civil rights.[47] In this way, Revels, a timid, accommodating African American who spent his political career ingratiating himself with white supremacists, is held forth as a role model of legitimate African American leadership for Texas children, be they African American or not.

From Whence Texas Standards' Neo-Confederacy?

Having demonstrated that the new Texas history standards are infused with a neo-Confederate version of the history of the Civil War and Reconstruction, the question remains as to where the members of the SBOE got the inspiration and information to embrace the Confederacy. Official records of the proceedings show no indication that the UDC or the SCV made the push—and they would have certainly announced the victory in their publications if they had indeed done so. There are two other venues by which neo-Confederacy would inform Texas conservative politics in regards to education: the textbooks used for homeschoolers and Christian private schools and the mainstreaming of neo-Confederacy into the Texas conservative movement.

The new standards might seem excessively pro-Confederate to public education scholars, but there is one group of textbook publishers to whom these standards would seem appropriately, or even possibly inadequately, pro-Confederate—conservative Christian publishers. It is instructive to examine a sample of these books.

Bob Jones University publishes an elementary level book, *The American Republic*, that refuses to use the term *Civil War*, preferring the term *The States at War* as a euphemism. The press's high school textbook *United States History for Christian Schools* treats the war in a chapter titled "The War between the States," which features a large sidebar titled "Stonewall Jackson: Soldier of the Cross" and minimizes the role of slavery in starting the war while asserting that "the central issue that sparked the Civil War concerned the nature of the Union." Contrary to historical record, Robert E. Lee is held to be antislavery.[48]

A Beka Books, housed at Pensacola Christian College, likewise embraces the Lost Cause. *America: Land I Love* does have a chapter on the Civil War—also loaded with Lost Cause ideology. A sidebar titled "Robert E. Lee: Great Christian General" explains that Lee opposed slavery, felt no tension in choosing the Confederacy, and freed his slaves (he did free some that he inherited under a will that required manumission after five years). The book presents Davis's farewell speech in the US Senate, portrays Jackson as a Christian leader, and identifies the Confederate army as a Christian army. Jackson's Sunday school for "black slaves" is brought up, and a section is devoted to his death and faith. The sidebar "The Civil War: Why Did They Fight?" explains the war as a question over whether states had a right to secede. Slavery is presented as a secondary issue, with the explanation that "the issues of states' rights became subtly intertwined with the issue of slavery," as if by accident. The book published for elementary grades, *The History of Our United States*, presents Lee as antislavery, discusses states' rights, and offers this rationalization for slavery: "By this time the South depended on its slaves. If Southerners freed their slaves, how would they be able to make a living? There was no easy answer to this question." Obscuring white exploitation of black slaves and writing with a racial identification with slave owners, the author revives the Lost Cause once again.[49] It would be worthwhile to compare other sections of the new Texas history standards to the textbooks put out by the Christian publishers.

Beyond textbooks used in Christian and home schools, neo-Confederate ideology has also found favor in some political circles in Texas. Not all Texas conservatives or Republicans are neo-Confederate or have adopted neo-Confederate ideas. However, there is an extensive involvement of neo-Confederates in Texas conservatism, and Republicans who are not neo-Confederate often feel it is necessary to pander to neo-Confederacy. The Texas neo-Confederates were largely hostile to George W. Bush during his political career, leading him to appeal to neo-Confederates. He was a sponsor of a Confederate ball for the Museum of the Confederacy. His campaign in 1996 paid for an advertisement in the *Confederate Veteran* to congratulate the SCV on their one hundredth anniversary. In 1996 in the *United Daughters of the Confederacy Magazine* issue for the centennial of the Texas Division is a full page with his photo and his letter of congratulation. When he ran for governor against Ann Richards, he worked to cultivate the endorsement of neo-Confederates, as revealed by *Dallas Morning News* conservative columnist Bill Murchison's endorsement of him in the leading neo-Confederate magazine *Southern Partisan:* "George W. Bush, who despite that name, is a man who strikes me (after conservations with him) as having authentic conservative convictions."[50] Governor Rick Perry has also seen fit to cultivate relations with neo-Confederate organizations. At the time of writing this chapter, it is expected in the media that he will appoint two members to the board of the Department of Motor Vehicles such that a majority will favor issuing a license plate for the SCV that would include a Confederate battle flag. He has also attended functions of neo-Confederate organizations.[51]

Though the sympathizers are perhaps concentrated in one faction, mapping out the involvement of the neo-Confederates and their conservative support would involve a lengthy paper in itself, therefore here only highlights will be mentioned. Phil Gramm and Dick Armey gave interviews to *Southern Partisan*.[52] William Murchison was a longtime contributor to the magazine and once a board member of the Texas League of the South.[53] Other prominent Texas conservatives, such as M. E. Bradford and Frederick D. Welhelmsen of the University of Dallas, were regular contributors to *Southern Partisan*. In Texas the magazine *Texas Republic* (not to be confused with the Republic of Texas movement) was published from 1993 to 1996 by the Landrum Society, named after a twentieth-century reactionary columnist for the *Dallas Morning News*. The debut of *Texas Republic* was announced in *Southern Partisan* in 1994 in an article by Murchison that explained that Texas identified primarily as a Southern Confederate state as opposed to a Western state.[54] The *Texas Republic* had a neo-Confederate point of view. In one of its article it pointed out that the Texas state flag has to be considered a Confederate flag and that if you oppose the Confederate flag, you would have to consider banning the state flag.[55] In another issue Morgan O. Reynolds of the National Center for Policy Analysis in Dallas wondered in the article "One Nation, Indivisible?" whether Texas would be an independent nation in 10 or 15 years.[56] It is interesting to note that there are an extensive number of Texas conservatives, many of them prominent, involved in *Texas Republic*. The masthead listed on the editorial board Cathie Adams, David Hartman, John Alvis, Charles R. Helms, William Caruth III, Joseph Horn, Marco Gilliam, William Murchison, J. Evetts Haley Jr., and Joseph Sullivan. US Senator Kay Bailey Hutchison sent them a letter praising their magazine.[57]

The issue for the purpose of discussing the Texas teaching standards isn't whether or how much the Texas conservative movement is neo-Confederate. The important issue is that the neo-Confederate movement and Lost Cause advocates have an extensive presence in the Texas conservative movement, and from them, neo-Confederate ideas can diffuse into and be mainstreamed into the Texas conservative movement and from there diffuse into the conservative movement's political positions and policies. Those who doubt that this diffusion of neo-Confederate politics has been extensive in Texas should consider Texas State Senate Resolution No. 526, passed in 1999, to lay out the principles for that year's Confederate History Month. Among the reasons given by a majority of the state's elected legislators for passing this resolution were that Texans had fought "for states' rights, individual freedom, and local government control" and that "politically correct revisionists would have Texas children believe that their Confederate ancestors fought for slavery when in fact most Texans joined the Confederate armed forces to defend their homes, their families, and their proud heritage as Texans."[58] In the interweaving of politics and history in Texas life and culture, neo-Confederate ideology is a dominant strand. In the twenty-first century, Texas hosts a global and multiracial society. Educating young Texans with white supremacist neo-Confederate historical narratives ill serves the students and the state and nation in which they will one day grow up.

Notes

1. SBOE meeting minutes, 1/14/10, 5/20/10, 5/21/10.
2. Euan Hague, Heidi Beirich, and Edward H. Sebesta, eds., *Neo-Confederacy: A Critical Introduction* (Austin: University of Texas Press, 2008); James Loewen and Edward H. Sebesta, *The Confederate and Neo-Confederate Reader: The "Great Truth" about the "Lost Cause"* (Hattiesburg: University Press of Mississippi, 2010); Euan Hague and Edward H. Sebesta, "The US Civil War as a Theological War: Confederate Christian Nationalism and the League of the South," *Canadian Review of American Studies* 32, no. 3 (2002): 253–84.
3. TEKS.5.b.4.E, TEKS.7.b.5.A, TEKS.8.b.8.B, TEKS.8.b.17.B (8/23/10).
4. Loewen and Sebesta, *The Confederate and Neo-Confederate Reader*, 3–21.
5. State of Texas Declaration (February 1861), quoted in William Winkler, "Journal of the Secession Convention," (Austin: Austin State Library, 1912), 61–65.
6. Alexander H. Stephens, "Address of Alexander H. Stephens," in *The Confederate Records of the State of Georgia*, vol. 1, ed. Allen D. Chandler (Atlanta: Georgia State Legislature, 1909), 183–205.

7. Edward Alfred Pollard, *The Lost Cause: A New Southern History of the War of the Confederates* (New York: E. B. Treat & Co., 1866), chapter 1 (states' rights), 51–62 (tariffs); Alexander H. Stephens, *A Constitutional View of the War between the States* (Philadelphia: National Publishing, 1868).
8. Mildred Rutherford, "The Causes That Led to the War between the States," *Miss Rutherford's Scrapbook*, January 1913, 8; Arthur H. Jennings, "The Causes of the War between the States," *Confederate Veteran*, December 1916, 566–67; Elizabeth Neal, "The Causes That Led to the War between the States," *United Daughters of the Confederacy Magazine*, January 1948, 20–22.
9. John S. Tilley, *Facts the Historians Leave Out: A Youth's Confederate Primer* (Montgomery, AL: Paragon Press, 1951), 47–48.
10. TEKS.8.b.8.C (8/23/10).
11. Jefferson Davis, "Inaugural Address of the President of the Provisional Government," in Dunbar Rowland, ed., *Jefferson Davis Constitutionalist: His Letters, Papers and Speeches* (Jackson: Mississippi Department of Archives and History, 1923), 5:49–53.
12. Jefferson Davis, "To the Confederate Congress," April 29, 1861, in Rowland, *Jefferson Davis Constitutionalist*, 5:67–85.
13. Rowland, *Jefferson Davis Constitutionalist*, 3:339–60.
14. "Jefferson Davis to the Confederate Congress," January 12, 1863, in Rowland, *Jefferson Davis Constitutionalist*, 5:396–415.
15. Mildred Rutherford, "Text Books—The South's Responsibility," *Miss Rutherford's Scrapbook*, September 1924, 13–15.
16. Mildred Rutherford, *Wrongs of History Righted: Address Delivered by Miss Mildred Lewis Rutherford, Historian General of the United Daughters of the Confederacy* (Savannah, Georgia United Daughters of the Confederacy Annual Convention, November 13, 1914), pamphlet: 18–29.
17. Mildred Rutherford, *Truths of History* (Athens, GA: self-published, 1920), 53–86.
18. John Barr, "Loathing Lincoln," (Cambridge: Harvard University Press, forthcoming). Prepublication chapter 3 supplied by Barr to the author. The book is based on his dissertation, which won the Hay-Nicolay Prize of the Abraham Lincoln Institute of Washington, DC.
19. "A Brief History of the Jefferson Davis Highway," *United Daughters of the Confederacy Magazine,* June 1947, 2, 26.
20. Carl May, "Jefferson Davis Park in Kentucky Gets Grant," *United Daughters of the Confederacy Magazine*, October 1958, 12.
21. Ruth Davenport Deiss, "The Whatnot," *United Daughters of the Confederacy Magazine*, August 1966, 8.
22. TEKS.7.b.5.C (8/23/10).
23. Randolph B. Campbell, *An Empire for Slavery: The Peculiar Institution in Texas, 1821–1865* (Baton Rouge: Louisiana State University Press, 1989), 247–51, 259.
24. Loewen and Sebesta, *The Confederate and Neo-Confederate Reader*, 203–5.
25. David E. Hayes-Bautista and Cynthia L. Chamberlin, "Cinco de Mayo's First Seventy-Five Years in Alta California: From Spontaneous Behavior to Sedimented Memory, 1862 to 1937," *The Southern California Quarterly* 89, no. 1 (Spring 2007): 23–64.

26. Wallace Hettle, *Inventing Stonewall Jackson: A Civil War Hero in History and Memory* (Baton Rouge: Louisiana State University Press, 2011), 12–15.
27. TEKS.8.b.22.B (8/23/10).
28. R. L. Dabney, *Life and Campaigns of Lieut.-Gen. Thomas J. Jackson* (1866; repr., Harrisonburg, VA: Sprinkle Publications, 1983).
29. Euan Hague and Edward, H. Sebesta, "The US Civil War as a Theological War: Confederate Christian Nationalism and the League of the South," *Canadian Review of American Studies* 32, no. 3 (2002): 253–84.
30. Mark W. Evans, "Battle for Truth," *Confederate Veteran*, November/December 2010, 12–13.
31. Martin G. Selbrede, "Geocentricity's Critics Refuse to Do Their Homework: A Special Chalcedon Position Paper by Martin G. Selbrede," *Chalcedon Report,* October 1994.
32. Steven J. Wilkins, "Christianity, the South, and the Culture War," *Chalcedon Report,* December 2000, 9–13.
33. Ben House, "The Rage of the Abolitionists," *Chalcedon Report*, December 2000, 21–22.
34. Douglas Kelley, "The Continuing Virtues of the Southern Heritage," *Chalcedon Report,* December 2000, 18–20.
35. Stephen Holden, "Film Review: Gory, Glory Hallelujah: Not Just Whistlin' Dixie," *The New York Times*, February 21, 2003; Ty Burr, "Civil War Pageant: 'Gods' Is an Epic Failure," *Boston Globe*, February 21, 2003.
36. Ted Baehr and Susan Wales, eds., *Faith in God and Generals* (Nashville: Broadman & Holman, 2003).
37. "Movies & Myths: A Conversation with the Maker of Gods and Generals," *Southern Partisan* 22, no. 6 (n.d.), 16–21.
38. *Warriors of Honor: The Faith and Legacies of Robert E. Lee and Stonewall Jackson* (Shawnee Mission, KS: New Liberty Videos, 2004); *Still Standing: The Stonewall Jackson Story* (Franklin, TN: Franklin Springs Family Media Presentation, 2007), 26:00–31:00.
39. Richard G. Williams Jr., *Stonewall Jackson: The Black Man's Friend* (Nashville: Cumberland House, 2006), 38, 43.
40. Frank Vandiver, *Their Tattered Flags: The Epic of the Confederacy* (New York: Harper's Magazine Press, 1975), 262–64; Edward H. Sebesta, "Frank Vandiver: A Life for the Confederacy," *The Touchstone* 11, no. 3 (Summer 2001); Edward H. Sebesta, "Neo-Confederate History Lessons: A Review of Frank Vandiver's Grimes County Speech," *The Touchstone* 11, no. 4 (September/October 2001).
41. James I. Robertson Jr., letter to the editor, *Southern Partisan* 10, 1993, 2; Christopher Sullivan, "Partisan Conversation, James (I. Know Stonewall) Robertson," *Southern Partisan* 17, 1997, 30–35.
42. Frank E. Vandiver, *Mighty Stonewall* (New York: McGraw Hill, 1957); James I. Robertson Jr., *Stonewall Jackson: The Man, the Soldier, the Legend* (New York: Macmillan, 1997), 191, 166–70; Hettle, *Inventing Stonewall Jackson*, 138–39.
43. James Henley Thornwell, *The Rights and Duties of Masters: A Sermon Preached at a Dedication of a Church Erected in Charleston, SC, for the Benefit of the Coloured Population* (Charleston: Walker and James, 1850).

44. TEKS.8.b.9.B (8/23/10).
45. James Garner, *Reconstruction in Mississippi* (1901; repr., Baton Rouge: Louisiana State University Press, 1968), 399–400; Robert Selph Henry, *The Story of Reconstruction* (New York: Bobbs-Merrill, 1938), 549.
46. Julius Eric Thompson, "Hiram Rhodes Revels, 1827–901: A Reappraisal," *Journal of Negro History* 79, no. 3 (Summer 1994): 297–393; Thomas Brown, "Hiram Revels," in *Encyclopedia of Free Blacks and People of Color in the Americas: The African American Heritage of Freedom,* ed. Stewart King (New York: Facts on File, 2011).
47. White Citizens Council, newspaper archive, available at http://www.citizenscouncils.com.
48. Rachel C. Larson, ed., *The American Republic*, 3rd ed. (Greenville, SC: Bob Jones University Press, 2010); Timothy Keesee and Mark Sidwell, eds., *United States History for the Christian Schools*, 3rd ed. (Greenville, SC: Bob Jones University Press, 2001); Alan T. Nolan, *Lee Considered: General Robert E. Lee and Civil War History* (Chapel Hill: University of North Carolina Press, 1991), 9–29.
49. Kurt A. Grussendorf, Michael R. Lowman, and Brian S. Ashbaugh, *America: Land I Love*, teacher's ed. (Pensacola, FL: A Beka Books, 1994), 281, 284–85, 291, 293, 298; Judy Hull Moore, *The History of Our United States*, 3rd edition (Pensacola, FL: A Beka Books, 1998), 206–7, 212.
50. "Donors to Fund Raising Events," *The Museum of the Confederacy Annual Report Fiscal 1997–1998*, 37; George W. Bush, letter to the Sons of Confederate Veterans, *Confederate Veteran* 3, 1996, 6; George W. Bush, letter to the United Daughters of the Confederacy, January 1, 1996, *United Daughters of the Confederacy Magazine*, December 1996, back cover; Charles R. Goolsby, "Partisan Conversation," *Southern Partisan* 14, 1994, 36–38.
51. Renee C. Lee, "Confederate License Plate a Vote Away from Approval," *Houston Chronicle*, June 25, 2011; "Division News," *United Daughters of the Confederacy Magazine*, December 2001, 22; *Confederate Veteran*, May/June 2008, 38.
52. Phil Gramm, "Partisan Conversation," interview by Donald Baldwin, *Southern Partisan*, Summer 1983, 30–33; Dick Armey, "Partisan Conversation," interview by Charles Goolsby, *Southern Partisan* 10, 1999, 26–29.
53. William Murchison, "Our Charming Speech Is Gone with the Wind," *Dallas Morning News*, March 13, 1996.
54. Bill Murchison, "Partisan Conversation," interview by Charles R. Goolsby, *Southern Partisan* 14, 1994, 36–38.
55. Charles Goolsby, "Rally 'Round the Flags," *Texas Republic* 2, nos. 5 and 6 (September/December 1995): 67–68.
56. Morgan O. Reynolds, "One Nation, Indivisible?," *Texas Republic* 2, nos. 5 and 6 (September/December 1995): 18–19.
57. Charles Goolsby, "Rally 'Round the Flags," Morgan O. Reynolds, "One Nation, Indivisible?," Kay Bailey Hutchison, letter to the editor, *Texas Republic* September/December 1995, 18–19, 67–68.
58. Texas Legislature Online, available at *http://www.capitol.state.tx.us/tlodocs/76R/billtext/html/SR00526F.htm*.

Figure 10 Parting the cloud of Western civilization
Translated into a word cloud, the Texas standards for world history reveal their foundation in a Western civilization narrative rather than world history methods and content.

CHAPTER 10

A Missed Opportunity for World History in Texas

David C. Fisher

Generate a word cloud from the text of the 2010 Texas standards for world history studies in tenth grade and the language of the standards is transformed into a graphic cluster of terms in fonts from minuscule to colossal corresponding to the frequency of their usage in the document. Unsurprisingly, "world," "history," and "civilizations" all appear in large font. Among world civilizations, "Europe" is the largest in the cloud, then "China," "Rome," "Greece," "India," "America," and "Soviet." World history themes emerge from the cloud as well. "Political" is in first place, followed by "war," "economic," "revolution," "society," and "culture." "Free" and "enterprise" pop up six times as do "Christianity" and "Constitution." Although none of the words in the cloud is out of place for a world history course, there is a curious pattern of emphases and absences. Why do "Greece" and "Rome" appear a collective 15 times but Africa not at all? "Economic" is prominent, near where the cloud includes "free enterprise," but not "capitalism," "socialism," or "communism." "Religious" pops up in a bold font along with "Christianity" and "Islamic," but other faiths and philosophies, such as Hinduism, Buddhism, polytheism, or Confucianism, do not appear, even in the smallest of fonts.[1] The standards, of course, do not ignore all these terms, but the cloud's representation of the most repeated vocabulary suggests that the tenth-grade social studies class is anchored in a Western civilization framework rather than a genuine world history approach. How did this happen and why does it matter?

The process of writing the standards, officially known as the Texas Essential Knowledge and Skills (TEKS), involved a number of parties with varying levels of influence. State legislators passed the Texas Education Code (TEC), which requires a "foundation curriculum" including world history as part of K-12 social studies. The TEC also stipulates an "enrichment curriculum" that includes "economics, with emphasis on the free enterprise system and its benefits" and "religious literature, including the Hebrew Scriptures . . . and New Testament."[2] The popularly elected members of the Texas State Board of Education (SBOE) are responsible for producing the TEKS in accordance with the TEC. The SBOE initiated the process of revising the world history studies TEKS in 2009 by appointing seven experienced public high school teachers to a review committee, often referred to as a writing team, to revise the TEKS that had been in place since 1998. To provide advice to the teachers and writing teams for other sections of the social studies TEKS, the SBOE also appointed six "expert reviewers" drawn from the ranks of university professors and non-academics with specialized interests in US history. Finally, the board members played active roles in shaping the TEKS by providing advice to the world history writing team, inviting public commentary at board meetings and writing and revising standards themselves. This conjuncture of state law, preferences for an emphasis on Western civilization, expert reviewers' lack of specialization in world history, and board members' tendency to pursue ahistorical political agendas produced TEKS that are fundamentally a reworking of traditional Western civilization courses rather than guidelines for an up-to-date, twenty-first-century world history curriculum.

What Is World History?

The goals of Western civilization and world history courses are different. "Western civ," as the field is affectionately known, spread through American universities beginning in the 1920s. It developed out of a need to explain the United States' links to Europe in the aftermath of the Great War and as a reaction to the political and cultural challenges of assimilating the millions of immigrants from southern and Eastern Europe who had been pouring into American ports since the 1880s. After World War II, Western civ served to differentiate free Europe and its cultural descendents, namely, North America, from the communist east by emphasizing what Ross Dunn has called "the West's cavalcade of freedom."[3] The traditional Western civ narrative in thumbnail sketch begins with Hammurabi's law code in ancient Mesopotamia and progresses westward to democratic Athens, republican Rome, and enlightened, industrialized Europe until it reaches fruition in the declaration of American independence and US victory in the Cold War. Western civ was a popular course in the twentieth century, the American Century, because it provides a rich and explanatory historical past for a relatively young United States. Yet to present Western civ as world history is a mistake. Western civ contributes useful material to explain how the United States became what it is today, but if we wish to know how the world became what it is, Western civ is a poor road to follow in search of answers. It is too narrow, short, and unidirectional. Indeed, world history courses began making inroads in American universities in the 1970s as historians found Western civ inadequate for explaining the increasingly complex political, economic, social, and cultural interconnections that characterize the world and its population.[4]

Although the fertile subject of world history is not the history of everything that happened everywhere, it does not lend itself to a singular definition. Nevertheless, the contours of the field are well drawn, and there is general agreement on what the field accommodates and what it does not. World history is not specific to a single civilization, society, or nation; its focus is on the history of humanity to explain why and how human societies have come to be what they are today. As the World History Association explains, "World history is macrohistory," and world historians study "phenomena that . . . have had a global or at least transregional impact."[5] Consequently, world history lends itself to thematic and comparative approaches to understand the shared human experience. Phenomena such as trade, migration, religion, epidemics, and war that explain connections and exchanges between people across societies are prominent world history themes. Comparative approaches, for example, may take up a singular issue like the arrival of tobacco in the Old World and compare its social impact on the diverse societies of Christian Europe and the *dar-al-Islam*. Thematic and comparative methodologies demonstrate world history's interest in examining how societies across the globe are similar and distinctive, integrated and differentiated across time and space. Consequently, world history accommodates the human experience from the Stone Age to the modern, from the earliest migrations of homo sapiens out of Africa to present-day globalization.

By its very nature, world history is inclusive in terms of its content, methods, and pedagogy. Ross Dunn notes in his influential publication *The New World History: A Teacher's Companion* that "world history is not so much a matter of deciding what data should be learned as it is a way of addressing historical problems that resists their being caged behind civilizational, national, or ethnic bars."[6] The "way of addressing historical problems" continues to expand. David Christian and others have pushed the boundaries of world history into "big history," which considers not just humanity's place on Earth but Earth's place in the cosmos.[7] On world history's complementary flank are scholars and textbook authors who focus on the individual or the local amid seemingly impersonal global and transregional themes of networks, connections, and exchanges.[8]

"Why learn world history?" is a question worth asking, and materials aimed at K-12 educators provide answers. The National Standards for History developed in the mid-1990s argue that "our increasingly pluralistic society and increasingly interdependent world" compel American students to have "a comprehensive understanding of the world." The benefits include appreciating "shared humanity and common problems" across cultures, inculcating empathy, and developing a sense of human identity grounded in a historical sensibility."[9] The pedagogical website *World History for Us All* explains that today's students find themselves as both national citizens and citizens of the world. "World history helps prepare [them] for . . . active participation in civic life," whether it be local, national, or global. Indeed, the "global citizen" is described here as "simply a national citizen who knows and cares about the history and contemporary affairs of all humankind" and shares a common cultural literacy with others educated in world history around the globe.[10] The implicitly stated value of world history is that global and transregional problems will require today's students and subsequent generations to develop global and transregional solutions. As education reformer Chester Finn of the Thomas Fordham Institute answers the question, "our students" require a sound education in world history because they "are growing up in a globalized world, and their future prospects . . . depend upon their ability to navigate confidently through a multinational environment . . . But without [state] standards that competently organize the subject's vast and trackless expanses . . . teachers won't know what to teach, students will be adrift, and parents will be bewildered."[11]

If expert advice from multiple quarters has been emphasizing the importance of a global world history, why did traditional Western civ prevail in the TEKS? Revision of the world history standards in 2009–10 went smoothly compared with the intense cultural warfare that erupted in the public debate over the US history standards. True, comedian Jon Stewart skewered board member Patricia Hardy for arguing to eliminate Archbishop Oscar Romero from a list of individuals who opposed political oppression because no one knew who he was anyway.[12] More notably, the dustup over whether or not Thomas Jefferson should be included in a list of Enlightenment thinkers received national media attention. Yet the debate here had more to do with how we conceive of Jefferson's place in American history than the influence of the Enlightenment in world history.[13] The more the world history TEKS emphasized Western civilization it seems, the less controversial they were. In part, this is because the Western civ narrative is familiar to Americans, and it speaks to our own national history in a positive way. It especially provides support for the dubious claim of "American exceptionalism," a key ideological point of view held by a conservative core of board members, and, I would argue, compatible with mainstream public sentiments on the political left and right. The emphasis on American exceptionalism was certainly no secret to those involved in revising the TEKS or to the American public following the Texas story in the news.[14] Western civ, rooted as it is in the notion that the West, especially Europe, is exceptional, prevailed in the TEKS because it provides a prehistory for the United States that supports the claim of America's unique identity and destiny.

The problem for world history is that despite the best efforts of its primary practitioners, the field's goals, methods, and content are not well known to the public, politicians, or policy makers. Consequently, there is little objection to standards in which a core Western civ narrative, with the history of other prominent civilizations along for the ride, stands in for genuine world history. This kind of ignorance seems odd because the practice of world history is not isolated in an academic ivory tower, but includes a broad and integrated range of scholars, college professors, and schoolteachers. Working together, they have created professional organizations with their attendant bulletins and journals, K-12 and collegiate world history curricula, textbooks, and curriculum-rich online sources. In short, one need not earn a PhD in historiography to develop a working definition of world history; high-quality material is readily available to teachers, parents, and policy makers.

Revising the TEKS: Alternative Models, Experts, and Teachers

The introduction to the 2010 world history studies TEKS defines the course as "a survey of the history of humankind." However, "due to the expanse of world history and the time limitations of the school year, the scope of this course should focus on 'essential' concepts and skills that can be applied to various eras, events, and people." Accordingly, the "major emphasis is on the study of significant people, events, and issues from the earliest times to the present" in "western civilization as well as in civilizations in other parts of the world." Student expectations are outlined as follows:

> Students evaluate the causes and effects of political and economic imperialism and of major political revolutions since the seventeenth century. Students examine the impact of geographic factors on major historic events and identify the historic origins of contemporary economic systems. Students analyze the process by which constitutional governments evolved as well as the ideas from historic documents that influenced that process. Students trace the historical development of important legal and political concepts. Students examine the history and impact of major religious and philosophical traditions. Students analyze the connections between major developments in science and technology and the growth of industrial economies, and they use the process of historical inquiry to research, interpret, and use multiple sources of evidence.[15]

Although there are welcome elements here of a world history course, the central position of Western civilization, with "other parts of the world" in supporting roles, is clearly stated. The themes of "political and economic imperialism and of major political revolutions since the seventeenth century," along with the evolution of "constitutional governments" and "industrial economies" keep the students focused on Europe and its offspring during the modern period. This is a missed opportunity to provide a conceptual foundation in world history for tenth-grade Texas teachers and students that reflects the best practices and developments in the study and teaching of world history. It is striking that although the standards and student expectations that follow this introduction have been thoughtfully expanded beyond the 1998 version, the 2010 introduction is fundamentally identical to the 1998 original.

Truly, it is challenging to conceptualize world history in a meaningful way that avoids the fruitless attempt to cover everything. Yet the influence of readily available and appropriate models for high school world history is not evident in the TEKS introduction to world history studies. The National Standards for History, published in 1996, suggest four possible frameworks for organizing a world history curriculum: comparative civilizations, civilizations in global context, interregional history, and thematic history. The National Standards also recommend a periodization scheme of nine eras, from "The Beginnings of Human Society" to "The 20th Century Since 1945: Promises and Paradoxes." Each era emphasizes two to seven content goals.[16] The recommendations of the National Standards have been influential in shaping state standards across the United States in part because of the broad authorial participation of scholars, teachers, and professional organizations and the support of the US Department of Education and the National Endowment for the Humanities. Professionalism, collaborative effort, and consensus produced a reliable and effective conceptual structure for balanced content.[17]

A related and practical outgrowth of the National Standards is the website *World History for Us All*, which aims to help teachers conceptualize world history pragmatically. Like the National Standards, this site is a collaborative effort of educators at the secondary and postsecondary levels as well as specialists in education technology. Among its primary goals is to help teachers avoid the pitfall of studying "various 'cultures,' each disconnected from the others."[18] Dunn, who is a world historian and one of the contributors to the site, wrote in 2000, "Teaching world history civilization by civilization . . . or region by region" does not offer a convincing "path to world scale understanding."[19] To achieve the goal of guiding student learning toward mastering "larger patterns of historical meaning and significance," the site offers educators a curriculum organized into nine "big eras" that "addresses history on the scale of humankind," rather than marching through one civilization after another.[20]

In addition, in the category of curriculum guidelines produced through collaboration, one might consider the College Board's Advanced Placement course description for world history. The College Board offers high school students the opportunity to earn college credit through a rigorous standardized exam based on the advanced placement (AP) world history course included as part of an enriched curriculum in public and private high schools. The AP course description and exam are "gold standards" for world history instruction, according to

Walter Russell Mead, author of the Fordham Institute's analysis of state standards across the nation. His report advises "states that are serious about world history" to consider the AP course as a model.[21] According to its 2010 course description, AP world history "highlights the nature of changes in global frameworks and their causes and consequences, as well as comparisons among major societies." The AP format divides the world history course into five chronological periods, each of which, save one, is covered in six weeks of class time. About 40 percent of the academic year is devoted to the premodern period (ca. 8000 BCE to 1450 CE), and the modern period (1450 to present) is covered in the remaining 60 percent. The AP course is also organized by five equally emphasized themes: interaction between humans and the environment; development and interaction of cultures; state building, expansion, and conflict; creation, expansion, and interaction of economic systems; and development and transformation of social structures.[22] The popularity of the AP approach to world history is indicated by the growth in the numbers of students taking the annual exam. More than 166,000 high school students took the AP world history exam in May 2010, double the number of examinees just four years earlier.[23]

The National Standards, *World History for Us All* website, and AP world history course description are only three of numerous guidelines for organizing a high school world history curriculum. Their attractiveness as models for state standards lies in the broad collaboration of scholars, educators, and policy makers and the resulting consensus that focuses on a balanced, global, and inclusive approach to the history of humanity. Unfortunately, the process in Texas was less a collaborative effort aimed at consensus than an advisory process after which a majority of the SBOE had the prerogative to determine the final text of the standards. Despite the lack of consensus and the unpromising introduction to the standards, the TEKS are not wholly divorced from effective approaches to world history. Indeed, the 2010 world history TEKS are significantly improved over the 1998 version in terms of their scope and detail.

The revision process began in early 2009 when the expert reviewers and the review committee began assessing the 1998 TEKS. The 1998 guidelines for high school world history studies list 24 knowledge standards, with attendant student expectations, in the areas of history, geography, economics, government, citizenship, culture, and the impact of science and technology on society, as well as three sets of skills standards in critical thinking, communication, and problem solving. In a 2004 study of high school world history standards from all fifty states, Robert Bain, professor of education and history at the University of Michigan, characterized Texas's 1998 TEKS as part of a "Western civilization plus" trend in US schools. This pattern of instruction revises the traditional Western civ course by adding "cultures and civilizations beyond Europe without dramatically shifting . . . the underlying narrative" about the "'rise' of the west."²⁴ Bain categorizes 27 other states in the same trend, thus making it the most common approach to world history in the United States, even though it is at cross-purposes with the goals of up-to-date world history scholarship and pedagogy.

The SBOE appointed six reviewers to independently assess the K-12 social studies TEKS, including world history studies, and to provide reports to the review committees that were working on revising the TEKS. The experts included four university professors—Jesús de la Teja, Daniel Dreisbach, Lybeth Hodges, and James Kracht, all PhDs in history or education—Presbyterian minister Peter Marshall, an advocate for Christian heritage, and David Barton, a public speaker and author of numerous works that emphasize the role of Christianity in US history. None of the social studies reviewers specialized in world history. The SBOE supplied them with a set of 12 questions to guide their assessments. Most of the questions directed the reviewers' attention to issues of accuracy, effective coverage of historically significant events and people, grade-level appropriateness, and clarity of expectations. More than one of the questions implicitly directed the reviewers to thoroughly examine the social studies standards in ways that are not applicable to world history. For example, question 1 asks if "the standards promote ideological neutrality by balancing people/events from various sides of the political spectrum."²⁵ This problematic question assumes that ideological neutrality, rather than evidence-based objectivity, is the goal that historians strive toward in their work.²⁶ It is actually more reflective of the heated culture wars playing themselves out around the TEKS revision process, rather than an effective approach to studying world history. Question 9 asks, "Do the standards promote an appreciation for the basic values of our state and national heritage?" Question 10 adds, "Do the standards promote citizenship, patriotism, and an understanding of the benefits of the free enterprise system?"²⁷ These last two questions are irrelevant for assessing world history guidelines, but are consistent with the TEC and help explain why the expert reviewers devote little attention to world history in their reports.

The first round of reports from the expert reviewers suggested that the high school world history course needed updating. Kracht, associate dean and professor in the College of Education and Human Development at Texas A&M University, also recommended considering "a two-year course of study for Grades 6 and 7" due to the "current level of world-wide communication, interdependence, and integration," but specific recommendations from the expert reviewers were few and largely at odds with current thinking among world history educators.²⁸ Reviewers Dreisbach, a specialist in American constitutional law and history at American University, and the late Reverend Marshall, then president of Peter Marshall Ministries, offered specific revisions for the world history TEKS that reflected their interests in US history. Dreisbach's recommendations centered on elements of traditional Western civilization studies, such as "Hebrew conceptions of representative government," that provide an ancient legacy for modern America. Reverend Marshall made no specific recommendations for world history studies but argued that "to study American culture in comparison to other cultures around the world . . . leads to the rejection of the idea that there is anything unique or exceptional about American civilization." He added that for the TEKS to comply with "educational mandates in the State of Texas," students will be required "to learn *why* America is the greatest country in the world."[29]

Unlike the expert reviewers, who worked in isolation from one another and produced uncoordinated reports, the members of the world history review committee collaborated as a group to revise the TEKS. The SBOE appointed seven high school educators to the committee. All were experienced world history teachers, many of whom offered College Board Advanced Placement courses in a number of social studies subjects.[30] The committee produced its first-draft revisions in July 2009. The revisions were guided by the committee's own experience, broad strokes guidance from the SBOE, efforts to align the TEKS with the recently published Texas College and Career Readiness Standards, and recommendations from the expert reviewers.[31] The committee produced a second revision the following October based on additional feedback from the SBOE, expert reviewers, and other "informal" sources, including public commentary.[32] The teachers made progress in nudging the Texas standards from a "Western civilization plus" framework toward a more up-to-date world history model.

Although the writing team did not revise the introduction to the world history standards, they did improve the knowledge and skills sections of the TEKS by largely rewriting them. The standards became more global in scope and, per the recommendations of expert reviewers, more specific. The review committee replaced 1998 standards such as the vague requirement "to identify the major eras in world history and describe their defining characteristics" with a specific periodization scheme of six chronological eras, influenced by the AP world history model, and brief, but specific descriptions of the six periods of study. For example, students will be expected to "identify . . . and describe . . . important turning points" in the era of "Connecting Hemispheres," 1450–1750, related to the rise of the Ottomans, the influence of the Ming Dynasty, European expansion, and the Columbian Exchange. The periodization also improved the TEKS in the second draft by eliminating the requirement to explain a list of dates centered in the history of Western civilization: "1066, 1215, 1492, 1789, 1914–1918, and 1939–1945."[33] The new chronological arrangement of the tenth-grade world history course also reflected common periodizations employed in college-level introductory textbooks, books written for the national market, rather than for a specific state's high school standards.[34]

The teachers' revisions then elaborated on the student expectations within each major era. The revisions effectively disaggregated overly comprehensive 1998 standards, creating clearer student expectations as recommended by the SBOE in its broad strokes guidance to the committee. For example, the 1998 TEKS pack the world wars, fascism, Nazism, communism, and the Cold War into a single student expectation under the topic of understanding the "impact of totalitarianism in the 20th century." The review committee replaced this topic with separate standards on the causes and impact of each of the two world wars, the global economic depression of the 1930s, and the Cold War. The inclusion of decolonization in the Cold War section, absent from the 1998 TEKS, particularly reflected a genuine world history approach in the new standards. Tenth graders are expected not only to describe the superpower rivalry between the United States and the Soviet Union but also to "summarize the rise of independence movements in Africa, the Middle East, and South Asia" as well.[35]

The expert reviewers responded only briefly to the review committee's first-draft revisions, but the tension between a global and Western civilization conception of world history began to emerge in their comments and the teachers' responses. In David Barton's 87-page review of the K-12 social studies TEKS, fewer than two pages addressed world history studies, and none of Barton's recommendations referred to world history topics. He noted only that state law mandates the observation of Celebrate Freedom Week in Texas schools, during which social studies classes must incorporate instruction on US founding documents and ideas, the American Revolution, the abolition movement, and the movement for women's suffrage. The review committee's draft already included this statement, but Barton encouraged them to add "identify Constitution Day as a celebration of American freedom" and "recite the Pledge of Allegiance to the United States Flag and the Pledge to the Texas Flag."[36] Dreisbach's comments contributed substantially to keeping the world history TEKS anchored in Western civilization by defending the inclusion of the Norman invasion of England in 1066 because "the impact of the conquest on English law, language, and civil government, and by extension American law, language, and civil government, is incalculable." The trend of Dreisbach's recommendations toward emphasizing America's legacy in the Western tradition was particularly evident in his suggestion that world history studies include the "Virginia Declaration of Rights (June 1776) . . . as the most influential declaration of rights in the founding era."[37] World history concepts were not at the center of Barton's and Dreisbach's few comments, and the review committee did not incorporate them into the second draft of the TEKS. Indeed, the committee noted that "the Virginia Declaration of Rights is more appropriately addressed in U. S. History," and despite Dreisbach's defense of the Norman invasion, the requirement to explain significant dates, including 1066, was completely eliminated in the second draft of the TEKS.[38]

Comments from other expert reviewers were similarly brief, but more than one reviewer questioned sections in the TEKS that emphasized Western civilization at the expense of global world history. "Western Civilization," noted Hodges, "has a key place in education," but "today's children and young people need to explore nations and cultures other than those with whom most of us identify."[39] In this spirit, she drew attention to the committee's decision to replace the expectation that students will "assess the degree to which human rights and democratic ideals and practices have been advanced throughout the world during the 20th century" with the nation-specific expectation that students will "assess the degree to which American ideals have advanced human rights and democratic ideas throughout the world."[40] Although Hodges commended the writing team for a number of improvements in the TEKS, she pointed out that the United States is not "the planet's only . . . democratic nation," and that "other free nations," like India, "have also influenced human rights and democratic ideas."[41] Nevertheless, the teachers rejected the recommendation to consider human rights and democratic ideas from a world perspective, noting the "committee feels that focus on American contributions to human rights and democratic ideals is appropriate in an American history classroom."[42]

Reviewer Kracht also raised questions about shortcomings in the revisions' commitment to a global perspective. He commented that the committee has a responsibility "to provide guidance" on "how the content of the Celebrate Freedom Week can or should be incorporated into the content of World History Studies." In short, Kracht implied that some imagination was needed here to place the American content of Celebrate Freedom Week in a global context, rather than further diminish the scope of world history studies. Kracht's comments also noted the drift toward Western civilization in the privileging of legal documents and political history over cultural history, evident particularly in Barton's and Dreisbach's reports. On their recommendation, the review committee eliminated the 1998 expectation that "the student understands the relationship between the arts and the times during which they were created" by identifying and analyzing "examples of art, architecture, literature, music, and drama" that are reflective of specific cultures or "transcend the cultures in which they were created and convey universal themes."[43] In response to Kracht's objections to removing this world history topic, the committee explained that the TEKS would "focus on legal documents as the foundation of study." Music, art, and architecture were moved to a list of source materials mentioned in the introduction that "should be incorporated" into classroom teaching but were no longer required.[44]

The exchange between the expert reviewers and the review committee was unproductive for sharpening a world history sensibility in the TEKS. The experts focused on their areas of specialization, US history primarily, and offered little to enhance the conceptualization of world history studies. None of the experts addressed the problematic contradictions in the introduction to the world history TEKS. In fact, Barton and Marshall argued that the notion of a global perspective diminishes students' identities as Americans. Both responded with incredulity to the expectation that social studies in the kindergarten and first-grade classrooms will establish "the foundation for responsible citizenship in a global society."[45] "Inappropriate," argued Marshall. "We should emphasize the uniqueness of American culture, and properly prepare our children for American citizenship."[46] "A *global* society?" Barton asked with underscored emphasis. The focus in Texas schools should be on "responsible citizenship," he argued, without reference to "global language."[47] Whether because of hostility, neglect, or simply a Western-centric frame of reference, the expert reviews constituted a missed opportunity to improve the world history studies TEKS. The SBOE shares responsibility here for not appointing an expert reviewer with a world history background to complement the cohorts' knowledge in US and Texas history.

World History Clothes on a Western Civ Body

The experts' lack of expertise in world history meant that the review committee's revisions to the TEKS were not vetted as carefully as they deserved to be. The most significant consequence was the poor conceptualization of world history in the introduction to the tenth-grade course. Closer scrutiny might have revealed the sections in the standards where a Western civilization approach comes to the fore in place of available world history methods of inquiry and content. Questioning these points individually is to quibble; observing them as a whole demonstrates the underlying foundation of a Western civ framework in the world history TEKS.

The standard and attendant student expectations for the period 8000 BCE to 500 BCE emphasize the development of early agricultural, river valley civilizations. Textbooks and teachers will no doubt address this topic by covering Mesopotamia, the Nile valley, Harappan society along the Indus, and the Yellow River valley of East Asia. The theme here of early complex societies and global geographic scope makes this a promising beginning for the tenth-grade course. Yet there are significant omissions of common world history content for this period: agricultural societies in Mesoamerica and the Andes, pastoral societies, as well as migratory peoples such as the Indo-Europeans. In the subsequent time periods, the standards increasingly focus attention on the traditional elements of a Western civilization course. The Roman Empire, for example, is the central focus of the one standard on the TEKS period of classical civilizations, 500 BCE to 600 CE. The first element of this standard is the expectation that students will be able to "describe the major political, religious/philosophical, and cultural influences of Persia, India, China, Israel, Greece, and Rome." Israel is an odd addition to this lineup of classical empires except for the contribution of Judaic monotheism to world religious history. Otherwise, the periodization is out of alignment—the last remnant of Israel, the kingdom of Judea, fell to the Babylonians in 586 BCE—and Israel possesses none of the hallmarks of the other states listed in terms of classical empire building, a common world history theme. Rome, of course, is an excellent example of classical empires, but the TEKS rely primarily on its history for the two remaining elements of the standard on the classical period. Students are expected to "explain the impact of the fall of Rome on Western Europe" and "compare the factors that led to the collapse of Rome and Han China." These are perfectly valid expectations, but they narrow the student experience with world history material to a familiar Western civilization trajectory beginning in Mesopotamia and continuing west through Hebrew society and on to Greece, Rome, and Europe. An alternative more consistent with world history methodology would focus on the comparative elements that explain the rise and decline of extensive empires.[48]

In the standards for the postclassical period, 600–1450, the theme of Christianity continues to emerge as a central thematic focus for Texas tenth graders. The trend begins in the standards for the previous period where, at the urging of board member Don McLeroy, the review committee explicitly named Christianity as one of the religious/philosophical influences to be covered in the material on Persia, India, China, Israel, Greece, and Rome. The reiteration is redundant here and odd because no other classical development of the era is singled out (Zoroastrianism, Hinduism, Buddhism, Confucianism, Daoism, Legalism, or Greek or Roman philosophy). Instead, this focus demonstrates the influence board members wielded on shaping the TEKS as a Western civilization course rather than a world history course. In the postclassical period standards, Christianity is posited as a unifying social and political factor in medieval Europe and the Byzantine Empire.[49] Christianity certainly did contribute to social and political stability in these areas, but the standard is tendentious rather than pedagogic. Medieval Europe is best characterized in world history during this period as fragmented and disorganized, especially when compared with Byzantium, the *dar-al-Islam,* and the Tang and Song dynasties in China. Indeed, the iconoclasm controversy that divided the church in Byzantium and distanced it from its Western counterpart suggests the limitations of characterizing Christianity solely as a unifying factor. A more effective alternative from a historical point of view and world history point of view would be the expectation that students explain the combination of factors (be they secular or nonsecular) that led to consolidation of political and religious authority in Europe and that maintained the Byzantine Empire in the face of Islamic expansion. Certainly, the role of the Christian church should figure prominently in such a standard, but to focus on one explanatory factor diminishes the application of historical methods to understanding the past. This flaw stands out particularly because the nine additional student expectations for the postclassical period are in harmony with the main trends in world history pedagogy.

The TEKS standards for the periods 1450–1750 and 1750–1914 place European developments at the center of students' attention rather than placing those developments in a global context. The Renaissance, Reformation, and European expansion receive emphasis, as they should, in the period of 1450 to 1750. Yet opportunities are missed here to include the global impact of European expansion on areas other than the Americas (conquest) and West Africa (Atlantic slave trade). The political and economic impact of European exploration and trade on African kingdoms, the Ottoman Empire, and South and East Asia could easily be included, but they are not. The expectation to "explain the impact of the Columbian exchange on the Americas and on Europe" does not need to be limited to the Atlantic world. New world crops, for example, impacted Afro-Eurasia as well.[50]

The loss of global context in favor of a focus on Europe is even more pronounced in the standards for the period 1750–1914, which emphasize the Industrial Revolution, imperialism, and political revolutions, all fascinating world history topics. Yet students are expected to "explain how seventeenth- and eighteenth-century European scientific advancements led to the industrial revolution" and "how the industrial revolution led to political, economic, and social changes in Europe." This is a monocausal explanation for the complex manifestation of industrialization in northwestern Eurasia. There are connections between the advances of the scientific revolution and industrialization, but developments in science explain far less about the beginning of the Industrial Revolution than do the conjuncture of global trade patterns, geographic and ecological factors, and pressures for technological innovation.[51] Furthermore, why limit study of the political, economic, and social impact of the Industrial Revolution to Europe when industrialization's impact is truly a worldwide phenomenon?[52]

The topic of Atlantic world revolutions (American, French, and Latin American) in the late eighteenth to early nineteenth centuries is commonplace in world history teaching. The Texas standards include this theme but undermine the expectation to "compare the causes, characteristics, and . . . consequences" of the revolutions by "emphasizing the role of the Enlightenment, the Glorious Revolution, and religion." Again we see a world history perspective narrowed by tendentious historical sensibilities and the desire to generate a Western civilization trajectory of ideas and values from Europe to the Americas in place of a world history approach. The emphasis added by the review committee casts this age of revolutions as predominantly ideological rather than as a conjuncture of economic, social, political, and ideological factors. The treatment of this period, 1750–1914, in the TEKS detours from a world history perspective even more significantly by neglecting to mention developments of any kind in Africa or Asia, such as the Meiji restoration in Japan.[53]

The period from 1914 to the present is divided into five topics centered on World War I, global economic depression, World War II, and the Cold War, including independence movements. One would expect a final topic here on globalization. Yet the final history knowledge standard addresses the development of "radical Islamic fundamentalism and the subsequent use of terrorism by some of its adherents." Islamism and terrorism fit well into a globalized perspective on the post–Cold War world, but the TEKS' narrow approach elevates Islamism to the same level of importance in the standards as the world wars and Cold War. The review committee missed an opportunity here to draw upon the rich scholarship and textbook narratives of the growing political, economic, social, and cultural integration of the earth's population. Islamism and terrorism are symptoms of this process, and to focus on them diminishes the opportunity students would have to develop an understanding of the benefits and costs of globalization.[54]

Why do these problems of balance appear in the TEKS? One cause is the very structure of the standards divided by disciplinary theme rather than simply by period. The goal of the SBOE is to create "vertical alignment" in all social studies classes from one grade level to the next, but the result can produce an "unwieldy tangle," as the Fordham Institute described the 2010 TEKS in US history.[55] The aforementioned standards fall into the history category and are followed by separate sections of standards on geography; economics, where one finds but a single standard related to globalization; government; citizenship; culture; science, technology, and society; and social study skills. This arrangement disrupts the interdisciplinary coherence, periodization, and explanatory power of a world history approach. For example, social history in general, and gender history in particular, fare poorly in the TEKS. The history of "women, children, and families" appears as an isolated standard in the culture section of the TEKS, rather than as a consistent element of social history integrated throughout the periodization of the standards.[56]

The Texas State Board of Education

Responsibility for shortcomings in the TEKS ultimately lies at the feet of the SBOE members. The expert reviewers neglected the world history standards and the review committee improved them, albeit with a number of missed opportunities, but the conservative core of the SBOE actively intervened to tilt the world history course toward a Western civilization narrative while the remaining members were at a loss whether to approve the standards or to question proposed revisions. The problem with the SBOE's influence on the TEKS is not that Christianity, free enterprise, and democracy are not part of a world history curriculum, but that these topics are not the central concepts for a world history course. Despite the political and ideological divisions on the SBOE that often pitted a ten-member Republican majority against a five-member Democratic minority, the world history TEKS were ill-served by board members on both sides unfamiliar with up-to-date world history scholarship and pedagogy. Board member Patricia Hardy is an interesting exception who demonstrates the hold of the Western civ narrative on Americans. Hardy holds a master's degree in history and taught world history and geography at the high-school level for thirty years,[57] yet many of the revisions she proposed contributed to the standards' Western-centric focus. The ideological positions that characterized the battle over the US standards (noncritical exceptionalism versus multicultural inclusivity) carried over into revision of the world history standards in muted form. These ideological approaches to world history revealed the largely ahistorical and Western-exceptionalist sensibilities of board members who motioned from the right to add more standards on Christianity and free enterprise and from the left for the inclusion of more American ethnic minorities. Frustrated by the conservatives' success at adding revisions to the K-12 social studies TEKS, board member Mary Helen Berlanga exclaimed, "They are going overboard, they are not experts, they are not historians . . . They are rewriting history, not only of Texas but of the United States and the world."[58] Indeed, the conservative members went "overboard," but liberals and moderates also lacked historical expertise and contributed to the emphasis on Western civilization and diminished comparative and thematic elements characteristic of up-to-date world history.

The SBOE particularly diminished a world history sensibility by adding to the introductory elements of the world history TEKS three new standards focusing on the American experience: "Identify the role of the U.S. free enterprise system within the parameters of this course . . . understand that a constitutional republic is a representative form of government whose representatives derive their authority from the consent of the governed . . . discuss how the actions of U.S. citizens and the local, state, and federal governments have either met or failed to meet the ideals espoused in the founding documents." These standards were added to the introduction of all K-12 social studies guidelines without significant division between board members but are clearly at odds with world history pedagogy.[59]

At SBOE meetings in March and May 2010, revisions to the TEKS proposed by Hardy, McLeroy, and Barbara Cargill reversed the progress the review committee had made at making the world history TEKS more global. For example, beginning with a motion from Hardy, an 8 to 7 majority of the board thwarted the best intentions of the writing team by replacing the ecumenical designations "BCE" (Before the Common Era) and "CE" (Common Era) with the Christian signifiers "BC" and "AD," despite the committee's explanation that "adherence to modern discipline nomenclature needs to be in Texas state standards."[60] Even a compromise motion from Mavis Knight to include both forms, "BC (BCE)" and "AD (CE)," failed.[61] Hardy cast the issue as maintaining tradition over deferring to "political correctness." Nevertheless, she and McLeroy continued to emphasize the Christian tradition, rather than comparative religious practices and influences, by proposing revisions that redundantly added monotheism, Judaism, Roman Catholicism and Eastern Orthodoxy to standards on the classical and postclassical eras.[62] Christianity is the only world religion that received added attention to its "history" and "sacraments." Fellow board members generally deferred to Hardy's years of teaching experience, but Lawrence Allen resisted her motion to remove a standard related to the Israeli-Palestinian conflict. "Just because I don't want it there" is not sound reasoning for a revision, Mr. Allen explained. Knight eventually felt compelled to ask the chair, Gail Lowe, to direct board members to explain the logic of their proposed revisions with historical justifications rather than evidence-free assertions of personal preference.[63]

Despite the chair's instruction, ahistorical attitudes continued to motivate revisions to the TEKS. McLeroy revisited Hardy's motion to strike the student expectation to "explain the origins and impact of the Israeli Palestinian conflict on global politics" and proposed replacing it with "explain how Arab rejection of the State of Israel has led to ongoing conflict." Asked by Lowe to speak to his motion, McLeroy replied, "It's true." Although the motion was challenged by Cargill, who quoted members of the review committee on the importance of retaining the original expectation, McLeroy's motions carried without measurable discussion or opposition.[64] Consequently, an effective standard that encourages historical thinking was replaced with a narrow and tendentious expectation that asserts a singular explanation for a complex historical and political situation.

A more prevalent obsession of the SBOE's conservative core was the superiority of the capitalist economic system, or free enterprise in their preferred terminology. Citing the TEC, Cargill made multiple motions at the SBOE's March and May 2010 meetings to add revisions emphasizing "the free enterprise system and its benefits." Here, as elsewhere in the TEKS, there is a cheerleading quality to the standards rather than a pedagogic one. Nevertheless, the SBOE inserted another six standards in this vein that expect students to explain "pro-free market factors contributing to the success of Europe's Commercial Revolution," "the benefits of free enterprise in the Industrial Revolution," and the superiority of "free enterprise" over "communist command" economies and communities.[65] The standards, phrased with foregone conclusions about the benefits of free enterprise, revealed a close split among board members. At the May 2010 meeting, members near the center of the ideological divide motioned to mitigate the cheerleading language in more than one standard. Liberals and moderates, including Hardy, succeeded in an 8 to 6 vote to change "benefits" to "effects" in the standard referencing the Industrial Revolution. The conservative core with the help of moderates, but not Hardy, succeeded in adding the phrase "the benefits of free enterprise in world history" to a standard on contemporary economic systems.[66] This devotion to the theme of free enterprise produced ahistorical expectations for students that turn inductive reasoning on its head. Instead of expecting students to assemble evidence and then draw conclusions, the standards assert one conclusion and require students to learn the supporting evidence for that outcome.

The debates within the SBOE over the benefits of free enterprise do not necessarily indicate differences based on an understanding of historical thinking in general or world history concepts in particular. Those ideologically opposed to the conservative bloc also lacked a world history sensibility as demonstrated in their efforts to amend the TEKS. For example, Democratic opponents of the conservatives, Berlanga, Knight, and Rene Nuñez, proposed motions at the March 10, 2010, meeting to add the expectation that students "understand the importance of Medal of Honor recipients including Private Cleto Rodriguez, Sergeant Alejandro Ruiz, and Lieutenant Vernon J. Baker." While Berlanga clarified the list of names to include, moderate Bob Craig offered an alternative using the phrase "including individuals of all races and gender" instead of personal names. A compromise motion included both Craig's language and Berlanga's list of names. The motions failed, but not because they were correctly viewed as irrelevant to understanding World War II from a global perspective. Rather, the motions and vote demonstrated how board members from both sides of the ideological divide were fighting the battle over ethnic inclusivity that characterized the highly charged debate on the US history standards. The group proposing multicultural inclusivity simply did not have the votes to amend the TEKS with the names of Latinos and African Americans.[67] The absence of compelling arguments for inclusivity from the left was further demonstrated by Rick Agosto's motion to "throw in a little color" by adding George Washington Carver to a list of "significant scientists and inventors." When Agosto learned that Carver was included in standards for other grade levels, he withdrew his motion, but no one pointed out that the lists proposed by Hardy did not include a single individual outside the societies of the ancient Mediterranean, medieval Europe, or Europe and the United States in the modern period.[68]

To the board's credit, revisions at the March and May meetings also made improvements to at least two standards. With broad support, Hardy motioned to reinstate the standard and student expectations on culture, which had been removed by the review committee on the advice of expert reviewers Barton and Dreisbach. The interdisciplinarity of world history was enhanced by restoring the requirement for students to understand "the relationship between the arts and times during which they were created." Also, Hardy successfully disentangled standards on Mesoamerican and Andean civilizations from standards on Europe and created a new standard and set of expectations that focused on a comparison of "the major political, economic, social, and cultural developments of the Maya, Inca, and Aztec."[69]

Public comment on revisions to the K-12 social studies TEKS overwhelmingly focused on the US history standards. Likewise, media attention emphasized the culture wars between the uncritical American-exceptionalists and the defenders of multicultural inclusivity. Appeals for a balanced approach to the past based on professionally accepted methodologies and historical sensibilities from teachers, academics, and others made little headway against the ideological positions and historical sensibilities of the SBOE majority and minority. A notable exception was the array of successful arguments made by representatives of the Sikh religious community to include Sikhism in the US and world history standards. The problem for world history was the absence of articulate defenders against easily digested claims that conflate Western civ with global history. Soviet émigré and Texas citizen of twenty years Vadim Anshelevich spoke before the board and demonstrated the common understanding that Western civ provides the backstory for an uncritical narrative of US exceptionalism. "American history," Anshelevich explained, "started much earlier than July 4, 1776. We are the heirs of Hammurabi's code . . . Greek democracy . . . the Roman republic . . . Magna Carta . . . European middle class . . . the Reformation . . . and the Enlightenment." These "milestones," Anshelevich concluded, mark a "road of history" that was "not always straightforward," but have led us to "America, the highest point of human civilization."[70]

Conclusions

In the end, the anemic guidelines for the Texas tenth-grade world history course were the result of a variety of factors: Texas education law, the sentimental appeal of American exceptionalism, lack of world history specialists among expert reviewers, and the Western-centered, ahistorical frame of reference among board members. The standards lack a sharp conceptual focus due to the ill-conceived combination of a Western civilization narrative with dutiful and generic appearances of non-Western societies. Students may gain an appreciation of the Western world's contributions to America's political culture and social values, but it is doubtful that they will understand much about the world we live in today, where India is home to the world's most populous democracy and China is the second-largest economy. Texas students will not be alone in their poor social studies preparation for college and the workplace. In Robert Bain's 2004 study of world history standards in the United States, only six states followed a global history approach similar to the AP course.[71] According to the Fordham Institute's 2006 ranking of the states' world history guidelines, only eight received an A. The 1998 TEKS earned a C, one letter grade above the median. If the institute's evaluation of the 2010 US history TEKS—"an unwieldy tangle of social studies categories and arbitrary thematic subdivisions"—is any indication, rankings for the world history TEKS, which follow the same organizational pattern as US history, will be mediocre.[72] The National Assessment of Educational Progress (NAEP) will test students' world history knowledge in 2018, and we will learn how Texas's tenth graders fare in a national comparison.[73] We know now through "The Nation's Report Card," produced by the NAEP, that Texas schoolchildren fall significantly below national proficiency in reading and math even though Texas state exams based on the TEKS deem the students proficient.[74]

For Texas students to succeed in world history studies, much depends on their teachers and the professors who train them. With a firm foundation in world history concepts and content received at the collegiate level, high school teachers may cast a skeptical eye on the curriculum and textbooks that the 2010 TEKS will produce and put in the extra effort to deliver a truly global world history course to their students. With a global word cloud of ideas and information to call on, high school graduates will be better prepared for the challenges and opportunities that face them in an increasingly complex and interconnected world.

Notes

1. TagCrowd website, http://tagcrowd.com.
2. *Texas Education Code*, Title 2, Subtitle F, Chapter 28, Subchapter A, Section 28.002.
3. Ross Dunn, ed., *The New World History: A Teacher's Companion* (Boston, MA: Bedford/St. Martin's, 2000), 5.
4. Dunn, *New World History*, 13–72.
5. World History Association, "What Is World History?," available at World History Association website, http://thewha.org/world_history.php.
6. Dunn, *New World History*, 6.
7. David Christian, *Maps of Time: An Introduction to Big History* (Berkeley: University of California Press, 2004); Fred Spier, *Big History and the Future of Humanity* (Malden, MA: Wiley-Blackwell, 2011).
8. Tonio Andrade, "A Chinese Farmer, Two African Boys, and a Warlord: Toward a Global Microhistory," *Journal of World History* 21, no. 4 (December 2010): 573–91; Valerie Hansen and Kenneth Curtis, *Voyages in World History*, 2 vols. (Boston: Wadsworth, 2008).
9. *National Standards for History* (Los Angeles: National Center for History in the Schools, 1996), 1.
10. *World History for Us All* website, "Why Learn World History," http://worldhistoryforusall.sdsu.edu/shared/thinking.php.
11. Chester E. Finn Jr., "Foreword," in Walter Russell Mead, *The State of State World History Standards* (Washington, DC: Thomas B. Fordham Institute, 2006), 5.
12. "Don't Mess with Textbooks," *The Daily Show* (Comedy Central), March 17, 2010.
13. United Press International, "Texas School Board 'Reinstates' Jefferson," May 21, 2010.
14. Don McLeroy, "Opposing View on Education: Teach Founding Principles," *USA Today*, April 12, 2010; Michael Soto, "Plagiarized Work," *History News Network*, May 10, 2010.
15. TEKS.10.b.1 (2010).
16. *National Standards for History* (Los Angeles: National Center for History in the Schools, 1996), 132–36.
17. Gary Nash, Charlotte Crabtree, and Ross E. Dunn, *History on Trial: Culture Wars and the Teaching of the Past* (New York: Vintage, 2000).
18. *World History for Us All* website, "The Idea Behind this Curriculum," http://worldhistoryforusall.sdsu.edu/foundations/idea_behind.php.
19. Dunn, *New World History*, 8.
20. *World History for Us All* website, "The Idea Behind this Curriculum," http://worldhistoryforusall.sdsu.edu/foundations/idea_behind.php; *World History for Us All* website, "The Big Eras," http://worldhistoryforusall.sdsu.edu/bigeras.php.
21. Mead, *State of State World History Standards*, 6, 31.
22. College Board, "*World History Course* Description," http://www.collegeboard.com/student/testing/ap/sub_worldhist.html. The 2011 course description is significantly revised from the 2010 version.

23. College Board, "AP Exam Scores," http://www.collegeboard.com/student/testing/ap/exgrd.html.
24. Robert Bain, "NAEP 12th Grade World History Assessment: Issues and Options" (commissioned paper for the National Assessment Governing Board, 2004), http://www.nagb.org/ publications/reports-papers.htm, 7, 27–28.
25. A complete set of the questions from the SBOE is available in Dr. James Kracht's report "Review of Current [1998] Social Studies TEKS" (2009), http://www.tea.state.tx.us/index2.aspx?id=6184.
26. Peter Novick, *That Noble Dream: The "Objectivity Question" and the American Historical Profession* (Cambridge, UK: Cambridge University Press, 1988).
27. Kracht, "Review of Current [1998] Social Studies TEKS."
28. Ibid.
29. Daniel Dreisbach, "Review of Current [1998] Social Studies TEKS" (2009), http://www.tea.state.tx.us/index2.aspx?id=6184; Peter Marshall, "Review of Current [1998] Social Studies TEKS" (2009), http://www.tea.state.tx.us/index2.aspx?id=6184 (emphasis original).
30. Texas Education Agency, "SBOE TEKS Review Committees, Social Studies, 9–12," http://www.tea.state.tx.us/index2.aspx?id=3643.
31. TEKS (7/31/09).
32. TEKS (10/17/09).
33. TEKS.10.c.1 (10/17/09). Kracht recommended elimination of this "quiz show" style of expectation in "Review of First Draft Social Studies TEKS," http://www.tea.state.tx.us/index2.aspx?id=6184, 10.
34. Jerry H. Bentley and Herbert F. Ziegler, *Traditions and Encounters: A Global Perspective on the Past,* 5th ed. (New York: McGraw Hill, 2011); Craig A. Lockard, *Societies, Networks, and Transitions: A Global History* (Boston: Houghton Mifflin, 2008); Robert W. Strayer, *Ways of the World: A Brief Global History with Sources* (Boston: Bedford/St. Martin's, 2011).
35. TEKS.10.c.7–8 (7/31/09).
36. David Barton, "Review of First Draft Social Studies TEKS," http://www.tea.state.tx.us/index2.aspx?id=6184, 85–87.
37. Daniel Dreisbach, "Review of First Draft Social Studies TEKS," http://www.tea.state.tx.us/index2.aspx?id=6184, 8.
38. TEKS.10.c.1, 19 (10/17/09).
39. Lybeth Hodges, "Review of First Draft Social Studies TEKS," http://www.tea.state.tx.us/index2.aspx?id=6184, 3.
40. TEKS.10.c.21.E (7/31/09).
41. Hodges, "Review," 5.
42. TEKS.10.c.21.F (10/17/09).
43. TEKS.10.c.20.C (7/31/09).
44. TEKS.10.b.2 (7/31/09); TEKS.10.c.19.B (10/17/09).
45. TEKS.K.a.1 (7/31/09).
46. Marshall, "Review," 1.
47. Barton, "Review," 8.
48. TEKS.10.c.3.C (10/17/09).
49. TEKS.10.c.4.A (10/17/09).

50. TEKS.10.c.6.D (10/17/09).
51. Robert B. Marks, *The Origins of Modern World History: A Global and Ecological Narrative from the Fifteenth to the Twenty-First Century*, 2nd ed. (Lanham, MD: Rowman and Littlefield, 2007).
52. TEKS.10.c.7 (10/17/09).
53. TEKS.10.c.8 (10/17/09).
54. TEKS.10.c.13 (10/17/09).
55. Sheldon M. Stern and Jeremy A. Stern, *The State of State U.S. History Standards* (Washington, DC: Thomas B. Fordham Institute, 2011), 141.
56. TEKS.10.c.23 (10/17/09).
57. Texas Education Agency, "SBOE Officers, Committees, and Members," http://www.tea.state.tx.us/index4.aspx?id=3803.
58. James C. McKinley Jr., "Texas Conservatives Win Curriculum Change," *The New York Times*, March 12, 2010.
59. TEKS.10.b.6, 8, 10 (5/10).
60. TEKS.10.b.2 (10/17/09).
61. SBOE meeting minutes, 3/12/10, 33.
62. Ibid., 34; SBOE meeting minutes, 3/10/10, 5; TEKS.10.4.B (8/23/10).
63. SBOE meeting minutes, 3/10/10.
64. SBOE meeting minutes, 3/10/10, 11.
65. SBOE meeting minutes, 3/10/10, 5/21/10.
66. SBOE meeting minutes, 5/21/10, 11.
67. SBOE meeting minutes, 3/12/10, 37–38.
68. SBOE meeting minutes, 3/10/10, 15.
69. SBOE meeting minutes, 3/10/10, 7–8, 14–15.
70. Amardeep Singh, President of the Sikh Coalition Before the SBOE, in SBOE meeting minutes, 3/10/10.
71. Bain, "NAEP 12th Grade World History Assessment," 11.
72. Mead, *State of State World History Standards*, 7; Stern and Stern, *State of State U.S. History Standards*, 141.
73. National Assessment of Educational Progress, http://nces.ed.gov/nationsreportcard/worldhistory.
74. Victor Bandeira de Mello and Charles Blankenship, "Mapping State Proficiency Standards onto NAEP Scales: 2005–2007" (Washington, DC: National Center for Education Statistics, 2009), 20, http://nces.ed.gov/nationsreportcard/pubs/studies/2010456.asp; Rick Casey, "TAKS Grade Inflation is Nothing New," *Houston Chronicle*, June 13, 2010.

Figure 11 An alternative to high stakes testing
The twenty-first-century Texas education system is overseen by politicians and driven by high-stakes standardized testing. More than a century ago, education standards were established through a mutually beneficial partnership between the University of Texas (shown on horizon) and high schools throughout the state.

CHAPTER 11

Standards before Standardization
The Affiliated Schools Program, 1885–1917
Linda J. Black

The headline in the *Washington Post* announced "Texas Passes Controversial Social Studies Standards." The accompanying article was one of many such news stories from both state and national news agencies that described the contentious debate surrounding the adoption of the revised academic standards in social studies in Texas, the Texas Essential Knowledge and Skills (TEKS), in August 2010 (see Chapter 1). The debate centered on issues of historical accuracy and interpretation as the social conservative majority on the Texas State Board of Education changed many of the recommendations made by teams of scholars and veteran teachers who had worked on revisions for more than a year, imposing its own views of what Texas students should know about history, geography, government, and economics.[1]

The TEKS, however, are only one of the sets of standards that govern teaching in Texas. In 2008, on the basis of persuasive data that Texas students were not sufficiently prepared for college, the state legislature mandated that the Texas Education Agency and the Texas Higher Education Coordinating Board develop an additional set of academic standards for core courses in English/language arts, mathematics, science, and social studies. Whereas the TEKS emphasize mastery of basic skills and knowledge, the resulting Texas College and Career Readiness Standards (CCRS) are designed to represent more in-depth knowledge and skills that students need in order to succeed in entry-level college courses, as well as in postsecondary careers. The Texas Education Agency was instructed to incorporate both sets of standards into the new high-stakes, statewide end-of-course assessments that begin in 2011–12.

This continued emphasis on using standards in high-stakes testing contrasts, however, with the beginning of academic standards in Texas a little over one hundred years ago. The development of the first state standards was a far different story, one that initially developed through a mutually beneficial relationship between the University of Texas and Texas high schools. This relationship was known as the Affiliated Schools Program and lasted from 1885 to 1917. An examination of the creation and development of these initial academic standards not only informs our perspective about the recent conflict over the state academic standards but also deepens our understanding of the role of government in education.

High Schools: From Private to Public in the Progressive Era

The affiliated schools movement developed during the Progressive Era, a time period from approximately 1885 to 1920 that "embodied a vast array of responses to the changes taking place in American society at the turn of the century." Industrialization, commercialism, urbanization, and immigration at home and abroad, coupled with economic opportunity, attracted large numbers of immigrants to the United States, resulting in a national population increase of 68 percent between 1890 and 1920. Texas also experienced significant population growth, resulting both from immigration and from rural-to-urban migration. In the span of one decade, from 1870 to 1880, the Texas population increased 94.5 percent, continuing thereafter with at least a 20 percent increase each decade through 1920. Historian Lewis L. Gould described the urban growth in Texas during this time: "There were 132 cities of 5,000 of more residents in 1910. But, after 1910, cities increased in population ten times faster than the countryside. Nearly one-third of the population lived in urban centers by 1919 and fifteen percent lived in Houston, Dallas, and San Antonio. By 1920, there were thirty cities with 10,000 or more people and Dallas, El Paso, Fort Worth, Houston, and San Antonio all had more than 50,000 residents."[2]

The population growth in Texas, particularly in urban areas, was a factor that favored the development of public schools. In fact, to meet the rising demand for education, the 1876 Texas Constitution decreed that any incorporated city could, by a majority vote of the property taxpayers, create and assume exclusive control of an independent public school district within its limits. By August 1884, there were a total of 208 independent school districts across the state, 65 in Texas towns and cities and 143 in rural areas. The 1876 constitution also allowed communities to establish either gender-separate or coeducational public schools according to the needs of the community. The continued growth in population led to an increase in the construction of schools in Texas, with the number of schools doubling from just over 5,000 in 1880 to more than 10,000 by 1910, primarily in urban areas.[3]

As Texas in the late nineteenth century experienced increased urbanization, parents and education leaders from school districts in Texas cities called for increased public education at the secondary level. In describing the reason for this development, historian of early Texas education Frederick Eby wrote, "The need for training beyond the elementary grades was felt especially in the growing towns, where the well-to-do and the ambitious desired to keep their children in school for a longer period of time." Public high schools slowly replaced the private schools or academies that had provided secondary education for Texas students since the settlement of the state.[4]

Although the first public high school in America appeared in Boston in 1821, the first public high school in Texas was not established for another fifty years, slowly replacing the private academies of the time. Beginning in the late 1870s, Texas towns and cities established the first coeducational public high schools: Brenham in 1875; Houston and Denison in 1878; San Antonio in 1879; Sherman in 1880; Austin and Weatherford in 1881; El Paso, Fort Worth, and Waco in 1884; and Marshall and Galveston by 1885. Separate high schools for African American students also opened in major Texas cities: Galveston in 1885, Dallas in 1888, Austin in 1889, and Houston in 1892.

The development of public high schools came to be viewed by Progressive reformers and parents alike as an important step in the American education system, what the administrator in charge of the Affiliated Schools Program in Texas referred to in his annual report of 1905 as "the nexus between the common schools and the University."[5] With the development and rapid growth of public high schools in Texas, some means of standardizing curriculum and assessing student progress, especially for students desiring to attend college, was needed. The Affiliated Schools Program not only strengthened this link between high school and college but also established the first statewide academic standards for Texas schools.

The Affiliated Schools Program

During the late nineteenth century, colleges and universities across the country admitted students based on their performance on examinations created by their own faculty members and/or administrators. These assessments varied widely among institutions. Not until 1900 did a handful of colleges and universities create a common college entrance examination that could be used by multiple colleges.[6] In 1870, however, the University of Michigan developed an additional method of admitting students, the first affiliated school program. This program enabled universities to admit students who had graduated from what the university referred to as affiliated high schools and became the model for other states in the Midwest.

The Michigan affiliated schools program included three components: a report about the high school sent to the university, samples of student work approved by university faculty, and a visit to the high school by a university faculty member.[7] This plan had two benefits for universities of the time: an increase in the number of students entering the university and the ability of university faculty to directly impact the curricula in high school classrooms by designating the subjects that were required to be taught. As the affiliated schools movement developed, university faculty began to evaluate other aspects of the school, such as the quality of teaching. In 1885, the University of Texas designed and employed a program similar to the Michigan affiliated schools model.

The Affiliated Schools Program in Texas

When the University of Texas first opened in 1883, there were few high schools in the state and, correspondingly, a small number of high school graduates. More important, though, many of the first high school graduates who applied for admission to the university were deemed by university faculty to be unprepared for college-level work. One of the issues in the uneven preparation of students was the variation in high school curricula. Although the Texas School Laws of 1876 and 1884 required that public schools teach orthography, reading, penmanship, English grammar, composition, arithmetic and mental arithmetic, physiology, history, and modern geography, there were few uniform curriculum requirements specifically for secondary schools, nor was there a standard method for assessing student achievement. For example, Eby reported that although "the better high schools of the state required English, mathematics, history, and some science," each school formulated its own courses of study.[8] The beginning of the University of Texas Affiliated Schools Program emerged out of the need to improve the quality of students entering the university and hence, the academic quality of Texas high schools.

In 1884, the Board of Regents of the University of Texas attempted to address the lack of preparation of high school students by considering different options, such as creating a preparatory department as part of the university and establishing its own high schools. The final decision by the board in 1885 called for encouraging the building of municipal high schools that would be affiliated with the university through faculty visitation of these "feeder" high schools. The university catalogue for 1885–86 described how a committee of faculty members would visit a high school upon request of the school board. The committee would then report back to the university about the competencies of the high school. If the high school met its "standards," or requirements for admission to the university, then its graduates would be admitted to the university without taking entrance examinations and the high school would be listed in the university catalogue as an affiliated high school.[9] This affiliation process established a relationship between Texas high schools and the University of Texas that continued for the next thirty years.

To begin the program of affiliating high schools in Texas, the University of Texas established guidelines for affiliation that reflected standard course requirements at the university and published these guidelines in university catalogues so that high schools, district administrators, and teachers could be aware of the required standards and adjust their courses and teaching accordingly. The next step was to publicize the process that schools were to follow to become affiliated. Published in 1885, the *Admission of Students without Examination* included the requirements of a visit to the high school by a faculty member and a formal letter of application from the high school describing courses of study and providing faculty/building information, presumably to facilitate the faculty's member visit. University faculty would then vote on the applicant school, and if approved, the school would be listed in the university catalogue. Also described in the publication was the university's justification for the Affiliated Schools Program, which included an explanation of how there was currently little "uniformity in high school programs" and how the affiliated high schools program would provide "a continuous course of study with no perceptible break between secondary and university programs."[10]

As the Affiliated Schools Program in Texas expanded over the next 32 years, the university modified both the affiliation process and the administration of the program. The standards for affiliation in 1892 included the subjects that were tested in the University of Texas entrance examinations of the time—for example, English, Latin, Greek, history, and mathematics. Between 1895 and 1905, high schools were allowed to affiliate in single subjects. Graduates of these high schools were exempt from taking the entrance examinations in the affiliated subjects but were still required to take the exams in the other subjects.

By 1891, there were 25 high schools affiliated with the University of Texas. By this time, the process also included the right of the faculty to conduct a new inspection of a school at any time and to terminate affiliation if standards were not met.[11] The number of affiliated high schools continued to increase each year: 37 in 1892–93, 55 in 1894–95, and 66 by 1895–96. In 1900, the faculty recommended that a four-year high school program be adopted in all Texas communities, though this would not be realized in rural areas for some time. The standards for the four-year plan included three to five 45-minute periods per week in English, mathematics, history, natural science, and foreign language.

In 1901, the standards for affiliation included the provision that at least two full-time teachers be employed. By this date, the specific process for affiliation included a formal application, specimens of student papers sent to the university for grading, a visitation by the president or his designee, and finally, faculty approval.[12]

In 1899, there were 84 affiliated high schools, and by 1907, there were 127. As the number of affiliated high schools continued to increase, the duties of the university faculty who volunteered to evaluate applications, grade specimen papers, and visit schools grew as well. To address this issue, the university made the first in a series of changes in the administration of the program. Before 1905, the affiliation process had been handled by the office of the university president. However, to better facilitate the affiliation process as well as to more efficiently handle the increased visitation workload, the Faculty Committee on Affiliated Schools was officially formed in 1905. All applications for affiliation had to go through this committee, which represented the major disciplines in the university.[13] The committee also asked faculty members for recommendations about courses and coursework, which served as guidelines/standards for affiliation and were printed in the university catalogues and bulletins. As a result, university faculty involvement in the program had the benefit of directly impacting the development of curriculum in Texas high schools.

Also in 1905, a standard form was developed for use by committee members in their visitations to the schools. The form required the inspecting committee member to obtain specific information at the time of the visit, such as number of students and teachers, organization of the school, length of class periods, number of books in the library, and specific courses and levels of study. Inspectors were also asked to evaluate discipline practices and "effective" teaching in the classes they visited.[14] Based on this information and the recommendation of the inspecting committee member, the faculty would then determine whether or not the high school was granted affiliated status. However, the demands of administering a full-time program that required regular visitation of schools statewide became increasingly difficult for faculty with other responsibilities. The university's Board of Regents sought to address this problem by the appointment of a Visitor of Schools, a full-time administrator whose responsibility was to take charge of the Affiliated Schools Program, including the inspection of schools.

The first Visitor of Schools to be appointed by the board in 1905 was Superintendent John W. Hopkins of Galveston, who held this position only part of the year. Dr. W. J. Battle, professor of Greek at the university, filled the position for the remainder of 1905.[15] In 1906, the board appointed Dr. J. L. Henderson, an experienced educator, who remained in the position until the end of the program in 1917. Dr. Henderson received both his master's degree and his doctorate from Columbia University, had served as teacher and principal at the elementary and high school levels, and worked as a superintendent in the Tyler school district before his appointment.[16] It was Henderson who, after surveying both the university's entrance requirements and the current affiliation process, made the final significant changes in the program.

Over the next ten years, the number of affiliated high schools continued to increase. As a result, Henderson requested and received an additional five staff members, "visitors," to help with school visitations, usually in specific subjects. Henderson described what the visitation process had come to involve by 1916, in response to a letter from an administrator in Illinois wanting information about the program: "It is impossible to visit all of the classes in all of the subjects. We strive to visit at least one class in each subject. At least one day should be spent in each school. When you go to Dallas or Houston, you would have different visitors for different subjects."[17]

In examining the Affiliated Schools Program during the period from 1910 to 1917, probably the most significant impact the program had—as well as a major difference in the standards program of that time and the standards program in Texas today—is in the relationship between the university and local school districts. With the reorganization of the Committee on Affiliated Schools into the Council of Affiliated Schools in 1913, the university began to directly influence curriculum and instruction in both secondary schools and the university as well as to facilitate the smooth transition of students into higher education, something that the current Texas College and Career Readiness Standards are still attempting to do. One faculty representative from each of the following fields was appointed to the council: English, ancient languages, modern languages, history, mathematics, physical sciences, biological sciences, physiography, manual training, domestic science, and business subjects. Council members analyzed the examination papers submitted by the high schools and provided specific feedback to high school teachers. They also advised other members of the faculty concerning the work of high schools and made university course adjustments, if necessary. "Finally, the council was responsible for writing and publishing bulletins that focused on the teaching of high school subjects, a valuable tool for many secondary teachers with little to no special training in their subject area. In summary, the purpose of the council was to address the entire field of college and high school problems."[18]

With the national adoption of the Carnegie unit as an unit of measure for high school courses, Texas high school students had to secure 14 units for full admission to the university without examination in the prescribed subjects of algebra, geometry, English, and history and in the elective subjects of French, German, Greek, Latin, Spanish, botany, chemistry, physics, physiography, and physiology. By 1916, the number of different subjects accepted for admission had increased to 30.[19][20]

Curriculum Changes and Vocational Education

With the dawn of the twentieth century came alternatives to the traditional subjects in the Affiliated Schools Program. With the increasing pace of industrialization, immigration, and urbanization in the late 1800s, certain business leaders and educators called for the school curriculum to reflect what they perceived as societal needs, especially the need for trained workers. These workers were not going to attend college and would not, therefore, need the same courses in high school as college-bound students. As a result, vocational and commercial classes that addressed the growing needs of business and industry were introduced into public secondary schools.[21]

Texas paralleled this national trend with the addition of vocational, commercial, and agricultural education in Texas public high schools between 1895 and 1910. The very first manual training department in a Texas high school was established in 1896 in Austin, with public high schools for whites and blacks in other Texas cities soon following. Domestic science courses provided instruction for female students in what is today referred to as home economics and were first offered in Texas at Fort Worth High School in 1903, with high schools in Austin and Dallas, San Antonio, and Houston adding such courses in 1904, 1905, and 1906, respectively.[22]

Additional business classes were added to the high school curriculum during this same time period. For example, the *Annual Report of the Public Schools of the Independent School District of the City of Houston, 1900–1901* stated, "Houston is a commercial and manufacturing city [and our] modern education needs the technical or industrial training to fit our youth for the battle of life, and lastly domestic service, which would prepare our daughters the better to fill their place in home life."[23] By 1904, the Houston school district had created a complete commercial department with six terms of work, including stenography and typewriting.[24]

Based on changes in the perceived goal of secondary education by parents and reformers alike and the subsequent growth of vocational courses in high schools across the state, the university added coursework in some vocational and commercial subjects in the second decade of the twentieth century. By 1913, school inspectors in the fields of domestic science, manual training, and agriculture were added to the Affiliated Schools Program at Dr. Henderson's request. By 1917, the Affiliated Schools Program, which had been created to benefit only those students planning to attend college, had evolved into a program that sought to provide all students with a quality education, one that would prepare students for either college or a career.

Transition to State Supervision, 1916–1917

Commenting on the significance of the Affiliated Schools Program in 1913, Henderson touched on concerns voiced by other education leaders in the state and, perhaps, foreshadowed the demise of university control when he wrote in his annual report, "When we consider that the University [Affiliate Schools Program] may not only serve its own perspective students but those of other colleges and those who will never enter college, the importance of the work becomes patent."[25] As public high schools throughout the state developed between 1875 and 1915, larger numbers of students of all classes were able to attend high school for the first time. With this change in student population as well as the growth of vocational education as preparation for work after high school, "the mission of the high school changed. It evolved from primarily preparing students for college to the additional or alternative preparation of preparing students for life and non-academic jobs."[26]

With the change in Texas high schools, the initial purpose of the Affiliated Schools Program of only preparing students for the university came into question by some parents, educators, and state officials. Added to this was the development of other colleges and universities, envious of the privileged position of the University of Texas in its relationship with Texas high schools and desirous of the impact the university had over curriculum and instructional decisions in local districts. In December 1916, concerned members of the Texas State Teachers' Association, representing educators, schools, and districts all over the state, addressed these issues and recommended "the inspection and affiliation of high schools under the direction of the State Department of Education, the legally constituted head of the school system of Texas."[27]

According to education historians Eby, Henderson (the final Visitor of Schools), and Cecil E. Evans, the transfer of the affiliated schools program involved negative feelings on the part of several groups. Evans described the situation in 1916 as a "fight for transfer of affiliation." Eby echoed the opinion of the teachers' organization: "On one hand, it was felt that the university was too conservative in recognizing the newer [vocational] subjects of the high school curriculum; and on the other, that the close connection with the high schools gave the university a disproportionate prestige." In his memoirs, Henderson described similar causes that he believed led to the transfer: the "disappointments" of schools that had not been approved for affiliation, the growth of the State Department of Education, and "the desire of the other colleges to have a place in the sun."[28]

Shortly after the Teachers' Association resolution, a committee representing both colleges and school districts was formed to "study the classification of high schools and report to the association one year from now its findings and actions concerning this work."[29] In February 1917, the members of the committee signed an agreement binding themselves and their member institutions to the State Department of Education to carry on the work of supervising the inspection and affiliation of high schools. The Committee on Inspection, Classification, and Affiliation of High Schools in Texas, which continued during the 1920s and 1930s, consisted of 12 members: 6 members representing colleges and universities and 6 members representing school districts.

In his 1916–17 report, State Superintendent of Education W. F. Doughty described the difference between the voluntary process of high school affiliation and the state system of classifying all high schools. Classification of high schools was based primarily upon schools meeting the minimum requirements in certain nonacademic standards: length of school term, number of teachers in elementary and high school, units required for graduation, cost of high school library, number of science courses requiring science equipment and the value of the corresponding science equipment, length of class periods, and maximum number of classes taught by each high school teacher. These standards varied with the type of high school at the time: two-year, three-year, or four-year.

Although affiliation was optional, schools were required to meet the classification standards before being allowed to apply for affiliation. Although classification was based on nonacademic standards, affiliation was "based upon efficiency of work," the description of which matched the Affiliated Schools Program of the University of Texas. This process included an application report, regular visitations by state supervisors, and grading of specimen papers. Reports by the State Department of Education supervisors included observations of classes and content of courses.[30]

Between 1919 and 1923, the process of affiliation and classification was adapted to fit elementary and junior high schools by State Superintendent of Education Annie Webb Blanton, thereby developing the first academic standards in those grade levels as well.[31]

The Impact of the Affiliated Schools Program

The Affiliated Schools Program in Texas had a significant impact on Texas high schools. It promoted the growth and development of secondary education throughout the state as well as the development of the state's first academic standards, standards that were both recognized and supported by university faculty. Writing in 1925, Eby described the mutual benefits of the program for both Texas schools and the University of Texas: "Affiliation with the university set up the only objective standard of excellence by which the high schools might judge their merits. The system guided the superintendents and boards in formulating their curricula, in judging methods of instruction, and finally it measured, in the only manner then known, the results attained. On its side, the university was called on to supply better trained teachers who could keep the standard of affiliation." School districts around the state actively sought affiliation; it was a "prize eagerly sought by all the schools."[32] The affiliation designation was also a source of community pride in that citizens believed that an affiliated high school not only demonstrated quality education for their children but also enhanced the reputation of their community, perhaps similar in significance to the "Exemplary" and "Recognized" displays seen on the front of many contemporary Texas school buildings that illustrate the state's current education ratings system.

Letters in the archives of the Affiliated Schools Program attest to the importance of the affiliated status and how school superintendents and principals actively sought affiliation. For example, F. E. Savage, Superintendent of the Floydada schools, wrote to Henderson in February 1915, saying, "We are very anxious for affiliation with the University this year. We are working hard for it." Correspondence from school districts to the Visitor of Schools asked about all aspects of the program requirements—curriculum, faculty, textbooks, buildings, and equipment—and anything else that would help schools become affiliated.[33]

Affiliation with the university also provided other benefits to local schools. For example, education historian Marsha Farney described university affiliation as having a dual impact on the Georgetown school district, both in the more clearly structured and aligned curriculum choices offered to students and in the development of a more positive public opinion of the school system by the town's residents. In fact, when the Visitor of Schools, Dr. Henderson, visited Georgetown High School in August 1914 and commented about the crowded conditions, his report prompted the district to build a new, larger high school building.[34]

By the end of the program in 1917, there were 188 affiliated schools with an enrollment of 36,661 students. Although the number of affiliated schools was only about a third of the total number of 541 high schools in Texas, the percentage of students enrolled in affiliated high schools was 69.61 percent of the total number of enrolled high school students. In other words, almost 70 percent of Texas students enrolled in high school received an education designed to prepare them for university-level work.[35] The Affiliated Schools Program produced changes on the university level as well. As high schools graduated students who were better prepared for college-level work, the university, in turn, was able to fashion new courses that reflected the changes in high school curriculum, such as vocational and commercial classes, as well as to increase the number of credits required for entrance, from 7½ in 1906 to 12½ in 1917.

Although the Affiliated Schools Program provided the first academic standards in Texas, the program did not meet the needs of all high schools and of all students, particularly in rural areas. In a period of little state financial support for districts, the program's requirements for things such as minimum numbers of teachers, textbooks, library books, equipment, and so on favored the large municipal high schools that were able to command the needed community support and financial resources. In fact, the program refused to affiliate any high school that lacked the resources to provide students with a fourth year in high school, even though it did provide information for small schools who wished to attempt to develop a fourth year. Thus there were no academic standards for schools that were not affiliated.

Nor did the Affiliated Schools Program make any effort to include the schools for African Americans in the affiliation process. Although the program favored the more affluent urban schools of the time, the lack of an affiliation process for African American schools reflected the historical context of a very segregated Texas society. After Reconstruction, issues of race and the need for cheap labor throughout the South combined to create a dual system of public education that continued until the *Brown v. Board of Education* decision in 1954. Segregated schools in Texas were part of the larger pattern of social, economic, and political segregation that developed in Southern society and was established by all-white legislatures during the late eighteenth century. Texas schools were legally segregated when the state legislature passed the School Laws of 1876 and 1884.[36]

As a result of this separation of school systems, schools for African American children lacked the number and quality of supplies, textbooks, equipment, desks, and teachers found in schools for white children. The main reason for this was inequity in funding. Although Texas law specified that "each race shall receive its just pro rate in each county, according to the number of children of each race," this rarely happened. For example, the State Superintendent's Report for 1909–10 showed local school districts spent an average of $10.08 annually per white student versus $5.74 per African American student. Even the State Superintendent of Public Instruction, Annie Webb Blanton, described this trend in her 1922 report: "The state apportions counties the same allowance for each colored scholastic as for each white scholastic, but, in many cases, the total apportioned by the state for negro education is not used [by the local authorities] for the support of the colored schools."[37]

Because of this inequity in funding, the number of teachers and school buildings provided for African American students and the amount of funds spent on furniture, specifically student desks, and other materials, such as science equipment, were not comparable to that spent on facilities, teachers, and materials for white students, as evidenced by data in the State Superintendent Reports of the period.³⁸ For African American students, the results of this segregated policy and the inequitable funding in Texas included substandard facilities, a lack of supplies and textbooks, shortened school terms, and either overcrowded facilities or a lack of facilities altogether. These factors also meant that African American schools could not meet the standards of the affiliation process during the period from 1885 to 1917.

However, by 1920–21, after the Texas State Department of Education had taken over the process for classification and affiliation of schools, the process was applied to African American schools. Unfortunately, the strengthening of school curricula, resources, and facilities that had taken place in some white schools as a result of the Affiliated School Program did not occur in the African American schools. Instead, the State Department of Education developed a different set of standards for the African American schools, one that did not address the inequity of school funding.³⁹ For African American students, the continued segregated school systems and the inequitable funding resulted in limited opportunities for education.

Although the Affiliated Schools Program did not address the needs of all Texas students, it did provide the first college and career standards for Texas schools and the foundation for later state accreditation and assessment programs. However, the current procedure of rating students and schools according to a single assessment of student knowledge of academic standards is quite different than the Affiliated Schools Program of a hundred years ago. The visit by the state supervisor included observation and investigation into multiple areas: school facilities and resources, such as the condition of the buildings, the library facilities, science equipment, and more; the organization of the academic departments; teaching loads; school discipline practices; and observation of classroom instruction. The program also assessed a variety of factors that impact student learning, including teaching qualifications, teacher content knowledge, and classroom practice. Specimens of student work assessed by university faculty included laboratory manuals from science experiments, written exams from various courses, and writing journals, very different assessments from today's emphasis on answers to multiple choice questions of standardized exams. But although student achievement was a significant part of the assessment of Texas high schools in the Affiliated Schools Program, it was only one of a variety of standards that involved all stakeholders—students, faculty, administration, and community members.

The state standardized the number and type of courses students had to complete to graduate from public high schools at the time, but there were no high-stakes state-standardized exams involved. If a student graduated from a nonaffiliated high school and wanted to attend college, then that student had to pass the specific entrance exam of that university. On a different note, the relationship of the university to local school districts in the Affiliated Schools Program was also mutually beneficial in that there was actual communication, if somewhat indirect, on an annual basis between educators from the two levels, something that rarely happens in the present-day world of academics.

Finally, the example of the original academic standards set by the Affiliated Schools Program of a hundred years ago raises some important questions: What if the local schools and districts of today had formal relationships with local colleges and universities in which university and high school faculty worked together on a regular basis? What if community members and local businesses were involved in not only supporting local schools but also helping to develop and then assess school programs? What if all these education stakeholders took part in designing, implementing, and then assessing the preparation of students? In today's climate of high-stakes standardized assessments, a multidimensional approach such as the Affiliated Schools Program is an interesting concept, one that might provide useful ideas and perhaps a much more equitable approach for evaluating the quality of Texas schools and preparing students for life after high school.

Notes

1. "Texas Passes Controversial Social Studies Standards," *Washington Post*, May 22, 2010; "Divided Board Makes Curriculum History," *Houston Chronicle*, May 22, 2010; "In Texas, Social Studies Textbooks Get a Conservative Make-Over," *Christian Science Monitor*, May 22, 2010; "Voting Over, Battle Isn't," *San Antonio Express-News*, May 22, 2010; Bill Steiden, "Social Studies Battle May Have Just Begun in Texas," *Atlanta Journal-Constitution*, May 23, 2010; "Texas, Textbooks, and Trouble," *Chattanooga Times Free Press*, May 25, 2010; "Politicized Curriculum in Texas," *The New York Times*, May 26, 2010.
2. Nancy S. Dye, "Introduction," in *Gender, Class, Race, and Reform in the Progressive Era*, ed. N. Frankel and N. S. Dye (Lexington: University Press of Kentucky, 1991), 1; Fredrick Eby, *The Development of Education in Texas* (New York: Macmillan, 1925), 178; Lewis L. Gould, "Progressive Era," in *The New Handbook of Texas*, ed. R. Barkley (Austin: Texas State Historical Association, 1996), 349; Thomas Woody, *A History of Women's Education in the United States*, 2 vols. (1929; repr., New York: Octagon Books, 1966).
3. Eby, *Development of Education in Texas*, 178, 208.
4. Eby, *Development of Education in Texas*, 246; David G. Taylor, "The High School, a Necessary Link in Our Public School System," *Texas School Journal* 5 (1887): 281–84; George T. Winston, "The Function of the High School," *Texas School Journal* 14 (1896): 460–62.
5. John W. Hopkins, *Annual Report of the Inspector of Schools*, May 25, 1905, box 4P323, folder 1, University of Texas Affiliated School Board Records (Dolph Briscoe Center for American History, University of Texas at Austin), hereafter Affiliated School Board Records.

6. College Board History, available at http://about.collegeboard.org/history.
7. Karon Nicol, "Establishment of Academic Standards for Early 20th Century Texas High Schools: The University of Texas Affiliated Schools Program" (PhD dissertation, University of Texas at Austin, 2004), 44.
8. Eby, *Development of Education in Texas*, 198, 250, 252; Joseph L. Henderson, *Educational Memoirs* (Austin: The University of Texas, 1940), 137.
9. University of Texas Catalogue, 1885–86 (Circular No.2).
10. Nicol, "Establishment of Academic Standards," 49.
11. Nicol, "Establishment of Academic Standards," 52.
12. Bulletin of the University of Texas, No. 3, 1900–1901.
13. Bulletin of the University of Texas, No. 47, *Questions Concerning Courses of Study and Methods of Teaching in High Schools*, July 1, 1905.
14. Nicol, "Establishment of Academic Standards," 57–58.
15. Henderson, *Educational Memoirs*, 140.
16. Henderson, *Educational Memoirs*, 71, 90, 98, 101, 129.
17. J. L. Henderson, letter to E. C. Phillips, May 25, 1916, box 4Q123, folder 1, Affiliated School Board Records.
18. Nicol, "Establishment of Academic Standards," 125–26.
19. The Carnegie unit is a time-based reference for measuring the amount of time a student has studied a subject. "A total of 120 hours in one subject, meeting four or five times a week for forty-sixty minutes, for thirty-six to forty weeks each year earns the student one 'unit' of high school credit." Carnegie Foundation for the Advancement of Teaching, available at http://www.carnegiefoundation.org/faqs.
20. Henderson, *Educational Memoirs*, 146.
21. Karen Graves, *Girls' Schooling during the Progressive Era: From Female Scholar to Domesticated Citizen* (New York: Garland, 1998); Woody, *History of Women's Education*, 2:52, 69.
22. Eby, *Development of Education in Texas*, 254.
23. W. W. Barnett, *Annual Report of the Public Schools of the Independent School District of the City of Houston, 1900–1901* (Houston: Morin, 1901), 5.
24. P. W. Horn, *Annual Report of the Public Schools of the Independent School District of the City of Houston, Texas, 1904–1905* (Houston: Gray's Printing Office, 1905), 85.
25. Report of the Visitor of Schools, January 15, 1913, 3–4, box 4P323, Folder 1, Affiliated School Board Records.
26. Nicol, "Establishment of Academic Standards," 115.
27. Cecil E. Evans, *The Story of Texas Schools* (Austin: Steck Company, 1955), 150–51.
28. Evans, *Story of Texas Schools*, 151; Eby, *Development of Education in Texas*, 261; Henderson, *Educational Memoirs*, 187.
29. Evans, *Story of Texas Schools*, 151.
30. W. F. Doughty, *Twenty-First Biennial Report State Superintendent of Public Instruction State of Texas September 1, 1916, to August 31, 1918* (Austin: Texas State Board of Education, 1918).
31. Annie Webb Blanton, *A Handbook of Information as to Education in Texas 1918–1922* (Austin: Texas State Department of Education, 1923).
32. Eby, *Development of Education in Texas,* 251.

33. F. E. Savage, letter to J. L. Henderson, February 9, 1915, box 4Q355, folder 1, Affiliated School Board Records.
34. Marsha L. Farney, "Promoting the Progress of Education: The History of Georgetown Public Schools, 1850–1966" (PhD diss., University of Texas at Austin, 2007), 124–25.
35. Nicol, "Establishment of Academic Standards," 129.
36. Darlene C. Hine and Kathleen Thompson, *A Shining Thread of Hope: The History of Black Women in America* (New York: Broadway Books, 1998); Frederick Eby, ed., *Education in Texas, Sourc e Materials: Education Series No. 1, The University of Texas Bulletin No. 1824* (Austin: University of Texas Press, 1918).
37. James D. Anderson, *The Education of Blacks in the South, 1860–1935* (Chapel Hill: University of North Carolina Press Anderson, 1988); Barnett, *Annual Report*; William R. Davis, *The Development and Present Status of Negro Education in East Texas* (New York: Teachers College Press Davis, 1934); Cynthia Neverdon-Morton, *Afro-American Women of the South and the Advancement of the Race, 1895–1925* (Knoxville: University of Tennessee Press, 1989); Eby, *Education in Texas*, 690; Seventeenth and Twenty-Second *Biennial Report of the State Superintendent of Public Instruction* (Austin: Texas State Department of Education, 1911, 1922).
38. Eighth, Twelfth, Thirteenth, and Sixteenth *Biennial Report of the State Superintendent of Public Instruction* (Austin: Texas State Department of Education, 1893, 1900, 1902, 1909).
39. H. Council Trenholm, "The Accreditation of the Negro High School," *Journal of Negro Education* 1 (1932): 34–43.

Figure 12 A revolutionary grab bag
The additions to the new Texas standards on the Revolutionary War include both Episcopalian Founding Father John Jay (left) and African American martyr Crispus Attucks (right) . . . and a Lutheran and a Catholic, two famous women, a black schoolteacher, a Peninsular Spaniard, and a Jewish financier. What is the logic behind this grab-bag approach to history education?

CHAPTER 12

A Perfect Storm in Austin and Beyond
Making the Case—and Place—for US History in Texas and the Nation

Linda K. Salvucci

"From Lone Star State to Laughing Stock State" lamented former Texas Lieutenant Governor Bill Hobby in March 2010 as Texas lurched toward producing its new social studies standards.[1] Expressing frustration and embarrassment at the ostensible trumping of history by ideology, this scion of a bipartisan Houston political dynasty reflected, and perhaps attempted to deflect, the negative reactions of so many inside and outside the state. Comedians and other critics had a field day, to be sure, but what transpired during the meetings of the Texas State Board of Education (SBOE) was no laughing matter. At the end of the day, with legitimate historians and experienced teachers effectively cut out of the process, the will of the social conservative majority triumphed. Although the history that Texas schoolchildren are now mandated to learn and be tested on does follow a conventional narrative in some respects, it also displays an odd blend of head-scratching particulars, misleading revisionism, and outright invention, wrapped neatly in the flags of American and Lone Star exceptionalism. Moreover, the 2010 standards overemphasize content—easily politicized—while paying scant attention to the skills associated with learning how to think historically.[2] In the end, the prescribed history reveals far more about the present than the past, much more about contemporary cultural politics than the nature and value of historical understanding.

Many external observers have argued that the stakes could not be higher, that these standards would weigh heavily on how history is taught across the entire nation because Texas is the largest unified purchaser of K-12 textbooks and publishers therefore must produce materials according to its specifications. Yet given the 2011 state budget cuts that likely will prevent Texas from actually purchasing new social studies textbooks until at least 2015, its wider influence appears to be less of a concern than in cycles past. Moreover, in many respects the 2010 SBOE so overreached that other states, such as California, will be in a stronger position to exert their own demands on the textbook market once they resolve their own fiscal problems.[3] Furthermore, with recent elections, the political composition of the SBOE itself has begun to evolve, so that the next round of standards and textbook adoption hearings could yield a different result. Nevertheless, in the short run, Texas students will be exposed to deficient history content and poorly articulated social studies skills that will not serve them well when they take tests such as the National Assessment of Educational Progress (NAEP), the College Board Advanced Placement (AP) examinations and the SAT Subject Tests.

But let us begin with the major shortcomings manifested in the debate over the Texas social studies standards and in the final product itself. Inclusion of too much content based upon ideological or idiosyncratic considerations, misapplication of the concepts of balance, historical context, and chronology, and a lack of attention to skills all reflect the SBOE's disdain for the expertise of professional history educators and historians. There was deliberate manipulation of the process to be sure, in the service of advancing particular agendas, but the interactions between the SBOE and the public also demonstrated a marked lack of familiarity with the principles and practice of historical thinking. There was a general failure to comprehend what standards for teaching and learning history are supposed to express. This last point is highlighted by comparing the 2010 Texas social studies standards with those produced nearby in Colorado in 2009. There is a popular advertising slogan that claims: "Texas. It's like a whole other country."® And the differences between its social studies standards and those of Colorado are indeed stark. Still, the detrimental actions of the SBOE place Texas squarely at the center of the modern perfect storm of the declining state of history education across the United States today.

Who's In, Who's Out: Don't Mess with Texas's Essential Knowledge and Skills

In both Texas and Colorado, the history of the United States up to 1877 is taught in grades 5 and 8 and from 1877 to present day in grade 11, so sustained comparisons will be developed for this subject only. However, it bears noting that these three levels of US history studies are incorporated, along with courses in world history, world geography, US government, psychology, sociology, special topics, and research methods, into the 2010 Texas social studies standards. On the website of the Texas Education Agency (TEA), there is a document of some 213 pages to wade through, although nearly half of these pages consist of the 1998 standards in effect until the amended version of August 23, 2010, is implemented, beginning with the 2011–12 school year. If this seems confusing, it is; the organization, language, and format make it extremely easy to lose one's place in this less than user-friendly document. For *each* social studies or history course at each grade level, there is an introductory section that lays out "eight strands of essential knowledge and skills for social studies . . . intended to be integrated for instructional purposes." These eight strands (history, geography, economics, government, citizenship, culture, science-technology-and-society, and a final category labeled "social studies skills") are repeated and filled out with very specific content directions in every subsection for each K-12 course.

These new introductory sections also assert that "the content, as appropriate for the grade level or course, enables students to understand the importance of patriotism, function in a free enterprise society, and appreciate the basic democratic values of our state and nation as referenced in the Texas Education Code." Just to be certain that the thrust of the previous message is not lost, the following requirements are likewise repeated in the introductory section for every course: "Students identify the role of the U.S. free enterprise system . . . and understand that this system may also be referenced as capitalism or the free market system. Students understand that a constitutional republic is a representative form of government whose representatives derive their authority from the consent of the governed, serve for an established tenure, and are sworn to uphold the constitution." Included, too, is another instruction to use "the founding documents" to assess whether "U.S. citizens and the local, state, and federal governments have either met or failed to meet the ideals espoused in the founding documents" as well as a mandate to "Celebrate Freedom Week" by having students in grades 3–12 "study and recite" text from the second paragraph of the Declaration of Independence.[4] Clearly, the SBOE subscribes wholeheartedly to the nineteenth-century notion of studying history principally to reinforce patriotic and nationalist values.[5]

For the one credit high school course called "United States History Studies Since Reconstruction," there is a five-page section of "Knowledge and Skills" in history that contains some of the most contested specifications of the entire standards controversy. Much has been written about the way that the Venona Papers were characterized by the SBOE,[6] so I will highlight another, slightly less-remarked-upon example of how one-sided and one-dimensional the prescriptions are. In the section that purports to cover the 1970s and 1980s, "The student is expected to *describe*" (italics added) the following: Richard Nixon's and Ronald Reagan's leadership, US support for Israel, the Camp David Accords, the Iran-Contra affair, Marines in Lebanon, the Iran hostage crisis, Phyllis Schlafly, the Contract with America, the Heritage Foundation, the Moral Majority, the National Rifle Association, and last—and undoubtedly least—"significant societal issues of this time period."[7] In the middle of this lopsided list is the lone insert "the student is expected to *compare* [italics added] the impact of energy on the American way of life over time." True, there was a conservative resurgence during these years, but these are the *only* individuals and events stipulated for these decades, mostly in the "including" (required) rather than the "such as" (suggested) categories. Without falling into the trap of adding to the laundry list of events worthy of attention, there is, for example, no mention here of Watergate, a notable constitutional crisis, or, more surprisingly, the fall of the Berlin Wall.[8] Nor is there mention of the spillover into the 1990s of some of the movements noted, reinforcing a sense of chronological disorientation. If there is bias in the content chosen, there is also an unsettling degree of historical mindlessness displayed. There is no sense of cause and effect, interconnections, or explanation—only the listing of particular figures and developments, which the student is most frequently instructed merely to "describe."

Other chapters in this volume stress the biased nature of the SBOE's content choices. Equally troubling, however, is the grab-bag approach to enumerating "essential" names and dates. For example, note the incredibly eclectic list of individuals from the era of the "constitutional republic," about which "the student is expected to explain the contributions of the Founding Fathers such as Benjamin Rush, John Hancock, John Jay, John Witherspoon, John Peter Muhlenberg, Charles Carroll and Jonathan Trumbull Sr."[9] I can identify these men because I earned a PhD in early American history and grew up on the East Coast. But I cannot offer a compelling explanation as to why these seven in particular would have been chosen to represent their contemporaries. What are the criteria for inclusion on this list? What meaningful characteristics do these individuals share? Think of who was omitted! To be fair, the high school US history course has 1877 as its starting date and treats the preceding eras only in an introductory review. Thus it is only reasonable to consult the new standards for grade 8, when the "social studies" course is supposed to focus upon "the history of the United States from the early colonial period through Reconstruction." One of these standards expects the student to "explain the roles played by significant individuals during the American Revolution, including Abigail Adams, John Adams, Wentworth Cheswell, Samuel Adams, Mercy Otis Warren, James Armistead, Benjamin Franklin, Bernardo de Gálvez, Crispus Attucks, King George III, Haym Salomon, Patrick Henry, Thomas Jefferson, the Marquis de Lafayette, Thomas Paine, and George Washington."[10]

I must confess that the name "Wentworth Cheswell" threw me for a loop. When I Googled him, up popped the website of the WallBuilders. So it is David Barton's group that has raised the profile of this New Hampshire schoolteacher as a black patriot. And what are we to make of the rest of this eclectic

Table 2 The Standards' Significant Individuals during the American Revolution

	1998 Standards	Added by Committees	Added by SBOE
Grade 11	None	None	Benjamin Rush John Hancock John Jay John Witherspoon John Peter Muhlenberg Charles Carroll Jonathan Trumbull Sr.
Grade 8	Samuel Adams Benjamin Franklin King George III Thomas Jefferson Marquis de Lafayette Thomas Paine George Washington	Abigail Adams John Adams Bernardo de Gálvez Patrick Henry	Wentworth Cheswell Mercy Otis Warren James Armistead Crispus Attucks Haym Salomon
Grade 5	Thomas Jefferson George Washington	John Adams Samuel Adams Benjamin Franklin Nathan Hale	Sons of Liberty

enumeration of historical characters? The comparable clause in the 1998 standards listed Samuel Adams, Benjamin Franklin, King George III, Thomas Jefferson, the Marquis de Lafayette, Thomas Paine, and George Washington.[11] Why were the Adamses, Cheswell, Warren, Armistead, Gálvez, Attucks, Salomon, and Henry added? Was the addition of two admittedly extraordinary white women, three lesser-known black men, a Peninsular Spaniard, and a Jewish financier, along with two radical-turned-conservative patriots, an attempt to appear inclusive or somehow balanced?[12] What is the logic behind choosing these people, not even presented in alphabetical or chronological order? There is a strange lack of ideological consistency, but more of historical reasoning in this list. What if some inquiring student raised the question of how and why these choices were made? How could a classroom teacher, a parent, or anyone familiar with the subject matter respond? Alas, we only know the "when"—the review committees appended Abigail and John Adams, Bernardo de Gálvez, and Patrick Henry to the 1998 list in July and October 2009. Members of the SBOE then added Mercy Otis Warren, Wentworth Cheswell, James Armistead, and Crispus Attucks during the January 2010 meeting. Being able to track the respective edits, however, still fails to shed much light on why these particular men and women were chosen.

Texas students are introduced to US history in grade 5, so it is also worth examining how the 2010 standards require this foundation to be laid. For the era of the American Revolution, the student is expected to "identify the Founding Fathers and Patriot heroes, including John Adams, Samuel Adams, Benjamin Franklin, Nathan Hale, Thomas Jefferson, the Sons of Liberty, and their motivations and contributions during the revolutionary period."[13] In the 1998 standards, only Jefferson and Washington had been named, and the only event listed for the period "prior to and during the American Revolution" was the Boston Tea Party, which is joined by the French and Indian War in the 2010 document. One wonders why Nathan Hale and the Sons of Liberty were added, only to be dropped in grade 8, when the Adams men, Franklin, and Jefferson were retained.

If professional historians have trouble recognizing or justifying several of the whos and whats that appear in the 2010 social studies standards, then classroom teachers undoubtedly will find the very short concluding sections on "social studies skills" for each course more than a bit problematic. Overall, the relatively brief skills portion of the 2010 Texas Essential Knowledge and Skills (TEKS) formulation remains remarkably similar to the 1998 version. At the end of each course description, following the subject strands, there appears a page or so of "social studies skills" that "the student" must demonstrate, ultimately to be assessed in the nearly phased-out Texas Assessment of Knowledge and Skills (TAKS) and new State of Texas Assessments of Academic Readiness (STAAR) tests and end-of-course exams. For US history studies since 1877, the 2010 standards include these general requirements: "The student applies critical-thinking skills to organize and use information acquired from a variety of valid sources, including electronic technology . . . ; communicates in written, oral and visual forms . . . ; uses geographic tools to collect, analyze, and interpret data . . . ; uses problem-solving and decision-making skills, working independently and with others, in a variety of settings."[14]

In the two to eight subsections under each of these four parts, these expectations are elaborated on to some degree, including that students "understand how historians interpret the past (historiography) and how their interpretations of history may change over time"; "use the process of historical inquiry to research, interpret and use multiple types of sources of evidence"; and "use correct social studies terminology to explain historical concepts."[15] With matters of *content* ("essential knowledge"), the 2010 standards are overly explicit while still managing to omit significant and basic people, events, processes, and trends. With matters of *process* ("essential skills"), however, the reverse holds true. The latter formulations are clumsy, undefined, and overly vague even in their itemization. What are "problem-solving and decision-making skills," "the correct social studies terminology," "appropriate skills," and "a variety of both primary and secondary valid sources"? What does "valid" mean? If the intent was to allow the teachers some flexibility outside the strict content guidelines—and it is not at all clear that this was the case—then there remains the vexing question of how Texas students can be prepared consistently and well to take district, state, or national tests that incorporate any measurement of *skills*. Attention to the principles of historical thinking, researched and applied by an increasingly large number of scholars and practitioners, is very much in order.[16] As it is, there seems little method to the madness.

So while much attention rightly has been focused on the mind-boggling battles over content (most often cherry-picked details) and the resultant sins of omission and commission, there is a more serious deficiency, the length of the TEKS notwithstanding, in terms of understanding the study of history as anything more than selective enumeration of facts, decided upon in a "mine versus yours" contest of opinion. In the minds of their creators, the 2010 social studies standards may have successfully reinforced some key ideological principles, but they do not provide an effective roadmap for the teaching and learning of history and the assessment of students' knowledge and skills. Sadly, the SBOE proved itself to be a body of controlling politicians whose vision of the past lacked historical, historiographical, and pedagogical expertise as well as integrity.

"Fewer, Higher, Clearer"—and Better: Colorado's Twenty-First-Century Standards

As Texans embarked upon revising their social studies standards from 1998, Coloradans were finishing their own efforts to replace guidelines dating from 1995. At the end of 2009, the state of Colorado released revised academic standards for social studies; they differ from the 2010 Texas social studies standards in several strikingly significant ways. To begin with, the 119-page Colorado document is carefully organized and smartly formatted, making it far easier to utilize.[17] For example, the first two pages present a concise "Overview of Changes" from the 1995 "Colorado Model Content Standards in History, Geography, Economics, and Civics." At the very outset, the "guiding principles" of the writing process are spelled out, mostly notably to "*begin with the end in mind* [italics added]; define what prepared graduates need in order to be successful using twenty-first century skills in our global economy" and to "align K-12 standards with early childhood expectations and higher education." Asserting that "change is necessary," the social studies subcommittees aimed to produce "fewer, higher, clearer" as well as "actionable" standards.[18] In another welcome nod to transparency, there then follows a one-page chart that serves as another "quick guide to changes in the social studies standards" from 1995.

In contrast to Texas's awkward intermingling of history and social studies themes, the 2009 Colorado document reduces 19 previous standards (more like topics or themes) in history, geography, economics, and civics to a single standard each for these four subjects. Standard 1, for history, affirms, "History develops moral understanding, defines identity and creates an appreciation of how things change while building skills in judgment and decision-making. History enhances the ability to read varied sources and develop the skills to analyze, interpret, and communicate." The purpose of studying the past is defined clearly and succinctly, with the focus placed squarely on acquiring skills rather than on amassing content. This approach incorporates Colorado's twenty-first-century and postsecondary workforce readiness skills, which are "intentionally integrated into evidence outcomes." Instead of benchmarks as articulated by grade *bands* (K-4, 5–8) in the 1995 standards, expectations now are clearly spelled out for each separate grade level, starting with preschool. Moreover, the overall number of benchmarks or expectations per grade level was reduced from an average of 27 to 10 for pre-K-8 and 17 for all high school grades combined. Colorado's purposeful, streamlined, outcomes-oriented approach, which emphasizes skills much more than content, is poised to drive instruction and learning in ways that stand in stark contrast to what is prescribed in the lengthy and meandering TEKS.

An additional "Continuum of State Standards Definitions" indicates how the social studies subcommittees kept the acquisition of twenty-first-century skills by pre-K-12 students at the center of their endeavor.[19] Defined skills include critical thinking and reasoning, information literacy, collaboration, self-direction, and invention. Three themes, used to illustrate necessary skills and competencies, are embedded and interwoven throughout the social studies standards: inquiry questions, relevance and application, and nature of discipline. For history, the "Prepared Graduate Competencies" are as follows: "(1) Develop an understanding of how people view, construct, and interpret history; and (2) Analyze key historical periods and patterns of change over time within and across nations and cultures."[20] No matter what the grade level, from preschool through high school, one of these two competencies appears at the top of each of the 22 pages of history standards. In other words, everyone involved in the education of Colorado's children, from parents to classroom teachers to assessors, knows precisely where the vertically integrated instruction is headed and what it is expected to accomplish. Even though Colorado is very much a local-control state, there is consensus regarding the ends of history education, with flexibility allowed to achieve these ends.

By now it should be clear that a fundamental difference between the social studies standards of Texas and Colorado revolves around the role accorded content versus the role accorded skills. In Texas, there were endless battles over—if not a near-total obsession with—particular bits of "essential knowledge." Ideological or idiosyncratic preferences, particularly relating to the inclusion of heroes and role models, determined most of the choices made. The lists grew longer and longer, resulting in a cumbersome code that turned every single social studies course into a multipage catalogue of prescribed, but essentially scattershot information, again with content specified in *each* of the eight strands for *every* course. In Colorado, by contrast, grade-level expectations are displayed in charts that range from one (preschool) to two (K-8) to three (all high school combined) pages in length for each grade. Whereas Texas starts with kindergarten and works up to grade 12, Colorado's standards are organized in reverse order; the high school ones appear first, thus reinforcing the results-oriented mentality.

For comparison with the eighth-grade Texas standards, let us examine Colorado's "Grade Level Expectation: Eighth Grade."[21] The first of two pages for this course in US history through Reconstruction addresses the "Prepared Graduate Competency" to "develop an understanding of how people view, construct, and interpret history." Students are expected to master concepts and skills associated with how to "formulate hypotheses about United States history based on a variety of historical sources and perspectives." There are six "Inquiry Questions" and two statements each on "Relevance and Application" and "Nature of History." Finally, there are four examples to indicate how "Evidence Outcomes" are manifested. Again, this format remains the same for every single page and every grade level; the skills of historical thinking thus become a habit and are consistent across levels. Yet it is the substance of the directions in these categories that demonstrates a most sophisticated approach to studying the United States' past. Very few specific events, movements, or documents are ever mentioned; moreover, these appear solely in the context of having teachers and students actually work with such facts or writings, rather than merely describing or identifying them.[22]

In essence, Colorado eighth graders are challenged to become historical thinkers, evaluating primary and secondary sources for purpose, audience, point of view, context, and authenticity and creating hypotheses and interpretations of events defended with supporting evidence. Content is not regarded as disembodied and sacrosanct bits of information; rather, it serves as the raw material used to practice history. Eighth graders are prompted to ponder such questions as "Should and can historians be completely impartial when writing about history?" and "What makes history different from literature?" At the end of this process, they recognize multiple and conflicting perspectives, critique data, and construct their own arguments. In short, they are "doing history," unlike their counterparts in Texas, who are condemned to trying to keep Wentworth Cheswell and Haym Salomon and Bernardo de Gálvez straight.

The foundation for the study of US history is laid in fifth grade where, as in Texas, Colorado students first encounter the subject. The expectations for this elementary course include identifying "different ways of dating historical sources to understand historical context"; creating timelines; and analyzing cartoons, artifacts, artwork, charts, and graphs.[23] All the readiness competencies for fifth grade involve perspective: "How do sources with varied perspectives help us to understand what happened in the past?" and "Some accounts of the American Revolution refer to the American patriots while others refer to American rebels." Under "nature of the discipline," it is affirmed that "historical thinkers examine data for point of view, historical context, distortion, or propaganda." The contrast in tone and substance with the 2010 TEKS could not be greater. In addition to acquiring broader skills, Colorado's fifth graders learn that studying American history involves much more than a forced march through unconnected and disparate material. The Colorado vision of history as a subject is dynamic, engaging, and insightful. Note the almost joyful justification of learning about the past that serves to introduce all the history standards: "History inspires by exposing students to the wonders and beauty of the past. The historical perspective prepares for an ever-changing future by helping to understand changes in the past. It allows students to gain perspective and develop better judgment by discovering and uncovering the complexity of human beings. This allows students to better understand themselves as individuals and their place in a complex and often confusing society. History provides examples of ethical behavior and the context for change, and illustrates the importance of responsible members of society in both our country and our world."[24]

So the obvious question is: how did these two states, Texas and Colorado, come to produce, within months of each other, such radically dissimilar requirements for the same courses taught at the same grade levels? Above all, the processes for generating the respective social studies standards were structured and executed in very different ways. In Texas, the SBOE controlled virtually every aspect, from beginning to end, of the drafting, consideration, and adoption of the standards; the SBOE has sole authority to change them and statutory authority to enforce them.[25] At the outset, each of the 15 members of the SBOE, elected to four-year terms, was allowed to appoint his or her own expert reviewers and review committee members. Some did, some did not (and, of course, there was vigorous disagreement over the definition of "expert"), leaving certain regions and districts across the state unrepresented. There were direct, often last-minute interventions by SBOE members all along the way. And what really matters is that, in the end, the full board had the authority to reject all *and any* recommendations. The members functioned effectively as judge, jury, and executioner.

Others have analyzed more thoroughly how the SBOE wielded its considerable power over every phase of revisions process, but suffice it to state that what the drafting committees produced was substantially altered, sometimes even word by word, at the board level up until the very last minutes of the very last meeting in May 2010. Moreover, participants followed the initial charge to merely revise the 1998 TEKS; they never considered that they might replace them. Essentially, then, writing standards became an additive process, resulting in the bloated final product, as more and more was included and very little was dropped. And there should have been meaningful input from university specialists, classroom teachers, and informed citizens, but such was not permitted to occur. In theory, of course, at selected points in the process, members of the public had opportunities to sign up to give three minutes of oral public testimony or to submit written comments online to the TEA. In practice, however, the registration website crashed, and links to the posted drafts for comment were sometimes broken. When registered witnesses did travel to Austin at their own expense on the appointed days, some had to leave before speaking because the public SBOE meetings would fall hours behind. For example, at the meeting on November 18, 2009, board members did not even turn their discussion to the social studies standards until 9:30 PM, some 12 hours after the session designated to incorporate such testimony had opened.[26] By May 10, 2010, the TEA website was flooded with more than twenty thousand public comments; one wonders how many of them were actually read by SBOE members before their final vote on May 20.[27] In the end, neither qualified professionals nor "the people" could make their voices effectively heard. Texas had first constructed and then adhered to the perfect system for manipulation by the few.

In Colorado, by contrast, a group of stakeholders (district administrators, superintendents, businesspeople, and other citizens appointed by the Commissioner of Education and the State Board of Education) selected a social studies standards committee through a name-blind process based upon merit. The resultant body was led by the former chairs of the National Council for Social Studies and the National Council for History Education, who worked with more than fifty subcommittee members chosen in a name-blind process that sought out relevant professional experience in history, geography, economics, civics, and personal financial literacy.[28] Rather than merely revising the 1995 Model Content Standards, the social studies standards committee worked within the context of Colorado's other well-defined education reform initiatives, framing its enterprise as outlined above and explicitly linking its standards to the twenty-first-century skills. Instead of an add-to-the-existing-code mentality, originality infused their efforts. As the social studies committee worked, and even consulted a "national expert reviewer" from outside the state, the stakeholders made very few suggestions before their first up-or-down vote.

Following their initial approval of the social studies standards, there was a period of public review and comment, both online and in a series of meetings held in locations across Colorado. The committee co-chairs were required to respond in writing to every public comment (more than one hundred), either changing the standard based upon input or explaining why they disagreed with the suggestion. Co-chair Fritz Fischer stated that the committee made few changes, instead mostly explaining why members chose to keep the standard as written. The stakeholders had a second up-or-down vote, and then Colorado's social studies standards went to the State Board of Education. In one of its meetings open to the public, Fischer presented the standards and answered a few questions from board members and the audience. At this point, the board members could have voted to approve, reject, or send back for adjustments—they voted unanimously to approve the social students standards on December 10, 2009.[29] The entire process was well conceived, transparent, and well executed; controversy was avoided, and there was general buy-in to fresh standards produced by qualified, experienced, involved, and outcomes-oriented Coloradans. The Colorado State Department of Education continues to produce toolkits to assist in standards implementation as well as updates on work on the new assessments to be put in place by 2014. Colorado's path to meaningful reform remains forward-looking and deliberate, professional and participatory.

A Perfect Storm for History Education, but Not Just in Texas

This tale of two standards has a bit of a twist. Although they are so dramatically different in genesis, substance, and style, neither the Texas and nor the Colorado social studies standards were well received by the coauthors of the Thomas Fordham Institute's *State of State U.S. History Standards 2011*. Not surprisingly, Texas's received a D. However, Colorado's were assigned an F.[30] What caused both of these very different sets of standards, along with those of 26 other states, to earn such poor grades? The answer underscores how and why history education is in peril, not only in Texas but also across the nation.

According to Sheldon Stern and Jeremy Stern, in response to sharp criticism of their Fordham Institute report, "standards are, or should be, the substantive guidelines for determining what a state intends (or at least hopes) its young people will know when they complete various grade levels. Clear and rigorous standards are the foundation upon which state history curricula, student assessments, and teacher training should be built."[31]

However, these evaluators then proceed to defend the view that permeates their own findings: standards are, first and foremost, about content (what students "will know," as opposed to what they "can do"). Despite some fairly harsh comments about the Texas standards, they still awarded them 2 points on a scale of 7 for "content and rigor" and 1 point out of 3 for "clarity and specificity." Colorado, in turn, received 0 points in both categories. Its standards were dismissed as a "jargon-laden snarl of nested categories" and graded poorly because "actual historical people, details and events never appear—just bits of historical flotsam in a maelstrom of social studies 'concepts.'" Yet, at the same time, the Sterns attack the Texas standards as "a bizarre amalgam of traditionally ahistorical social studies—combining the usual inclusive, diversity-driven checklists with a string of politically and religiously motivated historical distortions." Moreover, they write, "It is particularly ironic that the aggressively right-tilting Texas Board of Education embraced the mindset and methodology of social studies, traditionally the tool of a left-leaning educational establishment. The result is the worst of both worlds."[32] But so intent were they on condemning the "concepts" and "methodology" of social studies that the Sterns were willing to reward content that, by their own admission, contains "historical distortions"—not to mention that they seemed to miss the point entirely about the role of skills in history education. Whether their hostility to social studies is rooted mostly in ideology, as some critics of the Fordham report have suggested, or it reflects the decades-long uneasiness among professional historians with the way that history has been subsumed under social studies in the K-12 curriculum is beside the point.[33] The sad conclusion is that the evaluation, as well as the creation, of standards for US history in particular remains in need of improvement. Yet neither the consensus nor even the will to fix these shortcomings appears on the horizon.

    In the absence of national standards, each state produces its own set, which then drives the development of curricular and instructional materials, as well as those all-important assessments that determine future funding. This is a tremendous waste of energy and resources as every state repeats efforts to reinvent the proverbial wheel—with decidedly mixed, though only partially comparable results. For courses in US history, there is an intellectual issue as well because there is no collective effort made to articulate our common identity. In what ways are we "a people and a nation"? The meaning of "American," it seems, becomes subject to whether students reside in Massachusetts or Alabama, California or Kentucky, Colorado or Texas. But branches and agencies of the federal government, sensitive to a tradition of local control of education and/or skittish about reigniting culture wars, remain reluctant to lead reform in history education.

    Compounding the problem further is the fact that one of the unintended consequences of the 2001 reauthorization of the Elementary and Secondary Act, popularly known as No Child Left Behind, has been the drastic and well-documented decline of instructional time devoted to history, particularly at the elementary level.[34] Preparation for high-stakes testing in reading and math is the overwhelming priority, thus narrowing the curriculum and crowding out history and social studies. Across the country, teachers now spend mere minutes per week on these subjects, and course offerings themselves are being cut back.[35] Even in states where there are periodic required assessments in social studies, the temptation is to focus upon the students' acquisition of content rather than skills because content is easier, quicker, and cheaper to test.

How have the US Department of Education and Congress reacted to the crowding out of history in the curriculum? They have, by and large, ignored or dismissed the crisis while privileging and spearheading initiatives for STEM education; that is, they have sought to direct resources toward science, technology, engineering, and mathematics.[36] To this end, Secretary of Education Arne Duncan has pushed his scheme for a "well-rounded education," which involves consolidation of funding for formerly separate programs into one large pot; projects in history, the humanities, geography, civics, economics, the arts, and financial literacy henceforth will compete against each other for federal dollars. The bottom line is that Secretary Duncan has effectively removed history from the first-tier subjects and reduced it to the status of an optional add-on, which some states and districts might choose to prioritize while others will not. There are, quite simply, no incentives to focus upon history in his plan.

But wait, there's more, as the saying goes. Texas, along with Alaska, has made itself ineligible even to apply for Race to the Top and other federal monies because it is not part of the Common Core State Standards Initiative (CCSSI).[37] Texas Governor Rick Perry has spurned this movement, and HB 2923 was introduced in the last regular session of the Texas legislature to prohibit state education officials from participation in the CCSSI. This voluntary effort, coordinated by the National Governors' Association and the Council of Chief State School Officers (CCSSO), already has produced common standards in mathematics and English/language arts. The latter do include some brief guidelines on "Literacy in History/Social Studies, Science, and Technical Subjects" for grades 6–12, but professional organizations have called for the development of separate and full common standards in social studies. A coalition of 15 groups, including the American Historical Association, the National Council for History Education, the National Council for Social Studies, National History Day, and the World History Association has met four times to work toward this goal. These participants, of course, bring a level of professional expertise to the table that incorporates the latest scholarship on and best practices in historical thinking at the K-12 level.

Meanwhile, the College Board is working to revamp its AP examinations in US history, paradoxically the most popular AP subject, with some 387,000 test-takers. Its efforts are the closest we have at present to a national articulation of the content and skills that high school history students should master. And interestingly, the AP website now features "the redefined historical thinking skills and their components [that] provide an essential framework for developing historical habits of mind. These skills apply equally to all fields of history."[38] For the Texas social studies standards to give short shrift to historical thinking skills again puts the state's students at a comparative disadvantage.

But for top education officials at the federal level to devalue and defund the study of history is truly unfortunate, especially given the June 2011 release of the 2010 NAEP Report Card in US history.[39] In short, the nation's "report card" finds American students to be less proficient in their nation's history than in any other subject. Only 20 percent of fourth graders, 17 percent of eighth graders, and 12 percent of high school seniors achieved the rating of Proficient (the middle of three categories, the others being Basic and Advanced) on the examination. Changes in overall averages from previous years (2006, 2001, and 1994) were, for the most part, "microscopic," or statistically not significant. Of course, there was a brief flurry of media attention that bemoaned these poor results. Yet as Lee White, executive director of the National Coalition for History, so aptly put it, "they've narrowed the curriculum to teach to the test [in math and reading]. History has been deemphasized. You can't expect kids to have great scores in history when they're not being taught history."[40]

As if the decline in instructional time in history were not bad enough, there is another persistent issue, namely, out-of-field teaching in history classes. More than half of all public school students enrolled in history or world civilization courses in grades 7–12 are taught by teachers who did not major or minor in history in college.[41] Most preservice teachers continue to be trained primarily in education departments. Many receive a general or composite certification in social studies, which means that they have taken a variety of mainly introductory courses in various disciplines, such as history, economics, political science, geography, and psychology. An increasing number receives alternative certification or compressed in-house training, neither of which involves an in-depth study of history. Thus there is a crying need for professional development in history, much more so than in math, for example. For the last ten years, the Teaching American History grants program (TAH), administered through the US Department of Education, addressed this need, with sustained collaborations that bring together K-12 instructors, master teachers, university professors, and public historians (such as curators and archivists). Originally the professed goal was content deepening, but participants also are exposed to History's Habits of the Mind, and other approaches to historical thinking.[42] Yet the Obama administration, with support from the Democratic leadership in the House, collapsed TAH's funding into the consolidation pot, and then they and congressional Republicans succeeded in eliminating any new TAH grants. Over the last decade, hundreds of Texas teachers and thousands of their students have benefited from this program. However, the remaining projects are about to be phased out and there is nothing proposed to replace them. To compound the problem, given the recent billion-dollar cuts in state funding for public education, it is highly unlikely that local districts in Texas will be able to fund much professional development in history for the foreseeable future.

Without question, the social studies standards created by the Texas State Board of Education are deficient in many significant respects. Both the process and the product are deeply flawed and work against the proposition that all Texas schoolchildren deserve access to a quality education in history, one that prepares them for college, a career, and citizenship. However, against the added backdrop of decreased federal, state, and local funding for schools, incomplete education initiatives at the national level, the documented narrowing of the curriculum to crowd out history, questionable high-stakes testing practices, lackluster student performance on assessments, inadequate teacher preparation, and diminished opportunities for professional development, the standards' negative impact can only be magnified. At the same time, although Texas may well be "like a whole other country," the whole country itself must confront the dire state of history education today.

Notes

1. Bill Hobby, "Comment," *Texas Tribune*, March 12, 2010.
2. There was a separate, prior effort to produce readiness, skills-based standards that appeared in January 2008: Texas College and Career Readiness Standards, "Texas College and Career Readiness Standards," http://www.thecb.state.tx.us/index—.cfm?objectid=EADF962E-0E3E-DA80-BAAD2496062F3CD8. This document, prepared largely by professors and other educators, was ignored by the SBOE as it revised the TEKS, and thus is not discussed below. For a revealing analysis see Keith A. Erekson, *Bridging the Gap between K-12 and College Readiness Standards in Texas: Recommendations for U.S. History* (Arlington: Texas Faculty Collaborative for Social Studies, 2011).
3. John Fensterwald, "Texas Tales Won't Pollute Our Texts: Vetoed Bill Wouldn't Have Made a Difference," *Thoughts on Public Education*, September 30, 2010, http://toped.svefoundation.org/2010/09/30/texas-tall-tales-wont-pollute-our-texts.
4. TEKS.11.b.5–8 (8/23/10).
5. Peter Charles Hoffer, *Past Imperfect: Facts, Fictions, Fraud—American History from Bancroft and Parkman to Ambrose, Bellesiles, Ellis, and Goodwin* (New York: Perseus Books Group, 2004), 17–31.
6. Fritz Fischer, "The Texas History Standards: The Case of 'The Venona Standard' and Effective History Teaching," *History Matters*, 23, no. 1 (September 2010): 3–6; Michael Birnbaum, "Historians Speak Out against Proposed Texas Textbook Changes," *Washington Post*, March 18, 2010, A03.
7. TEKS.11.c.10.A–F (8/23/10).
8. See TEKS.11.c.19.C (8/23/10).

9. TEKS.11.c.1.C (8/23/10).
10. TEKS.8.b.4.B (8/23/10).
11. TEKS.8.b.4.B (8/23/10).
12. Gary Scharrer, "'Experts' Stir Controversy over Social Studies Textbooks," *Houston Chronicle*, July 16, 2009.
13. TEKS.8.b.2.B (8/23/10).
14. TEKS.11.c.29–32 (8/23/10).
15. TEKS.11.c.29.C–D, 30.D (8/23/10).
16. "Historical Thinking at the K-12 Level in the 21st Century: A Roundtable," *Historically Speaking: The Bulletin of The Historical Society* 12, no. 3 (June 2011): 15–25; "The Scholarship of Teaching and Learning and the History Classroom," *Journal of American History* 97, no. 4 (March 2011): 1048–88; Stéphane Lévesque, *Thinking Historically: Educating Students for the Twenty-First Century* (Toronto: University of Toronto Press, 2008).
17. Colorado Department of Education, *Colorado Academic Standards: Social Studies*, adopted December 10, 2009, available at *http://www.cde.state.co.us/cdeassess/UAS/COAcademicStandards.html*; hereafter CASSS.
18. CASSS, 1.
19. CASSS, 13.
20. CASSS, 21–23.
21. CASSS, 27–28.
22. CASSS, 28.
23. CASSS, 33–34.
24. CASSS, 23.
25. Keith Erekson, "Texas Social Studies *Simplified*," TEKS*Watch*, July 1, 2010.
26. Amy Jo Baker, email to author, November 20, 2009.
27. Kate Alexander, "SBOE Swamped by Comments on Social Studies Standards," *Austin American-Statesman*, May 20, 2010.
28. Anna Huffman, email to author, July 5, 2011.
29. Fritz Fischer, emails to author, June 27 and July 3, 2011.
30. Sheldon M. Stern and Jeremy A. Stern, *The State of State U.S. History Standards 2011* (Washington, DC: Thomas B. Fordham Institute, 2011), 33–34, 141–43.
31. Sheldon M. Stern and Jeremy A. Stern, "Run Down by Traffic in Both Directions: Is It Possible to Have a Rational Discussion of State U.S. History Standards?" *History News Network*, March 1, 2011.
32. Stern and Stern, *State of State U.S. History Standards*, 33–34, 141–43, 164–68.
33. Stern and Stern, "Run Down by Traffic"; Gary B. Nash, Charlotte Crabtree, and Ross E. Dunn, *History on Trial: Culture Wars and the Teaching of the Past* (New York: Alfred A. Knopf, 1997); *National Standards for History* (Los Angeles: National Center for History in the Schools, 1996).
34. Phillip Van Fossen, "'Reading and Math Take So Much of the Time . . .': An Overview of Social Studies Instruction in Elementary Classrooms in Indiana," *Theory and Research in Social Education* 33, no. 3 (2005): 376–403; Diane Stark Rentner, Caitlin Scott, Nancy Kober, Naomi Chudowsky, Victor Chudowsky, Scott Joftus, and Dalia Zabala, *From the Capital to the Classroom: Year 4 of the No Child Left Behind Act* (Washington, DC: Center on Education Policy, 2006).

35. Van Fossen, note 41; Andrea Koskey, "History Class Is History at San Francisco's Lowell High School," *San Francisco Examiner*, April 7, 2011; Norman Draper, "History Classes Might Be Taking a Back Seat in Minnesota," *Star Tribune*, July 4, 2011.
36. *A Blueprint for Reform: The Reauthorization of the Elementary and Secondary Education Act* (Washington, DC: US Department of Education, 2010); Allan Kulikoff, "A Modest Proposal to Resolve the Crisis in History," *Journal of the Historical Society* 11, no. 2 (June 2011): 239–63.
37. Lindsay Kastner, "Texas Shuns Common Standards for Schools," *San Antonio Express-News*, June 21, 2009.
38. See *http://advancesinap.collegeboard.org/historical-thinking*.
39. *U.S. History 2010, National Assessment of Educational Progress at Grades 4, 8, and 12: The Nation's Report Card* (Washington, DC: US Department of Education, National Center for Education Statistics, 2011), NCES2011-468.
40. Sam Dillon, "U.S. History Is Still Troublesome for U.S. Students, Nationwide Tests Show," *The New York Times*, June 15, 2011, A19; Stephanie Banchero, "Students Stumble Again on the Basics of History: National Test Shows Little Progress in Grasping Democracy, U.S. Role in World," *Wall Street Journal*, June 15 2011; Lee White, quoted in Joy Resmovits, "U.S. History Test Scores Stagnate as Education Secretary Arne Duncan Seeks 'Plan B,'" *Huffington Post*, June 14, 2011.
41. Richard Ingersoll and Kerry Gruber, *Out-of-Field Teaching and Educational Equality* (Washington, DC: National Center for Education Statistics, 1996), NCES 96-040, 23–24.
42. Rachel G. Ragland and Kelly A. Woestman, eds., *The Teaching American History Project: Lessons for History Educators and Historians* (New York: Routledge, 2009). For "History's Habits of the Mind," see *http://www.nche.net/document.doc?id=43*.

Notes on Contributors

Linda J. Black is an assistant professor of secondary education at Stephen F. Austin State University. She served from 1995 to 1998 on the social studies writing team that prepared the state's first standards, and she won the 2011 Selma Greenberg Outstanding Dissertation Award from the Research on Women and Education SIG of the American Educational Research Association.

Stephen Cure is the director of educational services for the Texas State Historical Association. He served on the Texas history review committee and later as an informal advisor throughout the revision process.

Keith A. Erekson is an assistant professor of history at the University of Texas at El Paso and director of the Center for History Teaching and Learning. He organized the TEKS *Watch* information and update service that monitored media coverage of the revision process and is the author of *Bridging the Gap between K-12 and College Readiness Standards in Texas: Recommendations for U.S. History* (Texas Faculty Collaborative for Social Studies, 2011).

David C. Fisher is associate professor of history at the University of Texas at Brownsville. He is the author of several articles on Russian and global history.

Richard T. Hughes is Distinguished Professor of religion and director of the Sider Institute for Anabaptist, Pietist, and Wesleyan Studies at Messiah College, Grantham, Pennsylvania. He is a graduate of San Angelo Central High School and Abilene Christian University and is the author of *Christian America and the Kingdom of God* (University of Illinois Press, 2009).

Laura K. Muñoz is an assistant professor of history at Texas A&M University in Corpus Christi and a 2011 National Academy of Education/Spencer Postdoctoral Fellow. She won the 2007 Claude A. Eggertsen Dissertation

Prize from the History of Education Society and served on the US history review committee during the revision process.

Julio Noboa is an assistant professor of social studies at the University of Texas at El Paso. He served on the US history review committee and is the author of *Leaving Latinos Out of History: Teaching U.S. History in Texas* (Routledge, 2006), as well as articles and book chapters on history teaching and standards.

Gene B. Preuss is associate professor of history at the University of Houston–Downtown and the author of *To Get a Better School System: One Hundred Years of Education Reform in Texas* (Texas A&M University Press, 2009).

Linda K. Salvucci is associate professor of history at Trinity University. She presently serves as chair of the National Council for History Education, as contributing editor to *Historically Speaking*, and as a member of the Board of Governors of The Historical Society. She is the coauthor of *Call to Freedom* (Holt, Rinehart and Winston, 2005), a US history textbook for eighth and ninth graders.

Edward H. Sebesta is an independent researcher and author based in Dallas, Texas. He coedited *Neo-Confederacy: A Critical Introduction* (University of Texas Press, 2008) and *The Confederate and Neo-Confederate: The "Great Truth" about the "Lost Cause"* (University Press of Mississippi, 2010). He also runs two historical reference websites: http://www.confederatepastpresent.org and http://www.citizenscouncils.com.

Jesús F. de la Teja is Regents' and University Distinguished Professor and former chairman of history at Texas State University–San Marcos. During 2007–8, he served as president of the Texas State Historical Association. He was an expert reviewer of the Texas Essential Knowledge and Skills Social Studies standards for the State Board of Education in 2009–10.

Emilio Zamora is professor of history at the University of Texas at Austin. He was involved throughout the revision process and is the author of the award-winning *Claiming Rights and Righting Wrongs in Texas: Mexican Workers and Job Politics during World War II* (Texas A&M Press, 2009).

Appendix for Teachers

This appendix highlights approaches and strategies that can be used to overcome the inadequacies in the Texas Essential Knowledge and Skills (TEKS).

Critical Thinking Skills

Ask about persons, groups, and perspectives that are not named in the standards, 113, 121, 185

Replace uneven analytical language, such as "examine the benefits of . . . ," with a more complete analysis, such as "examine the costs and benefits of . . . ," 12–13

Teach problem solving, analysis, and decision making as necessary preparation for college and careers, 13–14, 218

Historical Thinking Skills

Contrast the Texas vision of the past—rooted in nineteenth-century Manifest Destiny, rugged individualism, and social Darwinism—with the state's twenty-first-century urban, multiethnic, and global present, 13

Examine the benefits and limitations of structuring the narrative around concepts of exceptionalism, destiny, and enterprise, 118–20

Examine the full impact of a topic on American history; for example, religion influenced American government and the "American way of life" as well as prompted persecution, justified war, and fueled cultural debates, 13

Explore why and how historians identify events and periods as significant, 48–49, 51, 185

Help students see that the use of the term "free enterprise" already implies certain values and assumptions about the American economy, 63

Integrate the experience of minorities into the Celebrate Freedom Week requirement, 109

Move beyond listing the contributions of the individuals listed in the standards to see how they made choices and acted within the opportunities and restrictions of their times, 111–12

Place the names in the standards into wider relevant contexts, 13, 121, 161–62

Texas History

Contrast the reasons Texans gave for seceding from the union in 1861 with the reasons listed in the standards, 151

Place the actions of the confederate heroes listed in the standards within a wider context of war, patriotism, and civil crimes, 156–57

Resist the urge to identify a finite number of defenders of the Alamo, 82

US History

Consider why 1848 might also be considered a turning point in US history, 115

Contrast the vision of "Christian America" in the standards with the biblical vision of the kingdom of God, 127–29

Examine the influence of northern Mexican ranching on the American cowboy culture, 105

Examine the way the Founding Fathers approached religion as evidenced in the text of the Declaration of Independence and Constitution, 132–36

Debate the implications of describing US actions in the early twentieth century as *expansionism* or *imperialism*, 115–16

Explore the "Christianization" of America that occurred in the nineteenth and twentieth centuries through the Second Great Awakening and fundamentalist movement, 138–45

Question why Spanish colonization is not implied in the section on European colonization, 115

Use primary sources to draw a more accurate comparison between the ideas of Jefferson Davis and Abraham Lincoln, 153–56

World History

Apply Celebrate Freedom Week to global developments, 180–81

Examine the tension between narratives about Western civilization and world history, 171–75

Teach about colonization as a context for understanding the prescribed decolonization, 13

Appendix for Policy Makers

This appendix highlights approaches and strategies that can be used by policy makers to improve the process of designing education standards.

Process and Oversight

All amendments must be made with ample opportunity for review and editing, 7, 13

All aspects of the reform process must be clearly explained to the public and the media, 8

Everyone involved needs to understand the goals and objectives of education standards in light of classroom experience, 72

State governments should place the responsibility for designing education standards and curriculum in the hands of education professionals, 10, 44–45, 93, 186

Texas should recognize its own short-term and long-term history of working with university-based experts to define respectable educational standards, 195–96

The Texas state legislature should restrict the State Board of Education's curricular authority to the policy-making level, 72–73

Professional organizations—of historians, educators, or educational administrators—should be consulted for their collective expertise, 45, 77–79

Professional organizations should become engaged early and participate throughout the revision process, 76–77, 81–83, 86

Curriculum Design

Allow teachers, curriculum designers, and publishers enough flexibility to address the standards in ways that represent a range of geographic, demographic, and economic diversity, 72

The articulation of representative examples leads to bloating, repetition, and confusion, 62, 64–65, 71

Emphasize disciplinary goals and college readiness over polarizing content choices, generic learning activities (such as "description"), and de facto memorization of a laundry lists of names, 13–14, 216–18

Ideological "balance" is not a sufficient substitute for sound educational and historical concepts, 11, 71, 219

Replace the clumsy, undefined, and vague grab-bag standards with a document that is clear, concise, and well-organized, 219

K-12 education must be viewed in light of its multiple relations to higher education, 14, 96–97

School performance should be assessed not on a single measure of standardized test performance but on a range of measures that involve all relevant stakeholders, 207

Media Coverage and Analysis

Attention must be paid to the exercise of power, no matter how distracting or persuasive the sideshows, 6–8

Debates over curricula and schooling are best understood within broader historical and political contexts, 8–9, 20–21, 225–27

Media coverage must examine educational principles, student performance, and college readiness instead of culture war politics—even (or especially) when actors in the story try to frame their efforts in politicized terms, 7–8, 11

Media coverage must distinguish between the preliminary creation of standards and the subsequent application of those standards to textbooks, testing, and curriculum materials, 9, 62, 70

Index

A Beka Books, 163
abstinence, 9, 28, 46
Adams, Abigail, 108, 217
Adams, Cathie, 154
Adams, John, 133, 217
Adams, Samuel, 217
Addams, Jane, 108
Advanced Placement, 79, 176, 179, 214, 227
Affiliated Schools Program, 196–208
affirmative action, 12
Africa, 173, 185
African Americans, 31, 54, 150, 157, 206
   in the TEKS, 107–8, 111–13, 161–62
Agosto, Rick, 45, 150, 189
Alamo, Battle of the, 74, 82
Al Jazeera, xi
Allen, Lawrence A., Jr., 150, 187
Alvis, John, 165
American Educational Research Association, 42
American Historical Association, 31
Ames, Bill, 42, 44–52, 69
Amistead, James, 217
Anshelevich, Vadim, 189
Anthony, Susan B., 108
anticommunists, xii, 22–23
anti-intellectualism, 63
Arabs, 13, 187
Arellano, Dan, 90–92
Armey, Dick, 164
Asia, 184–85
Associated Press, 41
Atlantic world, 184
Attucks, Crispus, 108, 212, 217
Austin American-Statesman, 15n2
Austin, TX, 3–4, 19, 70, 76, 202

Bachmann, Michele, 11, 46, 119
Bain, Robert, 177, 190
Baker, Vernon J., 108, 112
Baptists, 132
Barton, David, 10–11, 14, 50, 119, 127, 130, 136, 178, 180–82, 189, 216
Beck, Glenn, 11, 119
Bell, Alexander Graham, 31, 65
Benavidez, Roy, 108
Berger, Dennis, 42, 44–45, 47
Berlanga, Mary Helen, 44–45, 61, 186, 188
Bible, 128, 133, 140, 142
   reading in classroom, 25, 46
bilingual education, 9, 27
Black, Linda J., xii, 231
Blanchette, Sue, 107
Blanton, Annie Webb, 206
Bob Jones University, 163
Bonhoeffer, Dietrich, 130
Bradford, M. E., 164
Bradley, David, 150
Brownback, Sam, 11
Brown v. Board of Education, 24, 52, 206
Bryan, William Jennings, 19
Burton, Britine, 42, 44–45, 49
Bush, George H. W., 32
Bush, George W., 9, 31, 144, 164
Byrd, Dave, 157
Byzantine Empire, 183–84

Calhoun, John C., 150
California, xi, 9, 32, 34, 214, 225
Calvin, John, 131–32
Campbell, Randolph B., 157
capitalism, 21, 47, 50, 118, 145, 171, 215

238 • Index

Career and College Readiness Standards (CCRS), 14, 44, 53, 78, 80–81, 179, 195, 201
Cargill, Barbara, 44, 72, 150, 187–88
Carroll, Charles, 50, 217
Caruth, William III, 165
Carver, George Washington, 65, 189
Catholics and Catholicism, 13, 68, 130, 132, 134, 141, 187, 212
Celebrate Freedom Week, 50, 109, 112, 180–81, 215
Chávez, César, 4, 12, 52, 70–72, 103, 107–8, 110, 127
Cheney, Lynn, 21, 31
Cherokee removal, 13, 113
Cheswell, Wentworth, 216–17
Chicano mural movement, 52
China, 171, 179, 182–83, 190
Chinese Exclusion Act, 110, 117
Chiras, Daniel, 34
Chisholm, Shirley, 108
Choate, Bronwen, 44–45, 47
Christian America, xii, 11, 128, 141, 143–44
Christian Coalition, 11, 136, 143–44
Christianity, 171, 183–84
Christians, 13, 53, 128, 136–38, 160
  evangelical and fundamentalist, 141–45
Christmas, 4, 7, 12, 65
chronology and periodization, 51, 66, 185
church and state, 4, 22, 69, 130, 134, 136
Cigarroa, Francisco G., 97
civil rights, movement, 26, 66, 102–3
  modern activist groups, 14
Civil War
  and religion, 150
  in Texas, 151
Clark, Suzanne U., 159
Clinton, Hillary, 54, 108
Clinton, William Jefferson, 31–32
CNN, xi
Cold War, 13, 18, 21, 49, 172, 180, 185
College Board, 176, 179, 214, 226
college readiness, 14
colonization, 66

Colorado, education standards in, xii, 214, 219–24
Columbian exchange, 179
Columbus, Christopher, 68
Comedy Central, xi
communism, 22, 23, 47, 143, 171, 180
Confederate flag, 4
Confederates, 11, 13, 149–65, 150
conservatives, xii, 8, 13, 98
  activist groups of, 3, 22, 25
  Christian, 4, 9, 11–12
  divisions among, 9–10
  governance by, 9
  New Right, 29
  political networks of, xi, 10–11, 14, 164–65
  on the SBOE, 107, 112
conspiracy, 10–11, 23–24, 69
Constantine, 129
Constitution, US, 31, 109, 151
  and religion, 135–36
Cornyn, John, 46
cowboy culture, 105
Craig, Bob, 44, 188
creationism, 9, 46
critical race theory, 120
culture war
  politics, 3–4, 8, 10, 12, 19, 21, 35, 62, 92, 159, 178k 189, 225
  storyline, xi–xii, 7–9, 11–12
Cure, Stephen, xii, 75–86, 231

Dabney, R. L., 150, 158, 160
Dallas Morning News, 15n2, 67, 164
Danish Broadcasting Corporation, xi
Davis, Jefferson, 148–50, 153–56, 161
DeBoe, David, 77
Debs, Eugene, 50
Declaration of Independence, 50, 132–35
Deism, 133–35, 137, 140, 142
Democrats, 3, 8, 45, 93, 119, 186, 188, 227
Department of Education, US, 226
Dies, Martin, 22
Dobson, James, 11, 136, 143

Doughty, W. F., 204
Douglass, Frederick, 108, 112
Dred Scott v. Sandford, 113
Dreisbach, Daniel, 178, 180–81, 189
dual-language instruction, 9
Du Bois, W. E. B., 108
Duncan, Arne, 226
Dunn, Ross, 172–73, 176
Dwight, Timothy, 140
Dwyer, John J., 159

Eagle Forum, 11, 14, 46, 52, 136
Edgewood v. Kirby, 52
Edison, Thomas, 31
education policy, xiii, 8–10, 25, 61, 63, 72, 92, 175, 177
education reform, xi–xii, 4, 8–9, 12, 97, 197, 216, 223–25. *See also* standards
Educational Research Analysts, 29
Edwards, Jonathan, 138–39
Einstein, Albert, 31
England, 180
Enlightenment, 184
Enola Gay, 4
Erekson, Keith A., xii, 96, 231
Evan, Mark W., 158
Evans, Cecil E., 203
Everson v. Board of Education, 22
evolution, 4, 9, 19, 33, 45, 76, 141–42
exceptionalism, xi, 47, 50–51, 110, 118–19, 174, 186, 189–90, 213
expert reviewers, xii, 5, 7, 10, 60–73, 81, 178–82

Falwell, Jerry, 11, 143
Feiffer, Jules, 29
Finn, Chester E., 34
Finney, Charles G., 140
Fischer, Fritz, 224
Fischer, Trey Martinez, 93
Fisher, David C., xii, 231
Florida, 8
Fort Worth Star Telegram, 67
Founding Fathers, xi, 50, 65, 67–68, 216, 218
 religion of, xii, 70, 126, 128, 132–38

Fox News, xi, 10, 11
Franklin, Benjamin, 133, 217
 Franklin Springs Family Media, 160
Fraser, Hugh Russell, 21
free enterprise system, 12, 20, 35, 47, 50, 60, 63, 118, 171, 178, 186–88, 215
Friedan, Betty, 51–52, 108
Fundamentalism, 141–45

Gabler, Mel and Norma, 25–31, 45
Gainesville, TX, 157
Gálvez, Bernardo de, 108, 114, 117, 121, 216–17
Garcia, Hector, 71, 108
García, Sylvia, 90
Garvey, Marcus, 108
Gay, Geneva, 119
gay, lesbian, bisexual, transsexual, and queer (GLBTQ), 51, 54, 116–117
geography, 12, 25
George III, 127
Gettysburg Address, 25
Gilliam, Marco, 165
Gingrich, Newt, 11, 20
Givens, Anita, 43
Glass, Herman A., 24
Gonzalez, Henry B., 71
Gorbachev, Mikhail, 13
Graham, Billy, 143
Gramm, Phil, 164
Grant, Ulysses S., 31, 162
Great Awakening, 138–39, 142
Great Depression, 13, 66, 180, 185
Great Society, 12
Greece, 171, 183
Green, Thomas, 150, 156
Guardian (London), xi

Hale, Nathan, 217
Haley, J. Evetts, 23
Haley, J. Evetts, Jr., 165
Hancock, John, 50, 217
Handbook of Texas Online, 85
Hanson, Abel, 22
Hardy, Patricia, 14, 44, 61–62, 78, 80, 84, 174, 186–87, 189

Harlem Renaissance, 52
Hartman, David, 165
Helms, Charles R., 165
Henderson, J. L., 200–203, 205
Henry, Patrick, 217
higher education, 96–97
historical thinking, 13, 51, 66, 218–22, 227–28
history, xiii, 20, 25, 62
Hobby, Bill, 213
Hodges, Lybeth, 178, 181
Holden, Stephen, 159
Hood, John Bell, 149, 156
Hopkins, John W., 200
Horn, Joseph, 165
Houston, TX, 22, 25
Houston Chronicle, 15n2, 67
Howard, Michael, 44–45, 47
Huckabee, Mike, 11, 20, 119
Huerta, Dolores, 71, 108
Hughes, Richard T., xii, 231
Hutchinson, Kay Bailey, 80, 165

imperialism, 30, 40, 49–50, 115–16, 118, 175, 184
India, 171, 181, 183, 190
Islam, 171, 173, 183–85
Israel, 13, 183, 187, 215

Jackson, Andrew, 13
Jackson, Thomas J. "Stonewall," 148, 150, 155, 157–61, 163
Jay, John, 50, 212, 217
Jealous, Benjamin, 3, 41
Jefferson, Thomas, 10, 21, 65, 71–72, 132–35, 140, 174, 217–18
Jenner, William, 23
Jews and Judaism, 13, 54, 133, 137, 141, 183, 187, 212, 217
Jindal, Bobby, 11
journalists, 3, 5, 7, 106

Kelley, Douglas, 159
Kennedy, James, 11, 136
Kennedy, Robert F., 49
Keteltas, Abraham, 139

King, Martin Luther, Jr., 49, 52, 102–3, 108, 112
Knight, Mavis B., 44, 52, 80, 187–88
Korea, 22
Kracht, James, 62, 178, 181
Ku Klux Klan, 28, 31

Lafayette, Marquis de, 217
Latinos, 105
  in the TEKS, 107–8, 114–16
Lee, Robert E., 31, 155, 163
Leo, Terri, 20
Lewis and Clark, 68
Liberal activist groups, xii, 3, 88–98
Liberty Institute, 5
Lincoln, Abraham, 25, 149, 153–56
Lippmann, Walter, 30
Loewen, James W., 33, 151
lost cause, 148–49
Louisiana Purchase, 20
Lowe, Gail, 14, 35, 44, 77, 80, 83–85, 187
Lubbock, Francis, 149

Magruder, John, 150, 156–57
manifest destiny, 114–15
Mansfield, TX, 24
Marshall, Peter, 19, 107, 127, 130, 178–79, 182
Marshall, Thurgood, 71, 107, 108, 127
Marty, Martin, 141
Maxwell, Ronald F., 159
McAndrew, William, 30
McCarthy, Joseph, 22, 31
McLeroy, Don, 10, 14, 42, 44–46, 48, 51–52, 79, 183, 187
Mead, Walter Russell, 177
media, xi, 5, 10–11
  circus-like coverage, xii, 2, 7
Mercer, Ken, 20, 161
Mesoamerica, 182
Mesopotamia, 182
Mexican American Legislative Caucus, 5, 71, 93
Miller, Geraldine, 44
Minnesota, 8
Moral Majority, 143

Moreland, William, 25
Mormons, 13
Muhlenberg, John Peter, 50, 217
multiculturalism, xii, 4, 8, 20–21, 25–27, 45, 53, 67, 106, 122, 189
  critique of TEKS, 105–22
Muñoz, Laura K., xii, 42–45, 49, 51, 53, 231
Murchinson, Bill, 164–65
Muslims, 13, 54

National Assessment of Educational Progress (NAEP), 32, 106, 190, 214, 227
National Education Agency, 28
National Governors Association, 31, 226
National Organization for Women, 31, 51, 66
Native Americans, 13, 66, 92, 94–95, 111, 112–14, 131–32
neo-Confederate ideology, xii, 11, 162–65
New Deal, 21
New Liberty Videos, 159
New York Times, xi, 21, 32
Nixon, Richard, 50, 215
Noboa, Julio, xii, 42–45, 49, 53, 232
No Child Left Behind, 9, 97, 225–26
North Atlantic Treaty Organization (NATO), 21
North Carolina, 8
Nuñez, Rene, 44–45, 61, 188

Obama, Barack, 49–50, 108, 112
  administration of, 9, 227
O'Connor, Sandra Day, 108
O'Keefe, Georgia, 108
Oñate, Juan de, 68
Organization of American Historians, 89
Ottoman Empire, 179, 184

Paige, Rod, 3, 41
Paine, Thomas, 217
Palin, Sarah, 54
Palmer, Benjamin, 150
Pampa, TX, 26

Parks, Rosa, 108
patriotism, 8, 22, 28, 48–49, 53, 60, 63, 178, 215
Pennington, Deborah, 42, 44–45, 49
Permanent School Fund, 6
Perry, Rick, 14, 46, 80, 96–97, 127, 136, 164, 226
Persia, 183
Pledge of Allegiance, 22, 27, 180
politicians, xi, 5, 8–11, 15, 40, 63, 93, 175, 194, 219
Pollard, A. E., 149, 152
Pope John Paul II, 13
Porter-Magee, Kathleen, 34
prayer, in school, 25
Presbyterians, 132, 137
Preuss, Gene B., xii, 232
problem solving, 13, 28, 218
Protestants, 141
protests, 2–3, 5, 28–29, 88, 98
psychology, 12
Public Broadcasting Corporation, xi
Puritans, 131

Race to the Top, 9, 226
Rangel, Irma, 71
Ravitch, Diane, 26, 27–28, 32–33
Reagan, John H., 149, 156
Reagan, Ronald, 9, 13, 50, 215
Reconstruction, 150, 161–62
Reformation, 184
religion, xi, 11–13, 22–23, 28–30, 44, 70–71, 93, 127–41, 150, 159, 173, 183
Renaissance, 184
Republican National Committee, 11, 136
Republicans, 3, 8, 9–11, 144, 20, 22, 42, 46, 80, 93, 136, 144, 163–64, 186, 227
Revels, Hiram Rhodes, 108, 148, 161
review committees, 4–5, 7, 63
  Texas history, 78, 150
  US history, xii, 40–54, 69–70
  world history, 11, 179
revolutions, 184
Reynolds, Morgan O., 164

Richards, Ann, 164
Rivas-Rodríguez, Maggie, 90–92
Robertson, Pat, 11, 136, 143
Rome, 171, 183
Romero, Oscar, 95, 130, 174
Roosevelt, Eleanor, 108
Rush, Benjamin, 50, 217
Rushdoony, R. J., 158
Rutherford, Mildred, 155

Salk, Jonas, 31
Salomon, Haym, 217
Salvucci, Linda K., xii, 232
Santa Anna, Antonio Lopez de, 95
Schaff, Philip, 141
Schlafly, Phyllis, 11, 14, 20, 51–52, 71, 108, 136, 215
Scopes Trial, 19, 30, 33, 143
Sebesta, Edward H., xii, 232
Second Great Awakening, 138–41
secular humanism, 25
Sierra Club, 31
Sikes, Melvin P., 27
Sikhism, 189
skills, teaching of, 13, 218–19
slavery, 140–42, 149
Smith, Edmund Kirby, 157
social studies, 13, 20–21
socialism, 20, 26, 47, 171
Sons of Liberty, 217
Sosa, Lionel, 108
Sotomayor, Sonia, 108
Soviet Union, 20, 24–25
standardized testing, 9, 72, 194–95, 225, 228
standards, 8–9
   national, 8, 18, 173, 176, 226
   for social studies, xi, 8, 12
   See also Texas Essential Knowledge and Skills
Stanton, Elizabeth Cady, 108
State Board of Education (SBOE), xi, 6–11, 14, 24, 29–30, 32, 34–35, 40, 43–44, 49–52, 54, 60–61, 69–72, 76, 81–82, 149, 186–89, 225
   meetings of, 2–4
   and neo-Confederate ideology, 162–65
   protests against, 2, 88
states' rights, 149, 151–53, 155, 163, 165
Steinem, Gloria, 51
Stephens, Alexander H., 152
Stern, Sheldon and Jeremy, 224
Stewart, Jon, 174
Stewart, Maco, 24
Stone Age, 173
Stonewall Riot, 51
students, 3, 6, 8, 12–15, 20–24, 27–28, 32–35, 42, 49–53, 62, 64–66, 71–72, 85, 94, 105–6, 174–77, 190, 197–203
Sullivan, Joseph, 165

tariffs, 151–53
teacher training, xiii
Teaching American History program, 227
de la Teja, Jesús F., xii, 62–73, 79, 178, 232
Tejano Monument, 91
Tejanos, 74
TEKS *Watch*, xiiin1, 15n2, 100n19, 123n4, 229n25, 231
Telford, Margaret, 44–45, 47
terrorism, 185
Texas Communist Control Law, 22
Texas Conservative Coalition, 5
Texas Council for the Social Studies (TCSS), 48, 76, 78
Texas Education Agency (TEA), 6, 26–27, 41, 43–44, 47–48, 51, 78, 90, 120, 195, 214
Texas Education Code (TEC), 6, 30–31, 35, 50, 171–72, 178, 188, 215
Texas Essential Knowledge and Skills (TEKS), xi, 40–41, 48, 54, 62–65
   compared to Colorado standards, 218–24
   multicultural critique of, 105–22
   for world history, 182–85
Texas Freedom Network, 5, 92–93
Texas Higher Education Coordinating Board, 14, 195
Texas Navy Association, 80, 82–84

Texas Public Policy Foundation (TPPF), 45–47, 79, 96–97
Texas Republican Party, 11, 136
Texas Social Studies Supervisors Association (TSSSA), 48, 76, 78
Texas State Historical Association, xii, 74–86
Texas State Legislature, 23, 30, 72
Texas Tech University, 23, 24
Texas Tribune, 15n2, 46
textbooks, 8, 33, 70
  controversy over, 18, 26
  publishing, xi, 25, 32, 34, 213
Theodosius the Great, 129
Thomas Fordham Institute, 14, 34–35, 107, 177, 190, 224
Thompson, Bill, 30
Thornwell, James H., 150, 158, 161
Tijerina, Andres, 90–91
Tilley, John S., 152
Title IX, 12
Tocqueville, Alexis de, 141
Trumbull, Jonathan, Sr., 50, 217
Tubman, Harriet, 31

Uncle Tom's Cabin, 140–41
Unidos de Austin, 90
University of Texas, 94, 96–97, 194, 198–208
USA Today, xi
US Senate, 23

Vickery, Richard, 81
Vietnam, 49
Voting Rights Act of 1965, 69

Walesa, Lech, 13
Wall Street Journal, xi, 31, 66
Walton, John, 45
Warren, Mercy Otis, 108, 217
Washington Monthly, 45
Washington Post, xi
Washington, George, 29, 31, 126, 217
Wayland, Francis, 141
Welhelmsen, Frederick D., 164
Wells, Ida B., 108
West Virginia, 18, 28, 30
Western civilization, xii, 49, 170, 172–75, 181–85
White Citizens' Council, 25
White, Lee, 227
Wilkins, Steve, 159
Willard, Frances, 108
Williams, Richard G., Jr., 160
Wilson, James, 137
Winfrey, Oprah, 108
Witherspoon, John, 50, 137, 217
women, 51
  in the TEKS, 107–11
world history, 172–75
World History for Us All, 174, 176
World Trade Center, 144–45
World War I, 13, 48, 185
World War II, 21, 51, 66, 92, 112, 116, 185, 188
Wright Brothers, 31

Young, Brigham, 68

Zaffirini, Judith, 97
Zamora, Emilio, xii, 89–98, 232

GPSR Compliance
The European Union's (EU) General Product Safety Regulation (GPSR) is a set of rules that requires consumer products to be safe and our obligations to ensure this.

If you have any concerns about our products, you can contact us on

ProductSafety@springernature.com

In case Publisher is established outside the EU, the EU authorized representative is:

Springer Nature Customer Service Center GmbH
Europaplatz 3
69115 Heidelberg, Germany

www.ingramcontent.com/pod-product-compliance
Lightning Source LLC
LaVergne TN
LVHW011812060526
838200LV00053B/3746